THE RELUCTANT PILGRIM

THE RELUCTANT PILGRIM

Defoe's Emblematic Method
and Quest for Form
in *Robinson Crusoe*

J. PAUL HUNTER

The Johns Hopkins Press
Baltimore

To Carolyn

*who came to a desolate
Island of Despair
and made a garden grow*

Preface

Despite the plethora of old and new "histories" of the novel, the flowering of prose fiction in the eighteenth century remains something of a historical puzzle. We seldom doubt the ultimate interest and value of the early novel, but its peculiar shape and unexplained "development" induce a chronic discomfort. The critical revolution that has, since World War II, reinterpreted most major Augustan works has barely touched the novelists (with a few exceptions [1]) and has forced the lines of literary history to be redrawn around the entire genre of prose fiction. In short, as the Augustan poetic has been reassessed, the novel has been almost completely left out of account.

But if we have suffered a critical lag in the study of prose fiction, it is less because of self-satisfaction than frustration. Laments are persistently heard about the state of our knowledge of the historical contexts of prose fiction, and about our failure to read the texts with the same critical sophistication we bring to, say, Pope; for it

---

[1] The recent publication of three Fielding studies promises a dialectic that might well bring revised estimates of more writers than just Fielding: see Martin Battestin, *The Moral Basis of Fielding's Art* (Middletown, Conn., 1959); Sheldon Sachs, *Fiction and the Shape of Belief* (Berkeley and Los Angeles, 1964); Andrew Wright, *Henry Fielding: Mask and Feast* (Berkeley and Los Angeles, 1965).

is not so much that we have confidence in the old generalizations as that we are uncertain about procedures to form new ones. For one thing, the novelists seem so comparatively "simple" (a comment earlier generations liked to make about Dryden, Pope, and Swift), and we never quite know how to talk critically about their work without seeming either truistic, on the one hand, or overly ingenious, on the other. For another thing, eighteenth-century prose fiction bewilders our notions about what a novel is, for its authors are notoriously misleading (or sometimes silent) about their intentions, and critics attempting to reconcile Defoe or Fielding or Sterne with Flaubertian or Jamesian theory have had to settle for unwieldy comparisons and terms that finally prove inappropriate. Then, too, treating long novels in the same manner as short poems requires a rather considerable devotion to the premise that the author and work are, ultimately, worth it, for several scores of lifetimes would be needed to give prose fiction the contextual solidity that we are now approaching for Pope. The condescension bestowed on eighteenth-century novelists by, on the one hand, Augustan critics, and, on the other, by students of the later novel suggests something less than the total devotion needed to undertake the task.

The difficulty of approaching fiction anew is illustrated by Ian Watt's *The Rise of the Novel*, perhaps the most impressive and influential such study of the last decade. Despite his fresh reading of individual authors and his often acute perceptions about specific techniques, Professor Watt manages to challenge received opinion surprisingly little, and his total study of relationships between authors affirms, rather than revises, the usual estimates of how fiction "develops." We could, of course, simply take comfort from such conclusions, but disquieting discrepancies remain between these conclusions and those arrived at by students of other eighteenth-century literary forms.

Much of the problem, it seems to me, derives from an implicit assumption about what a novel, or rather *the* novel, is. The metaphors commonly used to describe the early novel are very revealing. Critics speak of the "growth" of the novel, its "rise" and "development"; or they talk of the "family" of novelists, calling Defoe (or Richardson) the "father" of the form. Such terms barely disguise the assumption that the novel is organic, moving more or less predictably toward a realization of perfect form. Whether or not Aristotle is correct in describing the history of tragedy in this way, prose fiction moved too variously for such a definition to apply. We need, I think, less emphasis on similarities produced by the "English tradition" and more attention to the very substantial differences in the major early English novelists; we need a rather full reassessment of the various directions which prose fiction took in the hands of its early masters. And once we know more exactly what each individual writer was intending and accomplishing, we will then be able to define more fully the types of prose fiction and their relation to each other.

This study grew out of a desire to contribute to such a reassessment. I chose Defoe as my subject because I found his conscious artistry seriously maligned and because I found in his work qualities not usually thought to exist in early eighteenth-century fiction. *Robinson Crusoe* became the special focus of this book because I thought it to be defined and described inaccurately both by historians of fiction and by critics of Defoe and because I thought it not only the most undervalued, but ultimately the most important, of Defoe's works.[2] Exten-

[2] By *Robinson Crusoe*, I mean only Part I—*The Life and Strange Surprising Adventures of Robinson Crusoe of York Mariner*. The two

sive research has confirmed my conclusion and clarified
my reservations about traditional readings of *Robinson
Crusoe* in particular and of Defoe in general. Now I am
persuaded too that the artistic techniques in *Robinson
Crusoe* demand that we re-evaluate Defoe's contribution
to prose fiction and that we raise new, more sophisticated questions about the relationship between the cultural "mind" behind particular writers and the literary
forms that they produced.

Traditionally, the power of *Robinson Crusoe* has been
explained in three basic ways. One method describes its
appeal as that of "realism" and emphasizes Defoe's "circumstantial method" of making fiction seem like fact.[3] A
second, emphasizing the adventure plot and the "typical
Englishman" aspects of the hero, locates the book's appeal in the psychology of readers who, removed from
elemental physical struggles for survival, wish to identify with those so engaged.[4] A third considers the story
in terms of political economy, seeing its value either in
the social ideals of a "natural" civilization or in the
novel's representation of the rise of new economic ideals
and a new economic class.[5] Each approach has illumi-
nated important aspects of Defoe's art, and in proposing
a different version of Defoe's artistic power I do not wish

---

sequels, *Farther Adventures* and *Serious Reflections,* were published
later and seem, like *1 Henry IV* and *2 Henry IV*, to have been separately
conceived.

[3] Standard histories of the novel (Baker, McKillop, Wagenknecht,
Stevenson) discuss Defoe largely in these terms.

[4] See, e.g., Louis Kronenberger, "Defoe: The Great Materialist," *SRL*,
September 30, 1939, pp. 3, 4, 17; W. P. Trent, *Daniel Defoe: How To
Know Him* (Indianapolis, Ind., 1916).

[5] For various uses of this reading, see Rousseau's *Émile*; Ian Watt,
The Rise of the Novel (London, 1957); and such Marxist studies as that
of Brian Fitzgerald (*Daniel Defoe: A Study in Conflict* [London, 1954])
or Ralph Fox (*The Novel and the People* [New York, 1945], esp. p.
236). Watt's reading of Crusoe as *homo economicus* has been especially
influential, though recently this view has come under severe attack.

to minimize previous insights. But it seems to me that the traditional approaches have not suggested the full range and complexity of what happens in *Robinson Crusoe*, nor have they defined adequately the artistic technique which Defoe develops from Puritan thought patterns and a rich subliterary context.

Time has dealt rather more capriciously with Defoe than with many of his contemporaries. Once, *Robinson Crusoe* was regarded as his masterpiece, and even his enemies admitted its excellence.[6] But nineteenth-century scholars discovered unsavory facts about Defoe's life, and his image as a pious and zealous reformer, misused by his own generation, was rapidly redrawn into that of an unscrupulous hack. Recent years have raised to prominence works formerly ignored—*Moll Flanders* and *Roxana*, for example—and critics have suggested that Defoe was a writer whose real interests were different from his expressed ones.

The paradoxes of Defoe the man not to mention theoretical questions—have prevented me from taking Defoe's own assertions at face value, but I have allowed those assertions to point me toward contexts where relevant questions may be raised; finally, I have been led to conclusions about Defoe's art which are independent of his own articulation, perhaps even independent, in one sense, of his "choice," for finally I have tried to approach the question of how and why the materials that go into an artist's "mind" push him toward a specific form. Theoretical interests have thus ultimately become the motivating force behind this study, but I have tried not to let

---

[6] According to Joseph Spence, Pope called *Robinson Crusoe* "excellent" (*Anecdotes, Observations, and Characters of Books and Men* [2d ed.; London, 1858], p. 196). Samuel Johnson said *Robinson Crusoe* was one of only three books "written by mere man that was wished longer by its readers" (Joseph Epes Brown, *The Critical Opinions of Samuel Johnson* [Princeton, 1926], p. 305).

my attention to specifics be subordinated to these interests. I have had three simultaneous aims: to offer a detailed critical reading of *Robinson Crusoe*; to define and describe several kinds of Puritan subliterary materials; and to suggest the relationship between characteristic Puritan ways of thinking in the seventeenth century and the new prose fiction of the eighteenth.

Much of the old view of Defoe stems from assumptions about Defoe as a man and as a journalist who accidentally began to write fiction. In recent months there have been important indications that Defoe's artistry is being taken more seriously.[7] As my part of the exorcism of the old view, I have raised, in Chapter I, questions about the assumptions and conclusions traditionally held about the events which lie behind *Robinson Crusoe*. Chapters II, III, and IV define and describe several Puritan subliterary traditions which seem to me relevant to the mind and imagination that produced *Robinson Crusoe*. Some may find these chapters overly precise and my attention to detail tedious here, but those who regard works of art as cultural objects whose form is inseparable from the cultural mind which produced them will, I think, find much here to support later theoretical suggestions. Chapter V places the Puritan mind of the seven-

---

[7] Two books by Maximillian Novak (*Economics and the Fiction of Daniel Defoe* ["University of California English Studies," No. 24; Berkeley and Los Angeles, 1962], hereafter cited as *EF*, and *Defoe and the Nature of Man* [London, 1963]) have corrected a number of false assumptions about Defoe and have laid the groundwork for more adequate interpretation. See also his "*Robinson Crusoe* and Economic Utopia" (*KR*, XXV [1963], 474–90), and his "Defoe's Theory of Fiction" (*SP*, LXI [1964], 650–68), as well as the following essays by other hands: Robert R. Columbus, "Conscious Artistry in *Moll Flanders*" (*SEL*, III [1963], 415–32); Howard L. Koonce, "Moll's Muddle: Defoe's Use of Irony in *Moll Flanders*" (*ELH*, XXX [1963], 377–94); and William H. Halewood, "Religion and Invention in *Robinson Crusoe*" (*EIC*, XIV [1964], 339–51).

teenth century in a historical perspective and suggests how, and why, Puritan subliterary traditions look toward the symbolic novel, making it possible for an emblematic way of perceiving the world to be transformed into a literary style. In Chapters VI, VII, and VIII, I attempt to define Defoe's technique by offering a detailed reading of *Robinson Crusoe*. In an Afterword I have offered some tentative suggestions about how the ideas I express here affect other novels and novelists. If there is a certain audacity here in my unorthodox delineation of types of novels in the eighteenth century, I hope it will stimulate others to a more helpful retracing of the history of prose fiction than we yet have available.

Just as this book was completed, Princeton University Press issued G. A. Starr's admirable *Defoe and Spiritual Autobiography*. Professor Starr and I both regard Defoe's religious background as enormously important, and both of us offer readings of Defoe in terms of this background. We are not, of course, the first to suggest that *Robinson Crusoe* is ultimately about man's spiritual development,[8] but no one has considered the background as fully as we have. Professor Starr, however, traces Defoe's obligation to autobiography and is more concerned with the standard rhythm of conversion than with the literary background as such; he declines to characterize the background of Defoe's art as distinctively

---

[8] James Sutherland (*Defoe* [London, 1937]) and Sri C. Sen (*Daniel Defoe, His Mind and Art* [Calcutta, 1948]) take the religious element in *Robinson Crusoe* seriously; there have been several important studies of the subject: James Moffatt, "The Religion of Robinson Crusoe" (*Contemporary Review*, CXV [1919], 664–69); J. Harry Smith, "The Theology of Robinson Crusoe" (*Holborn Review*, n.s., XVI [1925], 37–47); Roger Lloyd, "The Riddle of Defoe: Impact of the Evangelical Challenge" (*Church Times*, July 16, 1954, p. 654); E. M. W. Tillyard, *The Epic Strain in the English Novel* (Fairlawn, N.J., 1958, pp. 25–50); and William Halewood's study, mentioned above (n. 7).

Puritan, and his major attention is to the first third of *Robinson Crusoe*.[9] My concern with fiction's quest for form, on the other hand, has led me to consider types of *public* literature which relate to Christian concern with conversion and ethical conduct but which (it seems to me) can be carefully distinguished from one another on the basis of distinctive aims and techniques and which lead us to important conclusions about the nature of Puritan art. I have been more concerned, too, to show how the tradition articulates itself in a conscious artistic technique, controlling the entire form of *Robinson Crusoe*. Professor Starr's argument about Defoe's intention reinforces my conception of the theme of *Robinson Crusoe*, though our differing interests and methods have led to quite different emphases and, ultimately, to very different conceptions about the relationship of intellectual background to fictive form.

October, 1965
Riverside, California

---

[9] My reservations about his neglect of the Puritan "mind" is implicit in Chapters II through IV and is crucial to my conclusions in Chapter V. Professor Starr also deals with *Moll Flanders* and *Roxana*; he mentions post-conversion changes in Crusoe, but his strategy does not permit him to give close attention to the many significant problems which follow Crusoe's conversion and which raise important artistic questions. His term "autobiography" evidently comprehends many literary forms.

Contents

Preface vii

Acknowledgments xvii

A Note on Texts xix

1. The "Occasion" of *Robinson Crusoe* 1

2. The "Guide" Tradition 23

3. The "Providence" Tradition 51

4. Spiritual Biography 76

5. Metaphor, Type, Emblem, and the Pilgrim
   "Allegory" 93

6. Robinson Crusoe's Rebellion and Punishment .. 125

7. Repentance 148

8. Deliverance 168

An Afterword 202

Index 213

Acknowledgments

In preparing this book, I have been more than usually fortunate in the debts I have accumulated; it was a pleasure to incur the debts, and it is a pleasure to record them. Grants from the University of California, Rice University, and the 1900 Fund of Williams College provided travel assistance and time to write. The staffs of the following libraries and collections were most generous with their time and resources: the McAlpin Collection at Union Theological Seminary, Princeton Theological Seminary Library, Yale University Library, Houghton Library of Harvard University, the Massachusetts Historical Society, the American Antiquarian Society, Chapin Library of Williams College, the Henry E. Huntington Library, and the Fondren Library of Rice University. To Richard Pacella at Union Seminary, Richard Archer at Williams, and Richard O'Keefe at Rice I am grateful for special favors. I must add a more general thanks to the many other libraries which made their holdings available to me by microfilm, photographic reproduction, or interlibrary loan.

To the following people I apologize for recording their contributions only in a list: Jackson I. Cope, Ralph Cohen, Robert F. Gleckner, Stefan Fleischer, Clay Hunt, Joseph N. Riddel, Alan D. McKillop, Carroll Camden,

Robert J. Allen, Donald R. Howard, Charles Thomas Samuels, C. Earl Ramsey, Cooper R. Mackin, Sheridan Baker, Rosalie L. Colie, and Ronald S. Crane. Each contributed personally and strategically to what I have done, although some will wish to argue my conclusions. I wish, too, to record my thanks to John Robert Moore, whose vast knowledge of Defoe has saved me time and effort, and whose personal kindness has been considerable. To Kathleen Williams I owe a special debt. Her judicious counsel was always rewarding, for her patience is inexhaustible.

My family must sometimes have thought they were the ones abandoned on an island; their endurance defies understanding, and the dedication expresses part of my gratitude.

One debt remains—to Aubrey L. Williams. Without him the study would not have begun; without his continuing counsel it could not have attained its present form. Under his direction I finished the original version of this manuscript in May, 1962. Since then he has encouraged, cajoled, and commanded a more precise and more comprehensive form, and his criticism has been unsparing but never unkind. What he touches he recreates. This is a debt which I will not be able to repay for a very long time.

A Note on Texts

The seventeenth- and eighteenth-century writers whom I have quoted in the pages that follow sometimes seem, to a modern eye, more quaint than clear, but I have risked that quaintness to preserve their flavor, for I consider that flavor important to our understanding of their thought processes and our appreciation of their rhetorical and formal influence on literature. I have therefore preserved (except in titles) their italics, spelling, capitalization, and punctuation, with a willingness to sacrifice surface consistency for a more accurate sense of their emphases and rhythms. To avoid distraction, however, I have provided the reader with these aids: correction of obvious printer's errors, transliteration of Greek titles into the English alphabet, and omission of Hebrew characters.

References to *Robinson Crusoe* are taken from the Shakespeare Head edition, published in London in 1927–28, which is the only accurate unmodernized text that is available. Because *Robinson Crusoe* appears in the later volumes of this edition and is spread over two volumes, I have designated references to the earlier volume simply by "A" (followed by a page number), and to the latter by "B"; exact citations are found in the text. For Defoe items not included in this edition, I have used the Maynadier and Aitken editions of Defoe. In citing critical works I have abbreviated two titles: *SA* refers to G. A. Starr's *Defoe and Spiritual Autobiography* (Princeton, 1965), and *EF* represents Maximillian Novak's *Economics and the Fiction of Daniel Defoe* ("University of California English Studies," No. 24; Berkeley and Los Angeles, 1962).

THE RELUCTANT PILGRIM

I

The "Occasion" of
Robinson Crusoe

———◆◆◆◆———

Interpretive problems in eighteenth-century fiction result not so much from a lack of historical interest and
knowledge as from a disguised antihistoricism in applying known facts, for it is often tempting to use history
rather than surrender to it. Defoe study has, I think,
more often settled for the illusion of history than for a
full, rigorous, and sensitive examination of the assumed
contexts of a particular work. Old generalizations have
often seemed more valid than they really are because a
façade of fact has obscured a flawed foundation of logic.
Such methodology has determined the greater part of
Robinson Crusoe scholarship, and I wish to examine
some of the assumptions of this methodology before
arguing another series of contexts which, it seems to me,
are more relevant to *Robinson Crusoe* and to the emergence of the novel as a form.

Knowledge of Defoe's political journalism has opened
some important windows to his art, but misuse of this
knowledge has also led to some serious misconceptions.
One such set of misconceptions involves the "occasion"
of *Robinson Crusoe*, for Defoe students (working upon
assumptions about Defoe's journalistic methods) have
reconstructed on the basis of conjecture the events
which inspired *Robinson Crusoe* and also those which
effected its ultimate form. Alexander Selkirk's four-year

1

sojourn on the desolate island of Juan Fernandez is thus usually considered to be the direct inspiration for *Robinson Crusoe*;[1] and travel books (such as those by Edward Cooke and Woodes Rogers, which give accounts of Selkirk's story) are regarded as formative influences on Defoe's art. This account of Defoe's procedure dates from a generation ago, but because neither its conclusions nor assumptions have been seriously questioned the received opinion is still that articulated by Ernest A. Baker in 1929: "The original incentive to write *Robinson Crusoe* and the central idea of a man left by himself on a desert island . . . came to Defoe from the actual experiences of Alexander Selkirk." The novel must "be considered as [a] fictitious narrative of travel."[2] This account of Defoe's design and procedure is, I think, inadequate and inaccurate; and it seriously misleads us as to the rich and complex traditions which nourish *Robinson Crusoe*—and which influence the form of an emerging genre.

The Selkirk conjecture dates from the middle of the eighteenth century and probably originated from rumors during Defoe's own lifetime.[3] Selkirk's adventure was, of course, well known to Defoe's contemporaries,[4] but

[1] Arthur W. Secord's assumption is typical: "Selkirk undoubtedly furnished Defoe with the central theme of the story,—a fact upon which too much emphasis cannot be laid and which I shall assume as fundamental" (*Studies in the Narrative Method of Defoe* ["University of Illinois Studies in Language and Literature," IX; Urbana, 1924], p. 31).

[2] *The History of the English Novel* (10 vols.; London, 1929–39), III, 147–48, 150.

[3] Late in the eighteenth century, James Beattie relates, as "the account commonly given," an anecdote about Defoe's taking advantage of Selkirk after hearing Selkirk tell his story personally (*Dissertations Moral and Critical* [London, 1783], p. 565). Another rumor during Defoe's lifetime insisted that *Robinson Crusoe* was really written by the Earl of Oxford.

[4] Accounts of it were published not only in standard travel books but

Selkirk was only the most recent of several persons who had endured long isolation in remote places. Many other "miraculous preservations" were recorded during the late seventeenth and early eighteenth centuries, and Defoe probably knew as much about some of them as he did about Selkirk. For example, two other men before Selkirk had been stranded at separate times on Juan Fernandez, one of them for five years.[5] Another castaway, Ephraim How, for nearly a year was supposed dead before he was found alone upon a "rocky desolate Island," where he and two companions had been cast in a storm. After his companions died, he had survived by using materials washed ashore from the shipwreck.[6] A fourth castaway, stranded near Scotland in 1616, had become so notable an *exemplum* that eighteenth-century writers still repeated his story.[7] A fifth spent two years alone on an island near the Isle of Providence after nine of his companions perished either on the island or in trying to swim to civilization.[8] A sixth, Anthony Thatcher, stranded with his wife in 1635 after a ship-

---

in a periodical (*The Englishman*, December 1–3, 1713) and a separately issued tract (*Providence Displayed* [London, 1712]). But Baker probably exaggerates in calling the incident "*the* great sensation of 1712–1713" (*History*, III, 148; italics mine).

[5] See Woodes Rogers, *A Cruising Voyage Round the World* (London, 1712), pp. 129–30.

[6] See Increase Mather, *An Essay for the Recording of Illustrious Providences* (Boston, 1684), pp. 58–64; and William Turner, *A Compleat History of the Most Remarkable Providences, Both of Judgment and Mercy, Which Have Hapned in This Present Age* (London, 1697), p. 110.

[7] See James Janeway, *Token for Mariners, Containing Many Famous and Wonderful Instances of God's Providence in Sea Dangers and Deliverances, in Mercifully Preserving the Lives of His Poor Creatures, When in Humane Probability, at the Point of Perishing by Shipwreck, Famine, or Other Accidents* (London, 1708), pp. 31–33. Janeway retells the story from Adam Olearius, *The Voyages and Travels of the Ambassadors*, trans. John Davies (London, 1662). For a discussion of Janeway, Mather, Turner, and similar books, see Chapter III below.

[8] See Increase Mather, *Essay*, p. 71, and Turner, *Remarkable Providences*, p. 110.

wreck had killed their fellow voyagers, survived by using clothing and debris from the wreck, much as Crusoe does.[9] Many castaways, in fact, underwent hardships much like Crusoe's, reacted to them much as he does, and recounted their experiences in a similarly detailed way.[10]

Any of these castaways might have provided some inspiration for Defoe, but, laying aside for a moment the issue of Defoe's possible indebtedness for facts or incidents, one may question whether any castaway event provided the major impulse for the creation of *Robinson Crusoe*. Selkirk's adventure is closer in time to the publication of *Robinson Crusoe* than are the other adventures I have cited, but almost seven years separate the publication of *Robinson Crusoe* from the publication of accounts of Selkirk. Because the Selkirk conjecture rests primarily on the assumption that Defoe usually "capitalized" on current news events, this seven-year delay would seem crucial. Pope and Horace may have thought a seven-year waiting period advisable, but no journalist would agree.[11]

---

[9] See Mather, *Essay*, p. 13.

[10] See, for example, Janeway, *Token for Mariners*, Mather, *Essay*, or Turner, *Remarkable Providences*.

[11] John Robert Moore's doubts about the Selkirk conjecture on first glance seem to represent an advance over received opinion, but although his conclusion differs from the usual one, his assumptions have the same weakness. Moore does not think that Selkirk's return to England in 1712 weighed heavily on Defoe's mind in 1719, but he does regard as significant the contemporary economic situation in South America. He points out that England's war with Spain had severed trade relations between South America and England's South Sea Company, and he argues that Defoe's interest in stimulating colonization near the Orinoco led him somehow to write *Robinson Crusoe*, though he is not explicit about how *Robinson Crusoe* delivers Defoe's economic message. Moore argues that "if [Defoe] wrote a novel in 1719, it would likely have something to say of the slave trade, of the jealousy between England and Spain, of pirates and mutineers . . . , and of an island near the mouth of the Orinoco River." He adds that "no one could have foreseen how Defoe would develop his hero's solitary life on the island," and concludes that the development was a "'strange surprise' to Defoe himself" (*Daniel Defoe: Citizen of the Modern World* [Chicago,

The assumption that Defoe's writings all stem from current happenings ignores an important distinction about artistic aim. An event often stimulated Defoe to produce a political tract, for his function as a news analyst for the Whigs and/or Tories often demanded that he interpret the current scene so as to influence the English public. But in other kinds of writing Defoe may well have worked differently. In *The Family Instructor*, for example, and in his other clearly moralistic works, he seems to begin with an ideological aim and to accumulate events (factual or fictional) as examples to support his ideology. The antithetical procedures of the journalist and moralist are only two of many authorial procedures in which Defoe may have engaged, for living by his pen cast him in a variety of roles. And to see what sort of role he assumed in writing *Robinson Crusoe*, one needs to determine what kind of book it is, for his procedures are much more likely to have been dictated by his aim in an individual work than by a standard scheme or method applied indiscriminately to his more than five hundred publications.[12]

The assumptions which, when pursued in one direc-

1958], pp. 223–24). Another recent critic, Francis Watson, has also been troubled by standard explanations of Defoe's delay in writing the novel; his reading of *Robinson Crusoe* is salutary, but he offers no new insights about the Selkirk conjecture ("Robinson Crusoe: Fact and Fiction," *Listener*, LXII [October 15, 1959], 617–19).

Earlier scholars suggested that a new 1718 edition of Rogers (which contained the Selkirk story) somehow prompted Defoe, but this suggestion does not seem very helpful unless it is meant to indicate that somehow Defoe's memory was jogged. Only briefly has it been suggested that the inspiration is tied to thematic concerns, and these suggestions have been related to biographical conjectures. Moore thinks that Defoe may have felt some concern for having left the calling (the ministry) for which he prepared at Morton's Academy, or that he may have been concerned with the rebellion of his own son, who showed little inclination to obey his father's wishes.

[12] Maximillian Novak has recently suggested that thematic concerns are primary in several of Defoe's works (see *EF*). Received opinion

tion, lead to the Selkirk conjecture, when pursued in another, lead to more serious misconceptions about *Robinson Crusoe*. Because it is assumed that Defoe began with factual information (largely from travel literature), wove various facts together, embroidered his by now fictional fabric with a semblance of truth, and, finally, tried to pass off the result as a true account, the conclusion is that Defoe desired to imitate his sources and that he wrote in the tradition of fictionalized travel literature. In "placing" *Robinson Crusoe* on the basis of assumptions about Defoe's method rather than on the basis of the book's text, Defoe students have diverted critical attention from relevant materials in other subliterary traditions and have instead defined a context which does a serious injustice to *Robinson Crusoe*, for while Defoe's novel bears some resemblances to travel literature, it differs from that literature in crucial ways.[13]

---

about Defoe is indicated by the response which Professor Novak's suggestion received. See, for example, the review by Michael Shugrue (*JEGP*, LXII [1963], 403–5), in which "Novak's conviction that 'Defoe created his fiction from ideas rather than from incidents'" is regarded as "perhaps the only disturbing note in an otherwise excellent discussion of *Robinson Crusoe*" (p. 404).

[13] At one time, Defoe students recognized that a wider context of traditions nourished *Robinson Crusoe*; they usually mentioned biography, picaresque romance, and moral treatise. But events of the late nineteenth century obscured this contextual richness. The eclipse of Defoe's moral reputation, based on discoveries about his political duplicity, was accompanied by decreasing attention to his ideas, especially moral and religious ones, and emphasis shifted quickly to the adventure-story aspects of his work. At the same time, a new consciousness of the novel as an art form stimulated the desire to evaluate Defoe's contributions to the history of fiction; this desire, combined with the shift of emphasis from ideas to events in Defoe, focused attention on materials from which Defoe could have obtained factual information.

For early discussions of the relationship of Defoe's fiction to other traditions in which he wrote, see George A. Aitken, General Introduction, *Romances and Narratives by Daniel Defoe* (16 vols.; London, 1895), I, xxix ff.; and W. P. Trent, *Daniel Defoe: How To Know Him* (Indianapolis, Ind., 1916), pp. 128, 135, 175. For the rationale behind Defoe source study, see Secord, *Studies*, p. 19.

Source studies of half a century ago are largely responsible for this definition of context. The search for sources turned rather naturally to travel books, for source hunters were first looking for sources of *information*, and travel books were the atlases and geographical encyclopedias of Defoe's day. But the search never really got beyond travel books, for the searchers never really looked beyond factual information, even though they implied that Defoe's dependence on travel books was almost total and influenced even the structure of books like *Robinson Crusoe*. Then too, they were greatly encouraged in their efforts by a strange and surprising bibliographical discovery of 1895.

Defoe's library had been sold a few months after his death in 1731, and although the *Daily Advertiser* for November 13, 1731, mentioned a sale catalogue, no copy of it had been found before 1895, when George A. Aitken located one in the British Museum.[14] The value of the find was considerably diminished, however, by the fact that Defoe's books were grouped with those of an Anglican clergyman, Philip Farewell, and the catalogue failed to distinguish individual ownership.[15] Announcing his find in the *Athenaeum*, Aitken admitted that because of the catalogue's grouping he was "in some cases . . . unable to say positively that a certain book was Defoe's," but he thought that "we shall not be far wrong if we set on one side certain classes of works as Dr. Farewell's and attribute the remainder to [Defoe]." On this assump-

[14] William Lee had noted the sale and lamented the apparent loss of the catalogue. See his *Daniel Defoe: His Life and Recently Discovered Writings 1716–1729* (3 vols.; London, 1869), I, 470–71.

[15] Besides, some of Defoe's books were apparently not sold through the catalogue. The fact that the Farewell-Defoe sale catalogue contains only a few of Defoe's own writings suggests that part of the library had been dispersed before the catalogue was printed. This possibility casts even further doubt on the reliability of the catalogue as a guide to Defoe's reading habits.

tion, Aitken proposed a partial list of Defoe's books, setting aside as Dr. Farewell's "the large array of theological and classical literature." He admitted that "in adopting this course we shall, no doubt, pass over not a few works of Defoe's, but this is unavoidable." [16]

Aitken listed more than three dozen travel books and maps as probably belonging to Defoe, and later source students seem to have trusted Aitken's list completely.[17] Although one cannot be certain, it is likely that Defoe did own most of the books on Aitken's list, but his background and interests make it equally probable that he owned many of the theological and devotional books passed over by Aitken. The authority of Aitken's list has never been seriously challenged, however, and its publication lent considerable support to the growing tendency to pass over Defoe's ideas and his intellectual background in favor of a quest for the sources of his facts in travel literature. During the next thirty years source students found enough "parallels" to "establish" the debt that they had anticipated, and since 1924 (when Arthur W. Secord's *Studies in the Narrative Method of Defoe* was published) their conclusions about Defoe's sources, his method of composition, and his aims have been accepted almost without dissent.[18]

[16] "Defoe's Library," *Athenaeum*, I (1895), 706–7.

[17] Not all scholars who have used Aitken's list have been careful to note the conjecture involved and Aitken's own reservations about the limitations of his list, and their footnotes often cite Aitken's list, not the catalogue itself. Secord and Baker assume the authority of Aitken's judgment. See, for example, Secord, *Studies*, pp. 25, 93, and 104 n.

[18] Since the late nineteen fifties there have been signs of a growing dissatisfaction with received opinion about Defoe (see the Preface to this volume), and, although the conclusions of students of the sources have not been attacked explicitly, the growing awareness of Defoe's artistic complexity has cast some doubt on the generally accepted account of Defoe's imaginative act. But for a recent example of the continuing prominence of source students' procedures, see Gary J. Scrimgeour, "The Problem of Realism in Defoe's *Captain Singleton*" (*HLQ*, XXVII [1963], 21–37).

The placing of *Robinson Crusoe* itself in the tradition of travel literature is ultimately the most misleading implication of such source studies, but an examination of the premises and procedures of such studies warns us to be wary of accepting even their general conclusions. Secord quotes approvingly the belief of Ernest Bernbaum that "originals will ultimately be found for all of [Defoe's] longer narratives,"[19] and although they do not say so openly, most Defoe source students seem to operate from such a premise. Often a subtle suggestion of Defoe's dishonesty hovers just beneath the surface of their analyses, and they seem anxious to attribute a very different role to Defoe's imagination than to the imagination of most writers. As a result, they often attach far too much importance to parallels which are either coincidental or indicate nothing more than the common knowledge of an age—errors which raise serious questions about generalizations we have come to accept.

Secord emphasizes Defoe's debt to Robert Knox's *An Historical Relation of . . . Ceylon* and William Dampier's *A New Voyage Round the World*; among the sources of *Robinson Crusoe*, he lists these as two of six "certain" ones.[20] Yet his conception of what their contribution was and his method of arguing Defoe's debt to them are most revealing. Knox's *Ceylon*, according to Secord, provided Defoe with a number of details about resourcefulness in the face of loneliness and hardship, for although Selkirk's adventure provided the inspiration for Defoe, it did not provide sufficient detail for a long story; Defoe therefore turned to Knox, for his *Ceylon* was "less known but more detailed, and more satisfactory to Defoe for both reasons."[21] Secord admits that

---

[19] P. 18. Secord says that Bernbaum offers this conjecture to explain Defoe's large number of publications.

[20] Knox's book was first published in 1681, Dampier's (in two volumes) in 1697 and 1699.

[21] P. 32. Assumptions about Defoe's deviousness seem clear here, as

Knox's external circumstances differ from Crusoe's—"It is true that Knox was a captive on a large and populous island, that he had a dozen or more fellow Englishmen with him so that occasionally they might converse, and that part of their time they were allowed to live together"—but he thinks these "external differences" may have "blinded investigators to the significance of Knox as a prototype of Crusoe. Both were on islands, both were lonely, and both had their existence to maintain under similar handicaps." Secord then notes the stylistic similarities of the two works ("It was now about the year 1673" [Knox]; "It was now the month of December" [Crusoe]), and he next illustrates Defoe's "borrowing" of events. He notes that "the island experiences of each, for instance, begin at about the same time": Knox's ship is disabled on November 19, 1659, and Crusoe is shipwrecked on September 30, 1659. Both have the ague, both wear out their clothes and try to replace them, Knox uses cocoanut oil in his acquired lamp while Crusoe makes a lamp and uses goat's tallow. After several pages of similar "parallels," Secord admits that "many of these similarities are not in themselves very convincing," but because he is sure that Defoe had read Knox he believes the similarities "become of more than superficial importance." "These matters," he concludes, "were known to Defoe and *could not fail* to find some place in Crusoe's endeavors to work out the problem of existence on his island." [22] Even if writers are a part of all that they have met, one may doubt the value of such source study when no specific debt can be discovered.

------

in Secord's statement elsewhere that "Defoe is compelled in the island story to go to . . . [great] lengths to disguise his materials borrowed from published sources so that those borrowings may not appear" (p. 26).

[22] Pp. 32–39. Italics mine.

As he begins to consider Dampier's *Voyages*, Secord indicates his conception of Defoe's imaginative act: "If we think of Selkirk as having suggested to Defoe the idea of writing a story of desert island life, and of Knox as having provided him with a concrete embodiment of that idea, we shall not go far astray. Defoe's next need would be a large storehouse of details of life under unusual circumstances from which he could clothe the skeleton furnished by Selkirk and Knox. Exactly such a storehouse of details is Dampier's 'Voyages.'" [23] One may doubt the accuracy of this description of creation, but Secord's suggestions about how Defoe used Dampier are even more startling. He does not distinguish clearly between facts and suggestions for episodes, and (as in the Knox argument) his case rests primarily on a long list of inexact parallels and a statement that Defoe must surely have read the book. Defoe might indeed have gotten information about South American geography, climate, and customs from Dampier, but he might just as well have gotten this information from a number of other sources, for to find such facts in both books hardly proves borrowing. As a political journalist aware of his expanding world, as a man of trade, and as a key figure in the formulation of the South Sea Company, Defoe might well have stored facts like these in his head; if not, the men with whom he conversed daily could have supplied him from memory with the kind of information found in Dampier. If one considers this sort of information as a literary source, there is no end of source study, for the encyclopedia and the dictionary (and how would one decide *which* encyclopedia, *which* dictionary?) would be

[23] Pp. 49–50. Secord seems to assume the primacy of printed materials as "sources," apparently believing that an author only makes use of oral information if there is no published word on the subject. Secord also assumes the primacy of English over non-English books, apparently on a similar theory, even though Defoe was conversant with several languages.

only the first sources studied in attempts to uncover an author's "materials." [24]

The rage for parallel passages as evidence of borrowing has blurred the one real contribution of source students: evidence that Defoe grounded his story on the geographical and cultural facts and beliefs of his contemporaries, just as he grounded the psychology and religion of his characters on contemporary belief.[25] But by overstating Defoe's debt to contemporary knowledge and by localizing it too exclusively, they have seriously misled us about Defoe's imagination. Once we are aware of the amount and variety of information available to Defoe about shipwrecks, castaways, and primitive life,

---

[24] The immoderate judgment of source students is suggested by Secord's discussion of two episodes—Crusoe's making of planks and his discovery of a footprint. He finds Crusoe's plank-making to be based either upon Dampier or upon information in the private unpublished journal of Knox, even though both Knox and Dampier describe how two planks are made from a tree and Crusoe is able to make but one. Such a derivation might still be possible if we assume Crusoe's more primitive method to be a part of Defoe's artistic strategy, but to regard these two accounts as the exclusive possibilities seems excessive, especially since the methods are rather obvious and would probably occur to anyone needing a plank.

Secord notes three narratives which contain footprint episodes and attaches much importance to one of them (in Dampier's *Voyages*) because the print evokes fear. Here is his description and interpretation of the incident:

> Dampier and some others, being ashore to kill cattle on the isle of Pines (near Cuba), landed on a sandy bay where they saw "much footing of men and boys; the impressions seemed to be about 8 or 10 days old." "This troubled us a little," said Dampier, who strongly suspected them of being the tracks of Spaniards; "but it being now their Christmas, we concluded that they were gone over to Cuba to keep it there, so we went after our game. . . ." The element of fear is, of course, mild in comparison to that in "Robinson Crusoe," but it is there.

One might, I think, more profitably consider the symbolic overtones of the footprint in *The Pilgrim's Progress*, though not as a "source" in Secord's sense.

[25] I have discussed this subject in my essay, "Friday as a Convert: Defoe and the Accounts of Indian Missionaries" (*RES*, n.s., XIV [1963], 243–48).

we are more likely to be impressed by his ability to distinguish the norm in the experiences of island castaways than to be convinced that he wrote with a specific incident in mind. And by generalizing about Defoe's method on the basis of inexact circumstantial evidence and specious logic, source hunters have successfully (but not accurately) promulgated an image of Defoe as a compiler whose art consists in the crafty fusion of unrelated anecdotes.[26] Lately Defoe's imagination and accomplishment have sometimes been viewed differently, but still too typical is the judgment of the Oxford literary historian of Defoe's time: *Robinson Crusoe*, he says, "is not so much invented as compiled from a number of reports."[27]

The artistry of *Robinson Crusoe* is most seriously maligned, however, not by viewing the novel's parts as somehow dependent upon travel books, but by considering its total form to be patterned on the travel tradition. Source hunters did not set out specifically to "place" *Robinson Crusoe* within any literary tradition, but, because they failed to distinguish between what Defoe worked from (sources) and what he worked toward (artistic aims), their conclusions have had the effect of defining *Robinson Crusoe* itself as a fictionalized travel

[26] The illustrations I have drawn from Secord are, I am afraid, too typical of the evidence and logic of Defoe source study; I choose my examples from Secord not because he is most vulnerable, but because he is the most articulate and detailed of Defoe source students. It now seems almost incredible that Secord's book has been the most influential study of Defoe in the twentieth century; my concern is that these conjectural conclusions have remained unchallenged for so long, have guided a majority of Defoe studies in our time, and have obscured aspects of Defoe's background which bear important implications for the novel as a form.

[27] Bonamy Dobrée, "The Matter-of-Fact Novelist," *Listener*, XLV (1951), 468.

book.[28] Such a definition has serious implications for the structure and meaning of *Robinson Crusoe*, as today's critical commonplaces about the novel clearly demonstrate, for, like the Selkirk conjecture, it suggests that Defoe's art is fact-centered rather than idea-centered. Because questionable assumptions and procedures have led to such a definition, the validity of the conclusion is at least doubtful, but ultimately such a definition has to rest (as Shakespearean studies ought to have taught us) not upon the matter of source materials at all, but upon questions of Defoe's aims and those of the travel writers. Examined on this basis, the categorizing of *Robinson Crusoe* as travel literature is even less valid than other conclusions of Defoe source studies, for (aside from a few surface similarities) *Robinson Crusoe* makes no attempt to follow the conventional pattern of the travel tradition.

Despite their subliterary status, travel books early in the seventeenth century developed a set of distinguishing characteristics almost as rigid as the conventions of a poetic genre: each book tried to answer the same kinds of questions and each was organized in much the same way. Travel books depended for their success on the continued interest of a buying public with specific expectations, and even when their stated purpose was to offer other benefits, travel writers usually fulfilled those expectations.[29] "I know 'tis generally expected," writes Woodes Rogers in his introduction to *A Cruising Voyage*

[28] Even Professor Secord fails to make this important distinction, and slips into a "placing" of *Robinson Crusoe* based on sources: " 'Robinson Crusoe,' finally, is not so much a fictitious autobiography . . . as it is a fictitious book of travel . . ." (p. 111).

[29] Reader expectation was, of course, largely determined by familiarity with Hakluyt, Purchas, and their seventeenth-century successors. For a good recent account of travel literature, see Percy G. Adams, *Travelers and Travel Liars* (Berkeley and Los Angeles, 1962).

Round the World, "that when far distant Voyages are printed, they should contain new and wonderful Discovries with surprizing Accounts of People and Animals,"[30] and like other voyagers, Rogers condemns this popular taste. But, also like others, he satisfies the very expectations which he rails against.

The expectations satisfied by the travel writers are of various kinds. For the reader interested in adventure and strange occurrence, a story like Selkirk's is often included, and though the story is advertised blatantly, usually on the title page, very sparing and professedly grudging attention is given to it in the book itself.[31] Other general readers, like those referred to by Rogers, sought encyclopedic information about exotic places and peoples. The writers, however, seem (or pretend) to be concerned with readers who expect more technical information, and they usually profess that their only desire is to disseminate knowledge which will benefit country and commerce. In practice, all these expectations are ministered to according to a procedural formula with little variation.

Basically, the formula may be described as chronological in movement from place to place, topical in describing the particulars of each place. Much geographical detail is given about the places and about the natives and their customs, but there is relatively little emphasis on event. When an unusual happening (like the finding of Selkirk) is described, the tone retains the same calm, dispassionate quality that characterizes the rest of the

---

[30] P. xiv.

[31] See the title page of Edward Cooke, *A Voyage to the South Sea, and Round the World* (2 vols.; London, 1712). It is always difficult to tell whether the travel writers are sincere in their protestations or whether they are simply repeating a conventional attitude toward reader expectations.

book, for "objectivity" of tone and style characterizes the tradition as a whole.[32] An important aspect of this objectivity is the absence of any informing idea or theme: chronology, replaced by topicality when the narrative is interrupted to describe a particular place, is the only organizing force in the books, thematic considerations being inappropriate to the "pose" or conventions of the form.[33]

Secord notes that Defoe has Crusoe "do a series of things well known in the literature of travel; suffer storm and shipwreck, endure slavery . . . , duplicate the experiences of desert island life, and participate in both commerce and travel," but the resemblances, as Secord's comparison would suggest, are broad ones.[34] Crusoe

[32] See, for example, the Hakluyt Society edition of Lionel Wafer's *A New Voyage & Description of the Isthmus of America* (ed. L. E. Elliott Joyce [Oxford, 1934]), in which the contrast between Wafer's "Secret Report" and the published version of his travels suggests the tone and manner expected of a narrator in travel literature.

[33] The typical narrative first states the author's credentials (previous sea experience) and explains the nature and purpose of the current voyage. The ship is described (size, number and type of sails), and often the more important members of the crew are introduced. The log of days at sea is detailed enough for a curious reader to trace the journey; masses of information are given about daily locations, winds, currents, and factors affecting the speed and direction of the voyage. Unusual events (storms, sighting of other ships, dietary problems, pirate encounters, crew changes) sometimes are given extended treatment, but such anecdotes seldom extend beyond two or three pages. On the other hand, topical descriptions of places and peoples visited are usually lengthy. The amount of detail for each place varies, of course, with the knowledge of the voyager and with the general importance of the particular place, but ordinarily such matters as the kinds of fish inhabiting the coastal waters or native methods of building huts get far more attention than any event. Such information may or may not have sold the books, but travel writers at least pretend to think it did.

[34] Secord, *Studies*, p. 109. The superficiality of the similarities suggests that instead of attempting to imitate the style and format of travel books (which the author of *The Shortest Way with the Dis-*

describes events in chronological order (after a rationale for the first voyage is established) until the "narrator" returns home from his longest, most arduous voyage. The style is matter-of-fact, and the book contains some of the same kinds of "fact" as do the travel books. When Crusoe is at sea, he frequently gives his position, speed, and direction; on land, he describes the animals and the weapons, food, and customs of the natives. About his island he gives full information, detailing its geography, climatic patterns, animal and plant life, and the sailing conditions around it.

But these superficial similarities lose their significance when one notes Defoe's very different emphasis and his considerably different use of similar materials. In *Robinson Crusoe* the facts about various places are never presented as information for its own sake; each fact is introduced because of its function in the narrative situation. Lions and leopards are described in Africa because they represent, in one case, danger to Crusoe and Xury, and, in another, their means of reciprocating the kindness of the natives. The description of the island accumulates gradually as the narrative unfolds; there is no tabular itemizing of descriptive facts. And the island is the only land area which receives anything like a full description. About Brazil the reader learns only a few things pertinent to Crusoe; during the voyage from Sallee, he is given only facts necessary to the narrative. Here, the description serves the narrative; in the travel books, the narrative often merely connects the various descriptions, which are avowedly the most important parts.

Failure to define the rationale and mode of the travel books has led to a general lack of discrimination between

senters could surely do, if he tried) Defoe used features like the title page simply to attract a particular kind of reader, one who was perhaps unlikely to be reached by *The Family Instructor.*

various kinds of books concerned with discovery.[35] *Robinson Crusoe* clearly is more like contemporary adventure stories than like the travel books; information is subordinated to event, and the movement is dramatic. Chronology, simply a convenience in the travel books, becomes for Defoe (as for adventure stories) a conscious device to dramatize development.[36] But even more important, *Robinson Crusoe* has a larger coherence than that produced by the narrative sequence—a coherence which ultimately separates *Robinson Crusoe* from both travel literature and adventure stories, for books in both the latter traditions lack an informing idea which gives a

[35] Throughout this study, I use the term "travel literature" to refer only to published reports of such explorers as Dampier, Rogers, and Cooke. This kind of literature was the chief type used by source students in their work; Secord, for example, lists ten such books as "certain" or "probable" sources of *Robinson Crusoe* and its two sequels. However, he also includes Defoe's *The Storm* and the anonymous *Providence Displayed* as sources of the same type. Their essentially different aims and forms are discussed in Chapter III below.

The term travel literature is sometimes used in a broader, less precise sense; a recent English Institute program on travel literature contained, for example, a paper on science fiction (as voyages of the mind). Under a broad enough definition of the term, *The Pilgrim's Progress*, *The Odyssey*, and almost every eighteenth-century novel could fit the category. But it is important to distinguish between different types of publications dealing with travel, and because source students have usually used the term "travel literature" to refer to reports like Dampier's, I have retained their term here. I use it, however, *only* to describe writings like Dampier's, not those with different aims and methods.

[36] Adventure stories often involve travel to far-off places, but travel books seldom involve much adventure. When writers like Dampier or Cooke do describe exciting events, they de-emphasize the action in accordance with their avowal that their only concern is information. Events only explain delays in the voyage or difficulties of exploration: they do not structure a sequential relation. Chronology is less a conscious structure than a convenience. Adventure stories—factual or fictional, episodic or unified—use chronology to suggest movement; they depend upon a world of time, for they are concerned with event, not fact. Even when based on actual happenings, they obviously filter and formulate experience, organizing it in a more or less dramatic manner; travel books, by contrast, pretend to be almost photographic. The difference is that between a story and a report.

meaning to individual events or to the sequence as a whole. These books seem to lack ideological content, and no thematic meaning can be abstracted from them. Some critics have insisted that *Robinson Crusoe* resembles them in this respect, that it is episodic and lacks fundamental unity. Secord states as a truism that *Robinson Crusoe* "imitates life in its very shapelessness." [37] This view, however, ignores the thematic structure of the novel, a structure set up by the artistic (and ultimately philosophical) rationale for all of Crusoe's wanderings.

Crusoe is never merely an adventurer who goes from place to place, participating in isolated events. Each of his experiences takes on meaning in relation to a pattern set in motion by his "fatal . . . Propension of Nature" (A2)—an irrational inclination to roam. His "rambling Thoughts" (A1) cause him to rebel against parental authority and against his divinely appointed "station"—a rebellion which he interprets as his "Original Sin" (A225). Crusoe views each subsequent tragic event as punishment for his rebellion, and at last concludes that real deliverance from his plight (both physical and spiritual) is only possible when he resigns himself completely to the will of God.

Robinson Crusoe is structured on the basis of a familiar Christian pattern of disobedience-punishment-repentance-deliverance, a pattern set up in the first few pages of the book. Crusoe sees each event of his life in terms of the conflict between man's sinful natural propensity, which leads him into one difficulty after another, and a watchful providence, which ultimately delivers man from himself. Crusoe's continual appraisal of his situation keeps the conflict at the forefront of the action throughout, for his appraisal is not the superficial, unrelated commentary some critics have described, but

[37] P. 232.

rather is an integral part of the thematic pattern set up
by Crusoe's rebellion and the prophecy of his father that
Crusoe "will be the miserablest Wretch that was ever
born" (A6). On the first page Crusoe plunges himself,
through disobedience by reason of pride, into the universal predicament of fallen man; the remainder of the narrative describes that predicament in detail and dramatizes Crusoe's attempts to confront his world—and his
God.

Despite its bias, Charles Gildon's criticism of *Robinson Crusoe* is historically valuable because it suggests
how Defoe's contemporaries viewed his aim and accomplishment. Gildon cites several improbabilities and historical inaccuracies, but his main objection is not to
Defoe's passing off fiction as fact, but to the book's moral
and religious point of view:

> I am far from being an enemy to the Writers of Fables,
> since I know very well that this Manner of Writing is not
> only very Ancient, but very useful, I might say sacred,
> since it has been made use of by the inspired Writers
> themselves; but then to render any Fable worthy of being
> received into the Number of those which are truly valuable,
> it must naturally produce some useful Moral . . . but this
> of *Robinson Crusoe* . . . is design'd against . . . publick
> good.[38]

A Roman Catholic turned deist turned Anglican, Gildon
was eager to defend what he now considered the orthodox faith, and his charges are directed primarily against
a theological point of view which seems to him unsound

---

[38] *The Life and Strange Surprizing Adventures of Mr. D——
DeF—— of London, Hosier* . . . (London, 1719), p. 2; reprinted
in *Robinson Crusoe Examin'd and Criticis'd*, ed. Paul Dottin (London
and Paris, 1923), p. 82. Gildon does not accuse Defoe of failing to
inculcate a moral, but of not pointing a *useful* moral.

and ultimately dangerous.[39] He attacks Defoe's use of
the supernatural, and (because he holds a very different,
much less orthodox view of God's role in human affairs)
he takes issue with almost every religious attitude in the
novel. Gildon's motives may have been those of personal
jealousy and party animus, but the charges themselves
are still revealing, for they suggest that Gildon viewed
the book in religious terms and felt that he must attack it
ideologically rather than simply expose its fictional
nature.

In his statement about *Robinson Crusoe's* popularity,
Gildon suggests that other contemporary readers also
saw the book in religious terms. People who buy the
book, says Gildon, leave it "as a legacy with the *Pilgrim's
Progress*, the *Practice of Piety* and *God's Revenge
against Murther.*" [40] The juxtaposition and implied comparison is a sneer at the level of Defoe's readership and
suggests (from Gildon's point of view) condemnation by
association, for the books he mentions all share a Puritan
view of morality and theology. Each of them was well
known to Gildon's contemporaries. By 1719, Lewis
Bayly's *Practice of Piety* (1613) had reached its fiftieth
edition and was probably the best-known Puritan manual of piety and conduct. John Reynolds' *The Triumphs
of God's Revenge against Murther* (1621–24) had gone

---

[39] For an account of Gildon's life and a discussion of his various
religious positions, see Dottin's "Life of Gildon" in *Crusoe Examin'd
and Criticis'd*. Dottin says that Gildon was resolved "to reap the ut-
most benefit from his conversion" (p. 22).

[40] P. x; in Dottin, p. 72. Because these words are placed in the
mouth of "Defoe" in a dialogue, one might suspect that Gildon was
simply being facetious—if he did not later attack the book for its
theological position on various matters.

In *Tom Jones*, Fielding suggests a similar contemporary classification,
even though (like Gildon) he holds very different religious and philosophical positions. Note the kind of books Fielding lists alongside
Robinson Crusoe in Bk. VIII, chap. v. For a brief discussion of Fielding's different artistic assumptions, see below, Afterword.

through fewer editions, but it was well known for assigning to providence a particularly active role in human affairs. Bunyan's book, then as now, seemed to epitomize the Puritan view of life.

Ultimately, *Robinson Crusoe* is much closer to *The Pilgrim's Progress* than to the other two books, but it bears a significant relationship to the traditions in which all three of the books belong. In his Author's Preface, Defoe gives two aims of *Robinson Crusoe*: (1) to present *"a religious Application of Events . . . [for] the Instruction of others by this Example,"* and (2) *"to justify and honour the Wisdom of Providence in all the Variety of our Circumstances . . ."* (Avii). These moral and ideological aims have often been regarded as Defoe's afterthoughts or rationalizations; modern scholars have seemed reluctant to take seriously a man who can "lie like truth." But Defoe's Preface, like Gildon's scornful comparison, suggests the connection with Puritan religious traditions; once examined, these traditions illuminate both the theme and structure of *Robinson Crusoe* and, ultimately, the development of the novel as a literary form.

II

The "Guide" Tradition

To many of his contemporaries, the period of Defoe's life (1660–1731) seemed a pivotal point in history. Behind lay the peaks of western culture, the golden years of the arts, of philosophy, religion, and morality, an inspiring heritage which many men began to fear was gradually eroding away. To many, it seemed that the vast changes taking place in the structure of their world indexed a breakdown of the traditional values which had guided the giants of the past. The breakdown seemed to exist on many levels. Men of letters like Pope and Swift envisioned the literary heritage of western man being pillaged and destroyed by swarms of dwarfish hacks, who, often ignorant of the cultural past and almost always disrespectful toward it, sapped its very life. Men of the church, confused and wearied by intestine wars, awoke to more fearsome challenges from without the church, challenges which questioned the very basis of the Christian faith. Political traditionalists viewed a nation racked by two "peaceful" revolutions, a government shorn forever of its once-clear seat of power, a new political system in which influence was wielded by a new breed of spies, pamphleteers, and backdoor advisers. The new science, a new economics, a shifting, tenuous social construct—all produced revolutions in traditional ways of thinking, and men became concerned about (and often confused by) the rapidity of changes which were shaking, to the very foundations, edifices which tradition had built. To many—however they might disagree about causes—Pope's vision of classical dedication diminished to bestial defecation, of Christian eschatology become secular scatology, seemed apt indeed.

Of particular concern to those who viewed the atmosphere of change was the decaying moral climate, for it seemed to many that morals were breaking down under the challenge to traditional ideas and values. A peculiar sense of moral urgency characterizes the writings of the period, and often they express a profound pessimism about the direction of both human ideals and conduct. From a later point of view, some of this concern may seem exaggerated and unwarranted, but the urgency with which the Augustan mind faced the situation is everywhere apparent. The cause of disorder was variously placed, but the diagnosis—whether by Swift or Defoe, Archbishop Tillotson or Dissenter Daniel Williams—was largely the same. "Surely," says Tillotson, "never in any Age was the sign of the coming of the Son of Man more glaring and terrible than in this degenerate Age wherein we live, when almost all Sorts of Men seem to have broke loose from all obligations to Faith and Trust." [1]

"Reform" became a popular watchword at the beginning of the eighteenth century, and popular "societies"

[1] *The Works of the Most Reverend Dr. John Tillotson* (9th ed.; London, 1728), Sermon XXII, p. 189. Defoe is now commonly regarded as a "liberal" or "modernist" who was in part responsible for the declining respect for tradition, but like his more conservative contemporaries he repeatedly shows strong concern about the loss of moral standards and the disruption of established traditions and institutions. Maximillian Novak has recently contended that Defoe's economic ideas were "unquestionably conservative" (*EF*). Something of the conflict between modern and traditional ideas within Defoe is suggested in Hans H. Anderson, "The Paradox of Trade and Morality in Defoe" (*MP*, XXXIX [1941], 23–46), and in Martin Price, *To the Palace of Wisdom* (New York, 1964). Defoe's attitudes are not always consistent, and sometimes his conduct contradicts his pronouncements; but those who wish to discover the "real" Defoe need to keep in mind

for the suppression of vice sprang up everywhere. A 1700 pamphlet says that thirty-nine of these societies were operating in and about London and Westminster, with ten others in Dublin.[2] Pamphlets denouncing such vices as swearing, drunkenness, and Sunday commerce were very popular during the later years of William's reign and the early years of Anne's; Trevelyan says that "scores of thousands of ['reform'] tracts" were issued and that "tens of thousands of successful prosecutions" followed.[3] Even if these estimates exaggerate the actual situation, they point to the popularity of "reform" and to the zeal with which reformers pursued their cause. English pulpits soon resounded with violent imprecations against decadent morality, and, according to many acute contemporary observers, so much emphasis was everywhere placed upon "manners" and conduct that Christianity itself was in danger of being reduced to a mere ethical system.[4]

The popular outcry against moral laxity flourished

---

the basic attitudes which guided Defoe in significant choices. Those who emphasize Defoe's disregard for tradition and the inherited social structure should be reminded that his family name was Foe, and that Daniel added the more "aristocratic" prefix, vaguely claiming that he was descended from an old French family—a claim which seems to suggest Defoe's ambivalence in desiring the authority of traditions while modifying these traditions within an inch of their lives.

[2] A Short Account of the Several Kinds of Societies Set Up of Late Years . . . [London, 1700], p. 1. For an excellent discussion of the moral concern of the late seventeenth century, see Dudley W. Bahlman, The Moral Revolution of 1688 (New Haven, Conn., 1957).

[3] G. M. Trevelyan, English Social History (London, 1942), pp. 327–28.

[4] Charles Morton, Defoe's mentor, advises ministers: "Let your Discourses be mostly Practical, both as to the Subjects, and Manner of Handling. 'Tis but a Crack, for young Divines to be much medling with Controversies" (Advice to Candidates, as quoted by Edmund Calamy in A Continuation of the Account of [Those] Ejected and Silenced after the Restoration [2 vols.; London, 1727], I, 206). Robinson Crusoe also shows disdain for detailed theological argument, reporting that "all the Disputes, Wranglings, Strife and Contention,

mainly during the first quarter of the eighteenth century, but a tradition of concern, largely designed by the Puritan mind,[5] had taken literary form long before. Throughout the seventeenth century, books such as Lewis Bayly's *Practice of Piety* offered directions to unbelievers for finding the path to the "celestial Canaan" and provided Christians with a guide to daily life and conduct. After the Restoration, as Puritan gloom about morality deepened, guide books of this type became increasingly popular. Bayly's book had reached a fifty-third edition by the time that Defoe published *Robinson Crusoe*, and

---

which has happen'd in the World about Religion, whether Niceties in Doctrines, or Schemes of Church Government . . . were all perfectly useless" to Friday and him and "to all the rest of the World" (B7). Typical of the concern over the new ethical emphasis is this lament by Dr. Philip Bisse in 1716: "Of late years a caution has been dinned into the ears of the clergy that they would do well to let alone the doctrinal and mysterious parts of religion, as nice, useless, and oftentimes contentious speculations, and instead thereof to preach to the people only good, plain, practical morality, upon good moral principles levelled to their capacities" (*Pride and Ignorance the Ground of Errors of Religion*, pp. 26–27, as quoted by Charles J. Abbey and John H. Overton, *The English Church in the Eighteenth Century* [2 vols.; London, 1878], I, 325).

[5] I use the term "Puritan" to describe an attitude toward life, that attitude best defined by Perry Miller's work on American and William Haller's work on English Puritanism. This attitude was often found within the Anglican community during the late seventeenth and early eighteenth centuries, partly because of political conditions and partly because some persons who were essentially Puritan in outlook never desired to leave the Established Church. Treatises and sermons by Anglican clergymen and even bishops sometimes take positions usually described as Puritan, and in this study I have quoted freely from Anglicans whose theological or ethical position supports the Puritan background out of which Defoe writes. Anglican and Dissenter are here used as opposites; Puritan never implies non-Anglican.

Starr (SA) de-emphasizes Defoe's Puritan heritage in order to support his claim that Defoe's structural debt is to a broader, less distinctive kind of spiritual history. While concern over contemporary morality and new philosophical challenges often produced a related response in Christendom generally, I find the distinctively Puritan formulations of concern most significant for Defoe and for the novel generally (see especially Chapter V below).

new guides were continually being written. Typically, these guides bewailed contemporary moral chaos and found it indicative of a deep-seated spiritual disease. Reform depended upon individual changes of heart which could be wrought only by Christian conversion and by individual efforts of the converts to increase their piety and to purify their conduct.[6] Guides usually began with an exhortation for the ungodly to repent and for Christians to dedicate themselves to renewed efforts of piety, and then went on to discuss the Christian's various duties during his sojourn on earth.[7]

Guide literature was the major outlet for practical divinity in the seventeenth century, especially as condi-

[6] Dedication to a spiritual life implied a reformation of conduct, and repentance and conversion came to mean approximately the same thing, for each term implied both a spiritual and moral change. According to Chillingworth: "Repentance if it be rightly understood, and according to the sense of the word in Scripture, is an effectual conversion from all sin to all holiness" (Works [Oxford, 1858], II, 470; quoted by H. R. McAdoo, The Structure of Caroline Moral Theology [London, 1949], p. 121).

Tracts written during the enthusiasm for the "reformation of manners" seem to differ in depth from earlier guide treatises and tend to attack individual abuses rather than underlying spiritual causes. It may be informative that Defoe, though he often shows interest in moral reform and wrote several guide books himself, was not very much interested in the societies. In 1707 he joined a society in Edinburgh, but soon stopped attending (see Charles Eaton Burch, "Defoe and the Edinburgh Society for the Reformation of Manners," RES, XVI [1940], 306–12). In The Review Defoe criticizes the societies for fighting results rather than causes: "It will be none of my business to exclaim against the poor despicable wretches, whose oaths, drunkenness, and other wickedness are the common subject of our Society for Reformation. . . . If you will reform the Nation, you that call yourselves reformers, bear with me to tell you, you must first reform yourselves" (VI, No. 4 [April 7, 1709], in the facsimile reprint edited by Arthur W. Secord [22 vols.; New York, 1938], XVI, 15–16).

[7] Sometimes a distinction was made between guides for the unconverted ("persuasion" treatises like Richard Baxter's Call to the Unconverted) and those for Christians ("direction" treatises like Baxter's A Christian Directory). See Baxter's discussion in Reliquiae Baxterianae: Or, Mr. Richard Baxter's Narrative of the Most Memorable Passages of His Life and Times (ed. Matthew Sylvester [London, 1696], p. 114). But in most treatises the aims were combined.

tions increasingly dictated (according to churchmen and moralists) a need for man's direction in the wilderness of this world. "Take heed, walke charily," advises John Welles in his *Soules Progress to the Celestiall Canaan*, "for the way is dangerous, craggy, and irksome, full of windings and turnings out, and many allurements in the way to hinder thy passage. . . ." [8] If man was to navigate successfully the narrow way to heaven, he needed a proper guide, like the Israelites moving toward their promised land. "I have determined," writes Richard Baxter at the beginning of *A Christian Directory*, "by God's assistance, to write . . . for the Use of . . . [those who wish to be good Christians], and to give them from Gods Word those *plain Directions*, which are suited to the several Duties of their lives, and may Guide them safely in their *Walk with God*, to Life Eternal." [9]

For his safe conduct during his journey, the Christian needed both awareness of his plight and arms for his warfare. Guide literature therefore warned man of the numerous evils he faced—the dangers inherent in his own depravity and in the hostile nature of his world, for even though God ruled the world by his providence, it was a fallen world, inimical to the aims of spiritual man. For protection against the forces of evil, guides offered the armor of God's word, reasoned argument against various temptations, and, occasionally, the instructive example of others who had avoided the most dangerous pitfalls.

Most guides described sources of difficulty common to all men: neglect of the ordinary duties of their station or place, discouragement due to failure or afflictions, uncertainty because of the conflicting advice of companions. But often, too, guides were designed for groups who faced particular kinds of problems and who could be

[8] Fol. B3ʳ.
[9] P. 2.

given more specific directions. Special guides advised, for example, tradesmen (*The Tradesman's Calling,* 1684), farmers (*The Husbandman's Calling,* 1668; *Husbandry Spiritualized,* 1669), weavers (*Weavers Pocket Book,* 1695), and seamen (*Navigation Spiritualized,* 1664; *The Sea-Mans Direction,* 1640; *The Religious Marriner,* 1700; *The Seaman's Monitor,* 1709). These more specialized guides often compared man's spiritual plight to physical situations common to the group addressed. The farmer, for example, was asked to visualize, while cultivating his crops, the necessity of nursing the seeds of his faith by watering them with meditation and by exposing them to the sun of God's word; the seaman was advised to interpret storms and tempests as emblems of spiritual danger, lest his soul "split itself upon some dangerous Rock" and "of Faith and conscience ship wrack make." [10]

Guides for seamen (to examine a single type) tried to minister to the problems of men whose typical experiences ("barren Desarts, and dark Prisons . . . Beds of Languishing and Storms at Sea") should "by an almost irresistable Necessity, drive the profanest and most profligate Wretches to their Prayers. . . ." [11] But in contemporary times, instead of being a cradle of devo-

[10] John Flavell, *Navigation Spiritualized; or a New Compass for Seamen* (Newburyport, 1796; first published, 1664), p. 48. The term "emblem" deserves special attention. In modern usage it has become a somewhat modish term to describe a variety of forms and procedures in literature and related arts. Seventeenth-century Puritans, however, use the term in a limited and usually precise way, to describe objects in the natural world which have spiritual significance. For Puritans, emblems become substitutes for icons. Unable to create objects to symbolize spiritual truths (because such action would usurp a divinely reserved prerogative), they permit themselves to isolate and interpret objects and events created by God. I use the term here, and throughout this study, in this Puritan sense; the concept behind the term is significant, for (as I shall argue in Chapter V) the Puritan habit of perceiving objects and events as emblematic becomes transformed into a fictional technique.

[11] George Stanhope, *The Seaman's Obligations to Gratitude and a Good Life* (London, 1699), p. 4.

tion, the sea had gained a reputation for "transforming Men into Infidels and Brutes." [12] A seaman had to be especially wary of companions who, like those on Crusoe's first voyage, would cause him to forsake high resolutions and lead him instead into debauchery and blasphemy. Even the slightest relaxation of his spiritual principles could be disastrous, for the wind and waves were under the command of a God who could, at any moment, require an account of the seaman's soul. He should, therefore, regard each deliverance from danger as a warning. "How should we think," exhorts John Ryther in his *Sea-Dangers and Deliverances Improved* (1683), "O what a Danger was I in at this time by such a Storm at Sea! by such a Sickness ashore! not only my Life in danger, but Lord, was not my Soul in danger? . . . Thy Souls danger was the greatest danger; hadst thou been drowned at such a time, thy soul had been shipwrackt to all eternity." [13] But if the seaman's station involved special dangers, it also provided exceptional opportunities; he could undoubtedly recall many instances of God's protecting guidance and care, and he should "witness" these experiences for the edification of others. His travels also gave him greater than usual opportunities to spread the Christian faith, and he ought to attempt to convert those whose lands he visited. Ultimately, of course, the seaman was reminded of the temporality of his "calling" and the fragility of his bodily existence; like men in all stations, he needed to employ his time and talents fruitfully so that when his earthly

---

[12] *Ibid.*, p. 23. Seamen's guides sometimes quoted, as an "ancient saying," *Qui nescit orare, discat navigare.* Flavell says the modern version might well read: "He that would learn to be profane, to drink, and swear, and dishonour God, let him go to sea" (*Navigation Spiritualized*, p. 4).

[13] Ryther's treatise was appended to the 1683 edition of *Mr. James Janeway's Legacy to His Friends.* The quoted passage is from page 96 of the combined edition.

voyages were completed he would be fully prepared for his inheritance on the shores of eternity.

During the moral crisis of the late seventeenth century, guide literature increased in both bulk and intensity, for the gloom of Puritan moralists was reflected in an increasingly frenzied effort to get at the source of moral disease, to placate a God who would surely punish the world severely for its wickedness. Guide literature had always been more or less aimed at youth (for it sought to provide direction for man's life from beginning to end), but shortly after the Restoration youth became a more explicit center of attention. Many guides were now addressed specifically to young people, urging them—in the name of God, country, and their own prudential well-being—toward an early commitment to a life of piety. Previous years had offered *The Plain Mans Pathway to Heaven* (by Arthur Dent, 1601), *Some General Directions for a Comfortable Walking with God* (by Robert Bolton, 1625), and *The Christian-mans Calling* (by George Swinnock, Parts I and II, 1662; III, 1665). More typical of later years are *The Young Man's Guide, through the Wilderness of This World to the Heavenly Canaan* (by Thomas Gouge, 1670), *The Young Man's Duty* (by Richard Kidder, 1670), and *The Young Man's Calling* (by Samuel Crossman, 1678). In the nineties, even greater attention was given to youth guides,[14] and the trend continued for at least two decades into the eighteenth century.

[14] See, for example, Daniel Williams, *The Vanity of Childhood and Youth* (1691); William Burkitt, *The Poor Man's Help and Young Man's Guide* (ca. 1692); Timothy Cruso, *The Necessity and Advantage of an Early Victory over Satan* (1693), and *God the Guide of Youth* (1695); Cotton Mather, *Early Religion* (1694); and Increase Mather, *Solemn Advice to Young Men* (1695).

Whether youth of this period were more impious and degenerate than those of other generations may be questionable, but many contemporary moralists thought that they were. "The days wherein we live are extremely Evil," says Timothy Cruso (a fellow student of Defoe's at Morton's Academy, Newington Green) in 1695,

> but yet we have a sad and doleful Prospect of the *next Age* becoming *worse,* if God do not by some effectual means stop the Wicked Course of the *Rising Generation.* We see such Crouds and Swarms of *young Ones* continually *posting down* to Hell, and *bringing up* so much of Hell in the midst of us, that both in compassion to them and to our Native Countrey, we cannot but use some Christian endeavors to open the Eyes of these *Mad Prodigals,* and to fetch them home.[15]

To others, equally concerned about an impending moral catastrophe, young people seemed the only possible hope for the nation's regeneration—if they could be properly stimulated and trained. But whether they considered youth the symbol of hope or despair, moralists agreed upon the urgency of stimulation and training. "Our youth will be the plague, or hope of this land, in this great crisis," writes Daniel Williams in 1691; "If our youth grow yet more profligate, God is about to leave us! If we recover our youth, we may hope he'll yet continue amongst us. Young ones, I would be earnest with you; for God indicates his mind to England by you." [16]

By the beginning of the rather general assault upon public "manners" and morals in the early years of the eighteenth century, a strong (and rather carefully defined) tradition of guide literature for youth had been established. Central to all of the treatises is the belief

---

[15] *God the Guide of Youth,* pp. 5–6.
[16] *The Vanity of Childhood and Youth,* in *Discourses on Several Important Subjects* (5 vols.; London, 1738–50), V, 283.

that proper guidance at the critical youthful stage of life sets the direction of future faith and conduct. "You who would make a safe and prosperous Voyage over this *deep and wide Sea* of Temptations," advises Timothy Cruso, "ought to be well-fortified against the tempter at your *first setting out*." [17] Most writers recognize that repentance may occur later in life and that a true conversion experience later will erase one's debt of sin, but youthful mischoice of a life course is blamed for the state of the nation's morals. Besides, neglect of early spiritual promptings can produce dire personal consequences. "*Those . . . who do not seek God Early*," says Benjamin Wadsworth, ". . . are Rebellious against God, and Injurious to themselves. . . . When Persons spend the Morning of their Days, their Youthful Years in neglecting to Seek God; they . . . lay a Foundation for unutterable Sorrow and Distress." [18] The crucial choices at the edge of adulthood are considered the major formative factors for later life, and most treatises thus aim for youth who are just beyond firm parental control.

All wrong choice represents tacit rebellion against God's will, for God's providential rule over the world extends to the life of every individual, and an individual's failure to follow that plan constitutes not a sin of omission, but active rebellion. But the choice of a marriage partner and the choice of a career are particularly crucial, for they commit one to a course which is not easily altered. In marriage, an individual should prayerfully seek divine guidance, heed the advice of others (particularly those, like his parents, whose stations are above his), and weigh carefully all personal and practical considerations, especially such matters as the spouse's religious commitment. The choice of a "calling"

[17] *An Early Victory over Satan*, p. 21.
[18] *Early Seeking of God* (Boston, 1715), p. 16.

is even more important. Youth guides often focus on this choice as the most singularly crucial one which a youth makes. Mischoice here can be fatal, and inexperience and pride make a young man particularly susceptible to mischoice. "Stubborn *pride* in chusing of *our own ways*," says Timothy Cruso, ". . . is the *plague of unbridled youth.*" [19]

The concept of the calling, while much talked about, has not always been clearly understood. Fundamentally, it means an insistence that all men's vocations are chosen for them by God and that every man is appointed to a specific place in the socioeconomic structure of his world. But the concept has taken on intense emotional coloration in most modern minds, for knowledge about it derives almost exclusively from the work of Max Weber and R. H. Tawney, who trace the flourishing of capitalism along social and geographical lines etched by Protestantism and who attribute to the concept of the calling a major influence. [20] The Weber-Tawney hypothesis places great emphasis upon the uniqueness of sanctifying secular vocation, regards this sanctification as a distinctly Protestant phenomenon, and assigns the concept a major role in bringing about modern economic, social, and political upheavals. Later scholarship has cast serious doubt on the entire hypothesis, [21] but regardless of the general validity of the correlation that Weber and

[19] *An Early Victory over Satan*, p. 25.

[20] Max Weber, *The Protestant Ethic and the Spirit of Capitalism*, trans. Talcott Parsons (New York, 1958); R. H. Tawney, *Religion and the Rise of Capitalism* (New York, 1958). For a good discussion of the concept's application in the seventeenth century, see William Haller, *The Rise of Puritanism* (New York, 1938).

[21] See, for example, Hugh Trevor-Roper, *The Gentry 1540–1640* (London, 1953); and H. M. Robertson, *Aspects of the Rise of Economic Individualism* (New York, 1959).

Tawney describe, their account of how the concept worked in the seventeenth century has been extremely misleading.

Weber traces the term "calling" (in German, *Beruf*) to Luther's translation of Jesus Sirach 11:20 and says that the concept develops gradually in Luther's thought and in that of his sixteenth- and seventeenth-century successors. But, as Weber's critics have pointed out, there is nothing really distinctive about the concept as Protestantism articulates it: medieval Catholicism teaches much the same idea, often in identical terms.[22] Ultimately, in fact, the concept derives from the social stratification of the Middle Ages and becomes a justification

[22] For an excellent rebuttal of Weber, see Robertson, *Economic Individualism*, esp. pp. 1–32.

The Weber-Tawney hypothesis has cast its shadow broadly and often strangely. Even such a fine scholar as Maximillian Novak once slips into this formulation of the concept's development: "Long before 1719 . . . Protestant sects had changed Luther's doctrine [of the calling] into a proof of salvation by works, or more specifically, by work. Because he believed that salvation and election depended only upon God's grace, the Protestant appealed to the evidence of worldly success as visible proof of God's favor" (*EF*, pp. 41–42). Here Professor Novak fuses four related but separate ideas: the concept of the calling, the doctrine of work, salvation by works, and prosperity as proof of salvation.

The prosperity which might result from diligence was sometimes, but not often, cited as evidence of election. Prosperity as proof of election was actually only an inference from a negative theological premise: those who did not labor faithfully were not chosen; but it did not follow logically that all those who did labor (and succeed) were chosen. Seventeenth-century Protestantism knew all about Job and about Lazarus' rich friend.

Protestant theologians—Puritan and non-Puritan—did often emphasize the secular benefits of Christianity and often used the prudential argument. Christianity, Tillotson says, "is the greatest friend of our temporal interests" (Sermon III, in *Works*, I, 409; quoted by Abbey and Overton, *English Church*, I, 333). But Tillotson knew well that material success was no evidence of election: "Outward Blessings are so promiscuously dispensed, that no Man can certainly be concluded to be a good Man from any Happiness he enjoys in this Life; and the Prosperity of good Men is usually on purpose . . . shadowed and mixed with afflictions . . ." (*Works*, Sermon XXIII, p. 207).

of that structure. The concept assumes a social world in which every man has a specific place or station (doctrine of "degree") and gives this order a teleologically oriented theological basis. Aiming to conserve a stratified society, the concept stresses the danger of defying God's plan and of thus destroying the order. This is the way Puritans applied the concept, at least until Defoe's time, for not even the fabled "medieval mind" was more concerned than they with preserving divine order on earth. Their emphasis is constantly upon the limitations which the concept puts upon the individual. Stay in your calling, they urge, for leaving it is rebellion against God's order. Significantly, their discussions of calling often lapse into discussions of station; they do not distinguish between the medieval Catholic formulation and the updated Protestant term, for their concern, like Luther's or Calvin's, is a conservative one.[23]

Youth guides place heavy emphasis upon preserving the social order through loyalty to one's calling. Whatever a person's station in life proved to be, he was expected to be faithful to it and remain content that he was fulfilling God's will for his life. Servants were as necessary to the divine order as kings, and everyone was expected to show Christian contentment with his lot. "Be well satisfied," John Flavell advises, "in that Station and

[23] The concept took support from both theology and philosophy. According to Stephen Charnock, "As there is a distinction of several Creatures, and several Qualities in them for the common good of the World; so among Men there are several Inclinations and several Abilities . . . for the common advantage of human society . . . ; one man is qualified for one Employment, another marked out by God for a different Work . . ." (Works [2d ed., 2 vols.; London, 1699], I, 222). Lovejoy points out that "the doctrine of the Chain of Being . . . gave a metaphysical sanction to the injunction of the Anglican catechism; each should labor truly 'to do his duty in that state of life'—whether in the cosmical or the social scale—'to which it shall please God to call him.' To seek to leave one's place in society is . . . 'to invert the laws of order' " (The Great Chain of Being [New York, 1936], p. 206).

Imployment in which Providence hath placed you, and do not so much as *wish* your selves in another . . . [for] Providence is wiser than you. . . ."[24] Avoiding or leaving one's calling could even cause God to inflict direct punishment. John Goodman, citing the parable of the prodigal son, describes discontent with one's place as "mutinous thoughts" which are "the seminalities of all rebellion." The prodigal, typical of sinful man, "grows male-content with his condition; and finding himself restrained, the proud waves of his passion rage and swell against all that bounds and checks them. . . . He finds his condition not to his mind, and . . . he is tempted to run upon adventures. . . ." The prodigal's dissatisfaction, notes Goodman, is like that of man's first parents.[25] The sin of Adam and Eve is, in fact, often described in these terms to emphasize the gravity (and disastrous consequences) of discontent.

In such a climate of seriousness, one did well to "choose" one's station carefully, for although "choice" simply meant ascertaining God's will and then abiding by it, one needed to proceed very carefully to discover God's plan. Youth guides devote a great deal of space to factors a youth must consider, for God normally revealed his will not through a dramatic supernatural "call" like that of Samuel (although he could) but in ways less dramatic and more subtle. Since his plan was not capricious but rational, he used men in stations for which their natural abilities and background prepared them. A young man should therefore prayerfully consider every

[24] *Divine Conduct: Or, the Mysterie of Providence* (London, 1678), p. 84. Italics mine. Flavell's statement is typical of the growing concern (of both Anglicans and Dissenters) with Christian contentment, as the social structure becomes more fluid.

[25] *The Penitent Pardon'd* (4th ed.; London, 1694), pp. 86–88. Under certain conditions, a person might change his calling with impunity. But he had to be certain that God now *willed* a change.

conceivable factor, and he should seek the advice of
elders whose experience tempered their judgment. Birth
and family were important considerations, for they influenced a person's qualifications, but a young person was
not advised to follow a particular occupation simply because his father did. Rather, he should weigh various
possibilities. According to *The Young Man's Calling*, the
wise young man should seek a calling which is *"in its
nature*, just and lawful. *In its discharge*, comporting
with a publick good, and serviceable to his private support. *In its kind* . . . in some measure suited to his own
abilities and inclinations." [26] The judgment of others,
especially parents, could aid the youth greatly, but ultimately the proper calling would become clear to the
youth himself if he considered rationally all factors and
sincerely sought divine guidance. And having reached
his decision in this manner, he could rest assured that his
calling was "the Sphaer and Station which God hath set
him in." [27]

The role of the parent in the decision is somewhat
ambiguous. Some writers rest the responsibility directly
on the youth's father; others picture the wise and God-
fearing father as more of a guide and counselor, a vehicle through whom God's will is clarified. But because
God revealed his will to those who sought to discover it,
the youth and his parent would inevitably reach the
same decision if both sought divine guidance; and, for
practical purposes, a youth could safely rely upon his
parents' wishes.[28]

[26] Samuel Crossman, *The Young Man's Calling, or the Whole Duty
of Youth* (London, 1683), pp. 63–64.
[27] *Ibid.*, p. 64.
[28] Professor Novak is technically incorrect when he says that Crusoe
refuses "to accept the position in life chosen for him by his father"
(*EF*, p. 39). Crusoe, reflecting typical Puritan doctrine, considers his
station chosen for him by "God and nature" and regards his father's

The general necessity of paternal respect and filial obedience is one of the most important emphases in youth guides, and young persons are urged to remain obedient even after reaching maturity and becoming technically free of parental control.[29] Obedience to an earthly father, God's deputy in the family, preserves the divine order, and rebellion against him is equivalent to rebellion against God. "God makes it a command . . . [to] *Honour our Father* and *Mother*," says William Fleetwood, "And to show us how fit it is to . . . obey our Parents, God calls himself throughout the Holy Scriptures our *Father*, and from that Title and Relation calls for our Obedience."[30] The parable of the prodigal son is frequently invoked to identify earthly father with heavenly Father; filial disobedience is emblematic, as in the parable, of rebellion against God. "You cannot sin against your parents [but] that you sin against *heaven* also," says Timothy Cruso. "Such as *obey their Par-*

---

advice as a result of this divine plan. Crusoe's father forbids him to go to sea but does not insist on a specific calling; throughout, Crusoe apparently regards his father as a divine deputy, and he nowhere implies that parental choice is the ultimate determinant of one's station. Charles Gildon (perhaps willfully) also seems not to understand this point, for he complains that parents should have no control over sons as old as Crusoe (see Paul Dottin's edition of *Robinson Crusoe Examin'd and Criticis'd* [London and Paris, 1923], pp. 84–85). Richard Steele, whose orientation is always practical rather than theoretical, says that choice of calling is "commonly under the direction of parents and guardians; though the inclination of the person to be disposed of, is not to be disregarded . . ." (*The Religious Tradesman* [Newburyport, 1780], p. 22); this American edition is a revised version of Steele's *Tradesman's Calling*, quoted heavily by Tawney.

[29] "*Obey* your *Parents* Conscientiously," Cotton Mather urges youth, ". . . though you should be as much above Twenty as Isaac was, when his Father had him Ly down upon his Altar. . . . For *this is well-pleasing to the* Lord" (*Help for Distressed Parents . . . and Warnings unto Children* [Boston, 1695], pp. 60–61). Mather here follows the tradition, reflected in medieval mystery plays, that Isaac was about thirty years old when his father offered him as a sacrifice.

[30] "Duty of Children to Parents," Discourse I of *The Relative Duties of Parents and Children* (4th ed.; London, 1732), p. 22.

ents in the Lord, do indeed obey the Lord in their Parents. . . ." [31]

Youth guides often evince a particular concern about youths who manifest their rebellion by running off to a far country, like the prodigal son, or to sea. "What's said concerning the Young Prodigal," writes Increase Mather, "is a description of the spirit which useth to prevail in Unconverted Young men. He was not willing to continue in his Fathers Family, nor under his Fathers inspection and government, but would be gone into far Countries. . . . Do we not see it just so in many Young men amongst our selves?" [32]

In seeking the fundamental cause of youthful waywardness, guide writers often focused upon the spirit of rebellion evidenced in filial disobedience and in failure to follow one's calling. They described rebelliousness as passionate and antirational—productive of horrible consequences, both physical and spiritual. Timothy Cruso, reflecting Proverbs 30:17, says that disobedient children may have "Their *Eyes pickt out and devour'd by Ravens and Eagles,*" or their undertakings may be cursed: "Nothing that you *set your hand unto,* shall prosper. . . . If you *sow much,* you shall *reap but little*; all your care and industry shall signify nothing. . . ." [33] Besides general promises of failure and torment, guides cite dramatic historical examples of divine judgments on wayward youths, and they record testimonies of reformed youths who had earlier suffered punishment for

[31] *God the Guide of Youth,* p. 20.

[32] *Solemn Advice to Young Men,* p. 21. Cotton Mather expresses similar concern: "Oh! That the Young Men, who follow the Sea and most of all, they that without a good Cause and Call run away to Sea, would very particularly consider . . ." (*Repeated Warnings, Another Essay, To Warn Young People against Rebellion That Must Be Repented Of* [Boston, 1712], p. [2]).

[33] *God the Guide of Youth,* pp. 21, 31.

their sins. "Example," says Cotton Mather, "has a singular Force to *Teach* and *Move* the Beholder of it." [34]

The guide writers assume man's natural depravity and find him apt to err in things little as well as great, so guide literature also discusses many lesser youthful pitfalls. All situations are seen as potentially dangerous, and man must study to know himself as thoroughly as possible so that he can guard against temptations aimed at his weakest point. Admission of weakness is, of course, the first step toward cure, but one ultimately needs divine interposition, for man is himself incapable of overcoming weakness, however sincerely he may try. "*Such is the corruption of our nature*," says Joseph Alleine in *A Sure Guide to Heaven*, "*that it utterly disables*" unless God intervenes to avert otherwise certain ruin.[35]

Deliverance is, of course, considered more likely in youth, before a person is habituated to a life of sin, and

---

[34] *Early Religion*, p. 72. Ordinarily, however, youth guides use "true histories" sparingly, relying instead upon exhortation. When used, *exempla* ordinarily are gathered in an appendix. See, for example, the collections of stories appended to *Early Religion* and to Crossman's *The Young Man's Calling*. William Turner's *A Compleat History of the Most Remarkable Providences, Both of Judgment and Mercy, Which Have Hapned in This Present Age* (London, 1697), also catalogues a number of judgments upon disobedient children. This latter book, in which the examples are rather overly dramatic (for example, a rebellious son has a serpent cling to his lip for the rest of his life), is discussed in Chapter III below.

Puritan writers were, of course, aware of the effectiveness of examples, particularly testimonies of those who themselves had had dramatic experiences. In an appendix to the *Young Man's Preservative* (Boston, 1701), Cotton Mather tells of a profane young man who becomes converted and on his wedding day converts his wife by giving his testimony: "He entreated her to sit down on the Couch by him; where he gave her the surprizing Story of his Life, and of what the *Grace of God* had been doing for him. . . . Now, as the Apostle *Paul* was an Instrument of Converting many, by giving a Relation of his own Conversion; such was the effect of this Young Gentlemans Relating what had befallen him" (p. 63). For a discussion of Puritan use of spiritual histories, see Chapter IV.

[35] Fol. A3.

man is best advised to choose the ways of piety in his youth, for he will then accrue a lesser weight of offenses against God and will not run the risk of being cut off from later repentance. While they recognize the possibility of repentance even as late as the moment of death (citing the example of the thief on the cross), guide writers emphasize the danger of procrastination. God can require an account from man at any time and may suddenly cut off his life without the opportunity for a last-minute change of heart. Certain special opportunities are provided for every man, however, and man ought to recognize and use them. "There are," says Flavell, ". . . seasons and gales of grace for our souls; golden opportunities of salvation afforded to man, the neglect of which proves the loss and ruin of souls. God hath given unto men a day of visitation, which he hath limited. . . ." [36] These special seasons are occasioned by divine interposition and usually show man his need in a dramatic way, often by stripping him of his goods or his health so that he may see his helplessness in the hand of God. "Times of affliction," according to Benjamin Calamy, are "particular Times wherein we are more especially called upon to review our Actions. . . ." [37] And even though repentance under stress is, in a sense, forced by God (like the repentance of the prodigal son),[38] man should accept the opportunity gratefully and acknowledge God's kindness and wisdom in prodding him to spiritual action which he is powerless to undertake alone.

Once converted, man still faces many trials and temp-

[36] *Navigation Spiritualized*, p. 63. For a discussion of the concept of "Finding Times," see Chapter VII.

[37] *Sermons Preached upon Several Occasions* (3rd ed.; London, 1700), Sermon X, pp. 290–91.

[38] See Robert Parsons, *A Sermon Preached at the Funeral of the Rt. Honorable John Earl of Rochester* (Oxford, 1680), p. 13.

tations, for repentance neither delivers him to heaven's gate nor renders him impervious to the world's snares. A true saint will, however, benefit even from his lapses. "The best of Beleevers," says Ralph Robinson in his *Safe Conduct, or The Saints Guidance to Glory* (1654), "have a spice of the Spiritual Falling-sickness, they stumble and fall . . . ," but God remains with them so that "when they sink into misery God will lift them up, and when they slip into sin God will restore them."[39]

The guides like to envision ultimate glory and describe its foretastes along the way, noting the privileges of heaven-born and heaven-bound souls. They describe the beauties of fellowship with other saints, the frequent (but by no means certain) temporal rewards brought by piety and godliness, and the pleasures of contemplating one's future estate by taking a "prospect" from the mount of heavenly meditation. But joy and privilege also bring responsibility, and the guides never stray far from their central task of reminding Christians of their duty. Because man's position in the world contributed to the divine order and somehow functioned in God's war against evil, every man had to perform his earthly work diligently (doctrine of work), but he should never let his temporal duties interfere with his eternal ones, nor let his concern with earthly well-being obstruct his passage to eternal bliss. "Let *Religion* be the *main business* and employment of your Lives," says Timothy Cruso in a typical exhortation. "Consider that your *General Calling*, as Christians, is of more concern, than your *particular*

---

[39] P. 36. In a prefatory section to the 1677 edition of *A General Martyrologie*, Samuel Clarke notes that "sometimes we shall find some of these Worthies at the first encounter (through the violence of temptation, and humane frailty) giving [going?] back: But . . . they (according to the nature of true grace) have gathered strength by their relapses. And no marvel though such weaknesses sometimes appear in the strongest Christians . . . ." (fol. a1ᵛ).

Vocation, as Men. Let *Spiritual* things have the constant precedency to *Temporal*." [40] Cruso's voice may have been a voice crying in the wilderness, but it did not cry alone. The multiplicity of such voices may have been occasioned by an intense struggle for material wealth, but the voices were heard far more often then (if not always heeded) than in modern times, when seventeenth-century grasping has been portrayed clearly, while the voices of pleading are heard hardly at all.

Defoe himself worked in the guide tradition, but his method differs from that of the typical Puritan moralist. *The Family Instructor* (published, in two volumes, shortly before *Robinson Crusoe*) shares the typical concerns of guide books, but it relies primarily on example rather than exhortation. "The Way I have taken," says Defoe in Volume I (1715), ". . . is *Entirely New*, and at first *perhaps* it may appear something *Odd*. . . ." [41] In Volume I, Defoe presents the spiritual history of an entire family, from the father's first attempt to Christianize it, up to the conversion or apparent damnation of each family member. The work is divided into sections dealing with specific problems, and each section has an introduction and commentary, but the major portion of the work is devoted to the story itself. Defoe emphasizes the essentially dramatic character of the work by having the story unfold through dialogue. "The whole Work being design'd both to divert and instruct," Defoe says, "the Author has endeavored to adapt it as much as possible to both those uses, from whence some have called it a Religious Play. . . ." [42] The story is complete as story

[40] *The Usefullnesse of Spiritual Wisdom with A Temporal Inheritance* (London, 1689), p. 19.
[41] I have quoted from the second edition (1715), p. 2.
[42] Preface to the second edition, fol. [A4].

(though perhaps not very compelling for the modern reader), but the emphasis is of course placed upon the lesson it teaches, rather like an extended *exemplum*. Volume II, published less than a year before *Robinson Crusoe*, employs a similar method to inculcate similar morals. The appeal of Defoe's "new" method of guiding Christians is attested by *The Family Instructor*'s popularity: Volume I had reached an eighth edition by 1720, and throughout the eighteenth century it was republished almost as often as was *Robinson Crusoe*. Later, Defoe wrote again in the guide tradition, publishing *Religious Courtship* in 1722 and *The New Family Instructor* in 1727. In *The Complete English Tradesman* (1725), *The Complete English Gentlemen* (published posthumously), and in several tracts his aims were apparently similar.

George A. Aitken has been criticized sharply for saying that the difference between Defoe's moral treatises and his novels is "one of degree rather than kind." "The difference [in the novels]" according to Professor Aitken, "lay chiefly in the prominence now given the story, which took the leading place, hitherto occupied by the moral." [43] While his statement oversimplifies the issue, it at least indicates a relationship which has been, during the last half-century, too often overlooked. *Rob-*

[43] General Introduction, *Romances and Narratives by Daniel Defoe* (16 vols.; London, 1895), I, xxix. Arthur W. Secord (*Studies in the Narrative Method of Defoe* ["University of Illinois Studies in Language and Literature," IX; Urbana, 1924]) finds this position extreme (p. 17). A half century ago, Charlotte E. Morgan noted the significance of Defoe's guide books in relation to the novel of manners; in her *Rise of the Novel of Manners: A Study of English Prose Fiction between 1600 and 1740* (New York, 1911), she briefly discusses *The Family Instructor*, but she does not suggest any relationship between guide books and Defoe's own fiction. For a more recent discussion which elaborates Miss Morgan's suggestion, see Alan D. McKillop, *Early Masters of English Fiction* (Lawrence, Kans., 1956). Few recent critics, however, seem aware of the relation of Defoe's guide books to his fiction.

inson Crusoe is, of course, far more than a guide for youth about to embark on life's journey. But it does bear important thematic affinities to treatises whose primary concern is religious and moral, affinities which would have been obvious to a contemporary reader who might well have grouped it (lacking a more precise category) with *The Practice of Piety*. Whatever the qualities that ultimately separate it from Puritan tracts, *Robinson Crusoe* speaks to the same concerns as do guide books, and it shares their theological and moral point of view. The 1715 volume of *The Family Instructor* introduces us to a son who tires of his father's efforts to tether him. "I'll be content to go to the *West-Indies*, or be a *Foot-soldier*, or anything, rather than be made such a Recluse," [44] he threatens. This rebellious young man might well be an embryonic Crusoe or Crusoe's brother,[45] and he himself may be descended from one or more of the rebellious young *exempla* who people seventeenth-century guide books. But whether or not Defoe proceeded gradually to thematic fiction from didactic treatise—whether or not *The Family Instructor* was his stepping stone to fictional form—the guide tradition provides one vital perspective from which to view fictional theme in *Robinson Crusoe* and from which to ask larger questions about the relationship between didacticism and literary form. More important than the "source" of *Robinson Crusoe* in another book or in several books is the *manner* in which ideas in the guide tradition become embodied in fiction. Rather than having an "original" somewhere in fact or fiction, *Robinson Crusoe* seems not to follow a specific "original," borrowing neither a particular incident nor a specific writer's attitudes, but rather concretizes in

---

[44] Pp. 135–36.
[45] Crusoe's second brother, who might well have provided an emblem for Crusoe, simply disappears after leaving home.

dramatic, symbolic particulars the saga of life as seen by the Puritan mind.

Once *Robinson Crusoe*'s relation to the guide tradition is noted, the name of its hero takes on added significance. Of the possible "sources" of the name suggested by scholars, the most prominent has been that of Timothy Cruso, though no one has explained why Defoe should have used the name of a former schoolmate.[46] Nothing is known of any personal relationship between Defoe and Cruso after their schooling at Morton's Academy, but Defoe must have known of Cruso's reputation as a preacher and casuist. Cruso was renowned enough to be selected for the famous Merchant's Lectures at Pinner's Hall (he delivered twenty-four lectures), and his bibliography of a dozen extant books includes three youth guides: *The Usefullnesse of Spiritual Wisdom with a Temporal Inheritance* (written specifically for a young man about to embark on his calling), 1689; *The*

[46] Defoe's latest biographer, John Robert Moore, simply says that "Defoe had a classmate at Morton's academy, Timothy Cruso or Crusoe, whose name (perhaps recalled by the island Curaçao [which Defoe spelled Curasoe] in the Caribbean) suggested the most famous name in all fiction" (*Daniel Defoe: Citizen of the Modern World* [Chicago, 1958], p. 225. Professor Moore had earlier (*N & Q*, CLXIV [1933], 26) suggested the possibility of Curaçao. Others have suggested that Defoe derived the name linguistically, through Creutznaer (Crusoe says that was his family name originally), from *kreutzen* (see Secord, *Studies*, pp. 42–43), or from Creutzinsel in Grimmelshausen's *Simplicissimus* (see Erwin Gustav Gudde, "Grimmelshausen's Simplicius Simplicissimus and Defoe's Robinson Crusoe," *PQ*, IV [1925], 110–20). Another argument, which I am unable to follow in detail, is given by Willard H. Bonner, *Captain William Dampier* (Palo Alto, Calif., 1934), p. 86 ff. Professor Bonner thinks that some connection exists between "Crusoe" and "cruise." In the nineteenth century quite a battle raged in *Notes and Queries* about the origin of the name Crusoe, and I should be content to leave it there, except that Timothy Cruso's writings seem to me to illuminate a tradition vital to *Robinson Crusoe* and to suggest new conclusions about Defoe's allusiveness. See Afterword, below.

Necessity and Advantage of an Early Victory over Satan, 1693; and *God the Guide of Youth*, 1695. Cruso's early death (brought on, according to his admirers, by his zeal for his work),[47] ended a writing career begun only eight years earlier, and there is no evidence that his work had a significant vogue later. But even though he was not of the first rank of Dissenting divines, his work was important enough that readers of 1719 might well be expected (especially in view of the rarity of his surname) to remember him and to associate Defoe's hero with his name.

One of Cruso's guides is particularly interesting, for although it is short (about the length of an average sermon) it deals with most of the major problems involved in *Robinson Crusoe*. In *God the Guide*, Cruso argues the necessity of early choice of God as guide so that one's life may be properly ordered. "The proper work of a Guide," he says, "is to *direct* the Ignorant Traveller in a strange Land, and unknown Countrey. Such is our Case during the *time of our Sojourning* here in this World; and it is the work of the *only wise God*, to *guide our feet*; *and direct our steps* for us, which he will do if we sincerely resign ourselves to him. That which undoes us, is not God's *unwillingness* to *instruct us*, but our own unteachableness. . . ." Cruso places heavy emphasis upon filial obedience: "It is very *becoming* to take [parents'] Advice in all weighty and eminent Cases; it is *necessary* to receive and perform their Commands in all things lawful. . . ." And he promises dreadful consequences for those who refuse God's promptings: "Tho you be placed in Lawful Callings, and prosecute them with the greatest *diligence*, I must denounce this Sentence against you in the Name of God, That the *fruit of your labour* will have a *blast* upon it . . . ; either your Undertakings, or your very *Blessings* will be *Curst*. . . . If

[47] But see the Afterword for additional information on Cruso's life.

your Voyage be successful, and you come home *richly laden*, yet God not being concern'd in the *steering* of your Course, your Misery will be the greater." [48]

One might argue that such a tract stimulated Defoe to stretch a story over its ideological framework and that, to pay his debt, he named his hero after his source of inspiration. It is possible that Cruso's language and metaphor prodded Defoe at some stage of conception or execution, but such a specific obligation would be hard to prove, especially since Cruso's guide (though more compact and pointed than many others), conveys ideas characteristic of the guide tradition generally. Or one might construct a wildly elaborate schematization of Defoe's psychological process of creation and imagine that he felt guilty for leaving the profession (the ministry) for which Morton's Academy prepared him, that he recalled his schoolmate's later success in discussing such problems, and that somehow he assuaged his guilt and ordered his mind by writing a therapeutic, somewhat "allegorical" account of his own life, with Cruso—now become Crusoe—as hero. Or one might speculate about Cruso's life and imagine that his children, about whom it is known only that they died before their father, were rebellious like Defoe's own son. And so on.

But we are, of course, unlikely ever to find out whether anything remotely like the processes described above occurred in Defoe's mind. What does seem certain is this: as a student with Timothy Cruso at a small academy, Defoe would have known of Cruso's later work and modest renown; as a writer of guide literature, Defoe would have been aware of themes, methods, and metaphors of the tradition; in naming his hero he could scarcely have forgotten Cruso and chosen the name by

[48] Pp. 12–13, **20**, **31–32.**

coincidence. It is more likely that he expected contemporary readers to recognize his allusion and associate the name with thematic aspects of his book, for one of his aims was certainly to deal with the problems which the guide tradition had previously faced. For the modern reader, the name provides a directional signal for a segment of ideological and subliterary background now largely forgotten. *Robinson Crusoe* ultimately is much more complex than any of the traditions which nourish it, but the complexity should not obscure the ancestry. Failure to recognize *Robinson Crusoe*'s relation to guide literature is to miss not only an illuminating segment of eighteenth-century background; it is to misinterpret significant developments in the narrative itself and to be misled on the tantalizing question of the relationship between the new prose fiction and the conventional didactic literature which helped form the minds of that fiction's first creators.

III

The "Providence" Tradition

———◆◆◆◆►———

Like Milton, Defoe sought to justify God's ways to man, but fifty years had made a difference. In 1719, a Christian apologist needed to justify not so much God's role as creator and lawgiver, but his role as governor of the universe. After the deistic challenge of the nineties (and the intellectual climate which produced it), one dared not assume too easily a God who maintained an active interest in his individual creatures and who oversaw their daily activities. Advocates of "natural," as distinguished from "revealed," religion had put theologians on the defensive regarding God's role in human history, a role about which an earlier generation could assume agreement, and churchmen attempted to define the precise nature of God's intervention. Different answers were proposed, and unanimity never emerged, but orthodox theists agreed on one thing: God was not an absentee landlord, as some charged, but the incumbent governor of the universe who in his benevolence specifically intervened for his subjects. During the first twenty years of the eighteenth century, many issues divided Anglican and Dissenter, but in this (as in other answers to deism and "other atheisms") they remained united. The challenge, Christians agreed, was aimed at the very foundations of Christian theology; if God failed to exercise provident dominion in a world where good and evil still battled, he was far less significant than even the deists said: he was really no God at all.

"Next to the acknowledgment of God's being," says Archbishop Tillotson, "nothing is more essential to Religion, than the Belief of his Providence." [1] For Tillotson and his contemporaries, as well as for Christian thinkers centuries before them, human history was purposeful, and (given man's depravity) only direct divine control could implement God's plan. And because his plan encompassed great and small, God governed even the humblest of creatures, the most minute of events. William Shelton summarizes: "The Providence of God governs the world, and extends it self to all Times, and Places, and Persons upon the face of the Earth. Interposes in all Events, has the Supremacy in all Affairs, so that nothing upon any pretense is remote or exempt from his Jurisdiction." [2]

To implement his plan, God ordinarily used the "natural" process of causation (although he could, of course, interpose by miraculous means), but his use of second causes should not obscure the fact that he was the ultimate cause of all events, and man should always "look beyond natural cause" [3] to see God's hand. Thankfulness for England's "deliverance" by William and Mary, for example, should go beyond thankfulness to human agents. "Whilst we give due Honour to the Instruments,"

---

[1] *The Works of the Most Reverend Dr. John Tillotson* (9th ed.; London, 1728), Sermon XXXVI, p. 330. Vincent Alsop offers this "commonly received" definition of providence: *"Providence is Gods most holy[,] most wise, most powerful ordering and governing* [of] *all his Creatures and all their Actions"* (*God in the Mount* [London, 1696], p. 20).

[2] *Divine Providence, the Support of Good Men under All Events* (London, 1680), p. 5.

[3] [Thomas Smith], *A Discourse Concerning Divine Providences, in Relation to National Judgments* (London, 1693), p. 12.

says Slingsby Bethel, "let us not forget ascribing the Praise and Glory due to Almighty God, as the Author and Principal of our Deliverance. . . ."[4] Man's actions were, in fact, always instruments of God's providence, even when the actions were sinful and were intended to resist God's will. Paradoxically, God's use of those actions was "without any restraint of, or prejudice to [man's] natural or moral Liberty"[5]—a position more effectively asserted than explained. Somehow, God brought about "the purposes of his *Providence*, by actions [men] design to other ends, nay sometimes by their sinful passions. . . ."[6]

Even events which seemed most tragic or evil were really controlled by God. Sometimes their tragedy was only apparent and masked a more important, further-reaching good. "No ship is cast away upon the Sea; no Sickness or Plague comes," says Bishop Patrick, "but God is perfectly pleased with it, and it is impossible that any should judge so well as he, what is most convenient. He sees it is most fit, and best for the whole World considered together . . . that those Things should happen, which we feel most grievous."[7] Sometimes, too, these "grievous" events were judgments upon man's sins and provided both punishment for past acts and a warning for the future. But a God who sometimes punished dramatically might also reward dramatically, and man ought to look to divine help for deliverance from divinely wrought affliction. "If God hath *in faithfulness*

[4] *The Providences of God, Observed through Several Ages, towards This Nation* (London, 1691), p. 35.
[5] Smith, *Discourse*, p. 10.
[6] *Ibid.*
[7] *Fifteen Sermons upon Contentment and Resignation to the Will of God* (London, 1719), Sermon X, p. 247. "Providence," says Ralph Robinson, "can carry a man to shore on a broken piece of a Plank, as well as in a long Boat. Some Providences are cross to us, but they are all direct to God" (*Safe Conduct, or the Saints Guidance to Glory* [London, 1654], p. 55).

afflicted us," asks Timothy Cruso, "why should we question his Faithfulness in releiving us? We that have felt the *lashes* of his angry *rod*, when we were running from him, shall undoubtedly experience the *succours* of his *mighty Arm*, when we come back to him." [8] The wisdom of God's ways might sometimes confound the finite reason of man, but man could remain certain that a divine purpose was nevertheless being served, and he ought to strive, to the limits of his ability, to understand God's message in all events. "Every Wind," Jeremiah Burroughs says in a sermon interpreting a tempest, "is as a messenger of God sent to us about some errand or other, and happy are wee, if wee . . . finde out what their message is . . . that they may never returne without doing the worke for which they were sent. . . ." [9]

Providence was considered especially active in bringing about the repentance and conversion of God's elect, for in a postlapsarian world man was impotent even to receive the proffered grace unless God interposed specifically to grant him special powers in a special situation. "In nothing," says John Flavell, "doth Providence shine forth more gloriously in this world" than in "*ordering the Occasions, Instruments and Means of* [man's] *Conversion*." [10] Once converted, man could count on even greater attention from providence, for even though God oversaw all of creation, he bestowed special attention on the righteous, granting continual providential guidance so that they remained on a heaven-bound course. Says Ralph Robinson, in *Safe Conduct, or the Saints Guidance to Glory*: "[The] Eye of God is never withdrawn from the righteous, but is continually fixed

[8] *The Churches Plea for the Divine Presence To Prosper Humane Force* (London, 1689), p. 14.
[9] *The Sea-Mans Direction in Time of Storme* (London, 1640), p. 17.
[10] *Divine Conduct: Or, the Mysterie of Providence* (London, 1678), p. 57.

upon them for their preservation and defence . . . , for
the preserving of them from wandrings, and for the
reducing of them when they do wander. The Starre
of providence is usefull for the guiding of the saints
feet. . . ." [11]

Divine intervention in history had, of course, been
assumed by orthodox Christianity since New Testament
times. At Christianity's very base was a special interposition of God, and Christian interpretations of history
had always assumed that God continued to intervene in
human affairs. Ideological developments in the seventeenth century, however, raised new questions about
Christianity's special claim to truth and suddenly focused the question of God's providence with new precision. Orthodox theologians quickly saw the potential
threat of new scientific discoveries and interpretations,
for orthodoxy necessitated a universe sustained by a God
who actively willed each event. As the universe began to
be imaged in terms of a self-sustaining, self-winding ma-
chine, churchmen feared a shift in the locus of order
from the creator to the created. And if the universe could
sustain and run itself, it needed no personal, prayer-
answering, governing father to oversee it. If the new
view (as interpreted by churchmen) were to triumph,
the traditional God would be dead.

The outbreak of deistic writings in the nineties clarified the challenges: they described an ahistorical God
who remained aloof from his creation, an impersonal
God who could be discovered in nature's unerring laws
without benefit of a special revelation. But theologians
were already on the defensive before deism marshaled
its full force. In 1678, John Flavell had found it neces-

[11] *Safe Conduct*, p. 12.

sary to write a treatise on *Divine Conduct: Or, the Mysterie of Providence. Wherein the Being and Efficacy of Providence Is Asserted, and Vindicated.* "It is the design of this *Manual*," he writes in the Preface, "to assert the *Being* and *Efficacy* of Providence against the *Atheism* of the times. . . ." [12] For more than half a century thereafter, the concept of providence remained at the center of theological and philosophical controversy.

Scientific and philosophical attacks on orthodox Christian doctrine were answered in kind, and a voluminous polemical literature resulted. In polemical discussion, Christian apologists sought to provide a philosophical basis for the doctrine of providence, and they tried to define the methods of divine control. At least equally important (much more important to the future development of literary form), however, was the popular literature which they produced to present their case to laymen on a less theoretical, more emotional basis. This popular literature depended less on argument than example: it consisted largely of accounts of events in which divine intervention seemed especially evident.

Theologians usually distinguished between general (or ordinary) providences—in which God simply watched over developments he had willed through his natural laws—and special (or extraordinary) providences, in which a specific act of interposition was involved. General providences involved the essential but undramatic sustenance of creation according to a predictable order—an order which many simply called "natural" law. But special providences were more dramatic and provided more effective "evidence" for a lay audience; those providences involved specific deliverance or punishment of individuals or societies. [13] Ordi-

---

[12] Fol. [A6]. Christian apologists usually called deism an "atheism."
[13] Perry Miller says that the idea of providence, as formulated by the Puritans, was meant as a "defense against mere blind vitalism" (*The*

narily, God interposed without violating or suspending
his "natural" laws ("miracles" were usually distinguished
from special providences). He could punish through
plague or shipwreck brought about in the normal course
of epidemic or tempest, and he could use men (physi-
cians) or other parts of creation (planks, boats, islands)
as instruments of deliverance.[14] The more unusual the
circumstances of the event, the more effective the illustration of God's power; the more numerous the occurrences, the more apparent God's concern and control.
Doctrinally, theologians found it easy to justify God's
intervention. He was committed to a watchful care of his
creatures and sometimes had to overrule man's depraved
will or aid impotent man in his struggle against evil.
Belief in prayer, they pointed out, presupposed God's
ability to alter circumstances to fit individual needs. Besides, man in his postlapsarian state often needed to be
reminded of his weakness and God's power. "God generally permits things to their natural Course," says Tillot-

New England Mind: The Seventeenth Century [New York, 1939], p.
15), and suggests that American emphasis on special providences resulted from the defeat of the idea of a national covenant. According to
Professor Miller, Increase Mather's _An Essay for the Recording of
Illustrious Providences_ (see below, p. 62 ff.) "was an attempt to show
that the wisdom of God does prevail, if not in general, then in particulars. . . . The book was a gesture against despair; it was a surrender
of the idea of national covenant, a strategic retreat to an atomistic, frag-
mental version of divine regulation. The Scale was no longer a coherent
sweep of history, but discrete 'magnalia'; not an over-all design working steadily through a predestined course, but simply this tempest or
that shipwreck, a deaf person who learned to speak, or so-and-so who
was possessed" (_The New England Mind: From Colony to Province_
[Cambridge, Mass., 1953], p. 145). This view, though persuasive, fails
to account for the almost simultaneous flowering of the providence
tradition in England, where covenant theology was already pretty well
dead by the sixteen eighties.
[14] Typical is the following distinction between the miraculous and the
natural: "Means and miracles are both the products of Gods mercy to
his people, and have both their place assigned: miracles come in when
means are wanting . . ." (Nathaniel Whiting, _Old Jacobs Altar Newly
Repaird; or, the Saints Triangle of Dangers, Deliverances and Duties_
[London, 1659], p. 39).

son, ". . . but then, lest Men should cast off religion
. . . God is pleased sometimes more remarkably to interpose . . . to make us know *that we are but Men*, and
that the Reins of the World are not in our Hands."[15]
Clearly, according to Tillotson and his contemporaries, if
God could sustain the entire world for the ultimate good
of mankind, he could sustain a nation or an individual,
either by directing his created instruments or by overruling them.

Emphasis on special providences was not, of course,
without theological pitfalls. The existence of such interventions might help answer opponents of a Christian interpretation of history, but emphasis upon their frequency invited religious interpretations of all events, and
inevitably these interpretations sometimes differed. A
plague might be seen as a national warning about the
future or as a punishment for the past; it could be interpreted as a judgment on lax individual morality, on national economic greed, on corrupt politics, or on mis-
taken theological ideas. If all Christians agreed that
God's hand could be seen everywhere, they differed on
the basis for his interventions. If they agreed that God
could interfere whenever he chose, they differed on how
often he interfered and in which cases.

Anglicans and Dissenters alternately accused one another of making God's providence suit their own beliefs
and causes. In his famous attack on Dissenters' academies, Samuel Wesley mocks the Dissenters for attribut-
ing the escape (after arrest) of Charles Morton "as is
usual with that sort of People, to a Particular Providence. . . ."[16] "Well," responded Samuel Palmer, ironi-

---

[15] Tillotson, *Works*, Sermon XXXVI, p. 335.
[16] *A Letter from a Country Divine to His Friend in London. Concerning the Education of the Dissenters, in Their Private Academies*
(London, 1703), p. 10. Morton was headmaster of the Newington
Green academy, which Defoe attended.

cally, " 'tis a Crime in Dissenters to admire Providence!
. . . And after all, this *scomma* is unpardonable from a
Party who have more than once made a *Weathercock* of
Providence, which they have varied to all the Points of a
Passive obedient Compass. . . ." [17] The attempt to present a united front to Christianity's challengers was
not always an easy one when Christians were themselves
fighting battles of interpretation like this one. Charges
that Dissenters misused the doctrine to exaggerate their
own importance in God's sight were especially common
in the late seventeenth and early eighteenth centuries,[18]
although (as Palmer pointed out) the critics were sometimes subject to their own criticism. Anglicans were,
however, generally more restrained in applying the doctrine of providence: most of the real vigor in defending
the doctrine against Christianity's rationalist and empiri-
cist detractors comes from Dissenting divines, and it is
the Puritan mind which is responsible for the major
polemical literature on the subject.

But no orthodox Christian dared deny that God intervened in human history, sometimes for reasons not altogether clear to human observers, and so the interpreters' battles largely involved questions of frequency
and emphasis. However they might accuse one another
of distortion or sectarian misinterpretation, Christian
apologists all agreed that complex and mysterious events
somehow were willed by God for his own purpose. "We
ought to be so modest," says Bishop Patrick, "as not to
censure God's Government, nor charge any Passage of

[17] *A Defence of the Dissenters Education in Their Private Academies*
(London, 1703), p. 17.
[18] Charles Gildon's complaint against *Robinson Crusoe* is typical:
Gildon finds Crusoe's interpretations of providential control exaggerated
and argues that if providence created storms and shipwrecks to punish
or deliver an individual, God would be unfair to large numbers of other
persons affected by those events. The quotation from Patrick on this
page represents the traditional answer to this traditional argument.

Providence with Injustice, or accuse him of any Partiality and ill Management; much less admit any suspicion, that there is no Providence at all." [19] Even the more rationalistic Anglican divines tried to give silent assent to the new emphasis, convinced of the contemporary dangers to the whole fabric of Christianity. "In no Age has the Being and Providence of God been more derided and scoffed at than in this," the defenders told themselves in the nineties.[20] While they debated their tormentors, they assured themselves that "it is beyond all debate, that there is a Providence of God always enfolding those in everlasting arms, that bear his Image." [21]

"To Record Providences," writes William Turner in 1697, *"seems to be one of the best Methods that can be pursued, against the abounding* Atheism *of this Age."* [22] During the four decades preceding the publication of *Robinson Crusoe* in 1719, Christian apologists zealously pursued the method advocated by Turner, and the accounts of special providences which they published form a specific type of polemic in the religious literature of their time—a type which might well be called the "providence tradition." Writings in this tradition aimed at convincing laymen of God's intervention in human affairs, and, rather than debating the issue on a theological or philosophical level, the providence writers simply recounted unusual happenings and defied the reader to explain them on any other ground than that of God's providence. "There are," says Increase Mather in a doc-

[19] *Fifteen Sermons,* Sermon X, p. 234.
[20] *A Sermon Concerning National Providence* (Oxford, 1694), p. 4.
[21] Flavell, *Divine Conduct,* fol. A4.
[22] *A Compleat History of the Most Remarkable Providences, Both of Judgment and Mercy, Which Have Hapned in This Present Age* (London, 1697), fol. b1ᵛ.

trinal defense published almost simultaneously with his anthology of special providences, "*Magnalia Dei*, things wherein the glorious finger of God is eminently to be seen. . . . There are eminent preservations and deliverances, which everyone may see the Name of God written upon them in legible characters." [23]

Because they expected the moral to be obvious, providence writers concentrated on the events themselves and carefully detailed the circumstances to make their accounts as vivid as possible.[24] Usually they concluded with a brief interpretative statement (a modern critic, removed as he is from the polemical world which the providence tradition reflects, is apt to consider these statements "conventional"), pointing to God's continuing interest in the affairs of men. Often the accounts were long and fully as dramatic as adventure fiction, but the propagandistic thesis of the tradition lent each story a thematic unity that was missing from contemporary fiction. Some providence books were wholly devoted to one story: *God's Protecting Providence* (1699), for example, recounts the deliverance of a ship's company "from the Devouring Waves of the Sea; amongst which they suffered Shipwreck: And also, From the cruel Devouring Jaws of the Inhumane *Canibals* of *Florida*." [25] and *Providence Displayed* (1712) describes the survival of Alexander Selkirk and argues that "nothing but the Divine Providence could have supported any man" in such is-

[23] *The Doctrine of Divine Providence Opened and Applyed* (Boston, 1684), p. 12. Providence writers usually cited events which *all* Christians could regard as providential, omitting events tinged with theological controversy (like that debated by Wesley and Palmer).

[24] Their use of detail probably was influenced also by a desire to be accurate in recording events of divine significance, for the role of these writers was not unlike the role of biblical writers (see Chapter IV below).

[25] Jonathan Dickenson, *God's Protecting Providence* (Philadelphia, 1700 [first published, 1699]). The quotation is from the title page.

land solitude.[26] Others, like Turner's *A Compleat History of the Most Remarkable Providences.... Which Have Hapned in This Present Age* (1697), or Increase Mather's *An Essay for the Recording of Illustrious Providences: Wherein an Account Is Given of Many Remarkable and Very Memorable Events, Which Have Happened in This Last Age* . . . (1684), anthologize and edit several stories to provide what is at once a heavily documented polemical argument and a reference guide for preachers who might wish to continue the controversy from the pulpit.

Providence writers utilized many kinds of stories, including those of divine judgments and punishments as well as of deliverances and "mercies." Increase Mather devotes a section of his anthology to persons punished by thunder and lightning; Turner, distributing his several hundred stories under 150 headings, records instances of "Remarkable patience," "Remarkable chastity," "Discovery of things secret or future by Dreams and Visions," "Divine judgments upon gluttony," and "Protection of the good in danger." Of particular interest to providence writers, however, were exceptional occurrences at sea, for these "sea providences" usually involved life-or-death situations with a dramatic interest and romantic appeal, and they offered exceptional opportunities for exploiting the favorite Puritan metaphor of life as a voyage.[27] Mather devotes his first two chapters to sea providences, and some anthologies (like James Janeway's *Token for Mariners, Containing Many Famous and Wonderful Instances of God's Providence in Sea Dangers and Deliverences*, 1708) are comprised entirely of such accounts. "Tho God's Wonders are every where visible," writes Janeway, "and his mercies no where hid

[26] As reprinted in *Harleian Miscellany* (London, 1810), V, 432.
[27] See Chapter V below.

from the Eyes of Man; yet more particularly are they Evident to *Seafaring-Men,* whose . . . Lives [are] exposed more than others to Innumerable Hazards and Dangers." [28] Providence writers considered themselves specially engaged to give attention to such strange and surprising accounts. "O what sweet musick doth it make in God's ears," says John Ryther, "that you thankfully record Sea-Mercies, and Sea-Deliverances." [29]

Many sea providences bear striking resemblances to *Robinson Crusoe,* and the survivors' reflections are much like Crusoe's. Both Turner and Mather describe one man's two-year stay on an island near the Isle of Providence. "This Solitary Person," reports Turner, "was encompassed with the Goodness of Divine Providence. Within three Days God was pleased to send this single Person (who now alone was Lord and Subject in this his little Commonwealth) [30] good store of Fowl, and to render them so tame, that the forlorn Man could pick and chuse where he list. Fish also were now and then cast up within his reach, and somewhat that served for Fewel, enkindled by Flint to dress them." [31] Mather in-

---

[28] Preface, fol. A3. *Token for Mariners* is an enlarged version of an earlier volume, *Mr. James Janeway's Legacy to His Friends: Containing Twenty Seven Famous Instances of God's Providences in and about Sea-Dangers and Deliverances* (London, 1674). Mather also places special emphasis on sea providences: "They who go down to the sea in Ships, that do business in great waters, see the works of the Lord, and his wonders in the deep. . . . It is meet that such Providences should be ever had in remembrance . . . that the God of Salvation . . . may have eternal praise" (*An Essay for the Recording of Illustrious Providences* [Boston, 1684], p. 2). Mather is echoing Psalms 107:23–24.

[29] *A Plat for Mariners: Or, the Seaman's Preacher* (London, 1672), p. 121.

[30] Cf. Crusoe's observations about being monarch of his island. One should note, however, that many instances of such remarks occur in providence literature and travel literature.

[31] *Remarkable Providences,* p. 110 (first alphabet). Turner's book is paged in four groups, with the pagination beginning again at the end of each alphabetic set of signatures.

cludes an account ("Thatcher's Relation") of a man who
was tossed from shipwreck to shore by providentially
controlled waves and who describes his underwater experience much as Crusoe does. Upon arriving on shore,
he finds that his wife has also been delivered there, and
he relates "God's goodness unto me in that desolate Island [which he later names "Thatcher's Woe"], on
which I was cast." [32] Another experience, recorded by
Janeway, involves eleven months of solitary despair on a
barren rock island ("a more wretched condition," according to the survivor, "than if swallow'd up by the
Sea"). "I . . . was resolv'd," the man tells his rescuers,
"to end my days in it, when God sent you to deliver me
out of the greatest Misery that ever Man was in. . . ." [33]

Like Crusoe, the sailors of the providence books attribute their miseries to previous wickedness and their
deliverances to divine mercy. Janeway tells of a stranded
shipful of men whose "wants and miseries were so many,
and great, that sometimes they brake forth into impa-
tient Speeches against the causes of them, but then their
consciences again minded them after their own *Evil
deserts*, and so they took it as a just hand of God in their
former wicked Lives, or that God intended to make them
examples of his Mercy in their wonderful deliverance. . . ." [34] Turner relates the experience of a Captain How, who, isolated on an island, "kept many Days
of Fasting and Prayer, wherein he did confess and be-
wail his Sins, the least of which deserved greater Evils
than any in this World ever were, or can be subject unto,
and begged of God, *that he would find out a way for his*

[32] *Essay*, p. 13.
[33] *Token for Mariners*, pp. 32, 33.
[34] *Ibid.*, pp. 64–65. Samuel Clarke recounts the same story verbatim,
saying that the account was written by one of the survivors (*A Mirrour
or Looking-Glass Both for Saints, and Sinners, Held Forth in Some
Thousands of Examples* [4th ed.; London, 1671], p. 516).

Deliverance." When he finally begins to thank God for past blessings, as well as plead for future aid, a ship immediately passes near the island and "providentially" rescues him.[35]

Like the more formal doctrinal defenses of providence, providence books had something of an earlier heritage, but their great vogue occurred during the last two decades of the seventeenth century and the early years of the eighteenth—just when Christianity was feeling the pressures which culminated in the deistic challenge. Early in the seventeenth century, books such as *The Triumphs of God's Revenge against Murther* (which documented thirty "histories" of divine retribution) and *The Theatre of Gods Judgements* (an anthology of examples of "the admirable Justice of God against all notorious sinners, great and small") used stories of divine intervention to urge good conduct.[36] Of course, the Judeo-Christian tradition has to some extent made use of such stories (written and oral) ever since Mosaic times. The ac-

[35] *Remarkable Providences*, p. 100 (first alphabet). Christian apologists also fought contemporary doubts about the orthodox God through the spectral evidence tradition, a tradition in which Defoe also wrote (see *A True Relation of the Apparition of One Mrs. Veal*, 1706). Richard Baxter defines the aims of the tradition in *The Certainty of the Worlds of Spirits* (London, 1691). Alan D. McKillop briefly discusses this tradition but does not distinguish its materials from those of the providence tradition (*Early Masters of English Fiction* [Lawrence, Kans., 1956], p. 10 ff.).

[36] John Reynolds (or Rainolds) wrote *God's Revenge ca.* 1621, and it was republished at least ten times before 1719. Its approach was also widely imitated. In 1680 John Tonge described the "providential" capture of two murderers, entitling his work *God's Revenge against Murther;* other collections noted God's judgments on other sins. *Theatre,* written by Thomas Beard and Thomas Taylor, was first published about 1610. While motivated differently, these revenge accounts, like providence books, emphasize the special intervention of God. In 1716 Pope parodied this kind of book in his *God's Revenge against Punning.*

counts of the sixteen eighties and after, however, are more specifically polemical in their purpose, and they argue with a poignancy and vigor that the earlier treatises lack. At the beginning of the seventeenth century, a Christian apologist might have wished to emphasize the difficulty of evading divine justice, but he would hardly have felt compelled to prove the existence of providence. Such a writer could begin by assuming God's providential control and go on to instance it in specific cases; by the end of the century, he felt it necessary to log specific examples of miraculous events and induce a providence from this evidence.[37]

The new polemical focus of accounts of divine intervention did not, of course, preclude the moral function which such accounts could perform, and (like the authors of *The Triumphs of God's Revenge* and *The Theatre of Gods Judgements*) providence writers expected their readers to be either morally inspired by examples of God's beneficence or terrified into good conduct by examples of God's wrath.[38] The Preface to *The Theatre of Gods Judgements* argues that *accounts* of God's judgment in history are more effective than biblical *threats* of divine action, for such accounts demonstrate that "the tempest of Gods wrath is not onely denounced, but also throwne downe effectually upon the heads of the mighty ones of the world, when they are disobedient and rebellious against God. . . ." It concludes that "everyone

---

[37] Collections such as Mather's and Turner's had been proposed by the middle of the seventeenth century, and Matthew Poole, a leading Dissenter, began a manuscript in the late sixteen fifties. But, significantly, the project was not brought to fruition until the intellectual currents of the next generation produced a specific polemical need and persuaded larger numbers of Christians that such Puritan *exempla* might serve a useful purpose. Both Mather and Turner say that they used Poole's manuscript.

[38] Early seventeenth-century treatises place the emphasis on punishment; later treatises, on deliverance.

ought to reap profit to himself by . . . examples . . .
which . . . are by benefit of History preserved from
oblivion." [39] "Why else doth the Lord strike others, and
spare us," asks Thomas Taylor, "but that we might be
wiser by other mens harmes?" [40]

Because special providences often carried special
meanings about God's will and required a specific sort of
resultant conduct, readers of providence books could
also gain new interpretive insights. Providence writers,
while warning that deliverances did not always indicate
God's approval of a person's actions, frequently delineated specific causes of divine judgments and told their
readers how to interpret their own reverses. Flavell admits that providences are sometimes "dark and doubtful"
and that sometimes a Christian finds it difficult to "discover the will of God and his own duty." But if he com-
pares the apparent message of the intervention with the
precepts of Scripture, consults his own conscience, and
prays for guidance, he can, according to Flavell, arrive
at God's will. [41] Writers in the guide tradition offered
further aid in interpreting such events. Noting that all
events are specifically willed by God, Jeremiah Burroughs advises seamen: "When thou art in any danger in
regard of stormy Winds, consider, advise with thy conscience what threat it is, against what sinne of thine the
word of the Lord is gone forth, that this stormy Wind

<hr/>

[39] Fol. a1. William Sherlock similarly comments on the dramatic
value of historical example; he says that the great London fire "is of
great use to keep up a lively sense of such Judgments upon our Minds,
which become the subject of Reason, of cool Thoughts, and wise Consideration, when the Terror and Frightfulness of them is over. Judgments could never make a lasting Reformation in the World, were we
concerned to remember them no longer than we feel their smart; but
they are intended both for Punishment and Instruction . . ." (*A Sermon Preach'd on the Second of September, Being the Fast for the Fire
of London* [London, 1699], p. 22).

[40] *The Practice of Repentance, Laid Downe in Sundry Directions*
(2d ed.; London, 1629), p. 14.

[41] *Divine Conduct*, p. 217 ff.

comes to fulfill. . . ." [42] In such cases, the sailor needed
to examine his past conduct carefully to find his "Jonah"
(the sin responsible for the distress),[43] even to the point
of evaluating his activities before he went to sea, for
punishment of sin, though certain, was not always immediate. "Punishments," says Ryther, "follow Provoca-
tions, sooner, or later. . . . Long forbearance is no for-
giveness. There will come a storm, a stroak, that will pay
for all. God will not let sin go unpunished. If punishments escape you at Land, they shall meet you at Sea.
. . ." [44] Readers ought, then, to heed the lessons of recorded accounts, for, as Thomas Taylor puts it, "It is just
with God, that those that will not *take* example, should
make examples; that if they will not bee bettered by
other mens harmes, others may be bettered by theirs." [45]

Just as divine judgments could *drive* man to God, deliverances might *draw* them to him. Providence writers
generally attributed an individual's deliverance not to
past merit, but to God's future plans for that individual.
In effect, a deliverance was a specific call from God—
usually simply a dramatic call for repentance, but sometimes a specific call to some kind of higher spiritual duty,
for the God who had delivered Jonah from the whale's
belly still had the same aims and could use similar
means. Because deliverances involved a divine singling
out, failure to respond spiritually to these experiences
was an especially serious sin; often, a deliverance
brought an individual's final opportunity to repent, for
God might well turn a deaf ear to anyone ungrateful
enough to remain spiritually unmoved after being physically rescued. As Flavell says in *Navigation Spiritualized*,

[42] *The Sea-Mans Direction*, p. 75.
[43] See John Ryther's discussion of how to find the "Jonah" (*Plat*, p. 170 ff.).
[44] *Ibid.*, p. 123.
[45] *Practice of Repentance*, p. 14.

Sometimes the Lord for the magnifying of the riches of his goodness upon you, drives you to such exigencies, that . . . *all hope of being saved is taken away*: Nothing but death before your eyes. The Lord commands a wind out of his treasury, bids it go and lift up the terrible waves; lock you in upon the shore, and drive you upon the rocks, so that no art can save you; and then sends you a piece of wreck, or some other means to land you safe: And all this to give you an experiment of his goodness and pity, that you may learn to fear that God, in whose hand your soul and breath is.[46]

Ryther, in a sermon appended to Janeway's anthology, puts it more simply: "Some have escaped Shipwrack of Soul, by Shipwrack of body." [47]

The real purpose of special providences was, in fact, not physical but spiritual, for God's plan aimed at man's ultimate salvation, not at a mechanical control of the physical world. As a physical deliverance may be the means of a spiritual one (Ryther calls this circumstance a "double deliverance"), physical rescue is ultimately emblematic of God's action in human life. An illustration prefixed to Janeway's *Token for Mariners* epitomizes the physical-spiritual implications of providences as interpreted in the Puritan myth: two men grasp a plank near a ship tossed in a stormy sea; in the sky above, a large, sun-like eye focuses downward, extending to the sea a beam which offers both deliverance and salvation.[48]

[46] *Navigation Spiritualized; or a New Compass for Seamen* (Newburyport, 1796 [first published, 1664]), pp. 55–56.
[47] *The Seaman's Preacher*, in *Token for Mariners*, pp. 120[for 118]–119.
[48] In the illustration, the eye takes the place of the sun and suggests a common Renaissance metaphor, that of the sun's beams extending to man to offer salvation, as the beams of the Son's cross had done. See, e.g., George Herbert's "Matins."

The joys of deliverance could easily blind a person to his debt of gratitude, and the providence writers duly warn of the dangerous ease of forgetfulness. Recipients of God's mercy were of course obligated to morally upright conduct ("Each Person," says Stanhope in *The Seaman's Obligations to Gratitude and a Good Life* [1699], "ought to make his diligence in pleasing God hold proportion with the marks of his having been the peculiar Care of his Providence"[49]), but two rather more specific duties also engaged them. First, they must keep any promises they had made in distress, for if they did not, even more terrible dangers would result. This obligation was especially urged upon those who had escaped disasters at sea, for seamen were notorious for making rash promises in distress, but, like Crusoe and his comrades on the first voyage, for breaking them once danger had passed. "You are delivered from the tempest, doe not now sinne more," exhorts Burroughs. "When you have escaped one ship-wracke, take heed of a worse shipwrack, namely that of faith, and of putting away conscience. . . ."[50] Promises in distress are considered the "seeds of a godly life,"[51] and the degree of distress determined what quality of moral response was demanded, so that dramatic sea rescues induced a rather greater than usual moral obligation.[52]

A second duty involved the continual remembrance of one's deliverances and the devotional contemplation of

[49] P. 20.
[50] *The Sea-Mans Direction*, p. 79.
[51] *Ibid.*, p. 80.
[52] This address to seamen is typical: "Consider what engagements ly upon you to be singularly holy, from your singular deliverances & salvations. . . . Sometimes [seamen's] ships have been cast away, & yet they themselves wonderfully got safe to shore upon planks, yards, masts &c. I might be endless in enumerating their deliverances from drowning, from burning, from slavery, &c. Sure (*seamen*) your extraordinary salvations lie more than ordinary engagements upon you, to praise, love, fear[,] obey and trust in your saviour and deliverer" (T. M.'s "Epistle to Seamen," in Flavell's *Navigation Spiritualized*, p. 21).

them. *"It is the duty of the saints,"* says Flavell, *"especially in times of straits, to reflect upon the performances of Providence for them in all the states, and through all the stages of their lives."* [53] Recalling these events was not only spiritually rewarding in itself but was also morally efficacious, for it revivified the magnetism of goodness in a world where sin's appeal was likely to be overpowering. "O, Labour to keep the sense of [deliverances] fresh upon your spirits," says Ryther, "[for] when we lose the sense of the mercy, then we are easily drawn into sin." [54] Some immediacy could be gained by reading vivid accounts of the experiences of others, and providence writers advertised the merits of their tradition by enjoining readers to reflect upon all recorded experiences, though they admitted that vicarious remembrances were always less effectual than one's own experience.

Because man's memory was not wholly to be trusted and because one man's deliverance could benefit others, recipients of God's mercy ought not only to *recall* but to *record* their experiences. "Trust not your slippery memories," says Flavell in a Postscript to his *Divine Conduct,* "with such a multitude of remarkable passages of Providence as you have, and shall meet with in your way to Heaven. . . . Written memorials secure us against that hazard; and besides, makes them useful to others when we are gone. . . . Certainly it were not so great a loss, to lose your Silver, your Goods and Chattels, as it is to lose your Experiences which God hath this way given you in this world." [55] To authenticate their demands,

[53] *Divine Conduct,* p. 8.
[54] *Plat,* p. 94.
[55] *Divine Conduct,* pp. [268–69]. Josiah Woodward advises seamen similarly: "Record the special Mercies of God in some Book for that Purpose; which will be a Thing of great Pleasure and Advantage to you. For, by reading them over as you sit in your House, and in rehearsing them to your Relations and Friends in your Discourse, you will have a Fresh Taste of God's Goodness, which will tend to enliven

the providence writers drew upon the example of the Bible [56] and upon the long-established reasons for keeping a diary or a spiritual autobiography. But the public theological and moral function of the providence tradition deepened the dimension of its demands. The following rationale for recording special events might well serve as an epitome of the aims of the entire tradition:

First, in regard of *God.* It is an especiall meanes of continuing and propagating the honour of God, arising from such memorable matters, longer and further than otherwise it would be. . . .
Secondly, in regard of *our selves.* By such memorials our faith, hope, feare, and other like Graces, may be the better preserved, quickned, and strengthned. . . .
Thirdly, in regard of *others.* A ground of faith and hope in Gods goodnesse, power, prudence, and other excellencies is hereby afforded to succeeding ages.[57]

---

your Affections and Thankfulness to the gracious Preserver of Men. . . . These Demonstrations of God's Being, and his gracious and special Care of Men ought to be recorded in some Public Register, or however, to have been set down in your Journals and Diaries" (*The Seaman's Monitor; or Advice to Sea-Faring Men* [8th ed.; London, 1776; first published, 1703], pp. 39–40).

[56] They noted, for example, that after God had providentially sent a ram as a substitute sacrifice for Isaac, Abraham named the location "Jehovah Jireh" as testimony of divine deliverance, so that the name (meaning "God will provide") was an emblem for subsequent generations. Providence writers also noted that the many events marking the deliverance of the Hebrews from Egypt (which they interpreted as a "type" of mankind's deliverance from the bondage of sin) were meticulously recorded by biblical writers. This deliverance from Egypt, according to William Gouge, "was one of the most famous deliverances that ever God gave to a people. . . . No wonders are more frequently repeated and brought to the mindes of Gods people in the Old Testament than these" (*Mercies Memoriall* [London, 1645], p. 4). The relevance of the Israelite deliverance for contemporary England is discussed in *A Memorial of God's last Twenty Nine Years Wonders in England* (London, 1689). For a discussion of Puritan preoccupation with this "type," see Chapter V below.

[57] Gouge, *Mercies Memoriall,* p. 12. Many writers offered elaborate lists of reasons. See, e.g., Ryther's five reasons (*Plat,* pp. 98–100) and Flavell's ten (*Divine Conduct,* pp. 163–205).

In surveying the providence literature before 1719, one might easily beguile oneself into errors made by students of sources, for the providence tradition affords many parallels to *Robinson Crusoe*. But ultimately the striking thing is not the similarity of fact and event between *Robinson Crusoe* and its analogues, but the similarity of meaning given to stories of physical and spiritual castaways. Factual accounts in both providence and travel literature reflect events which recur again and again in an age of increasing maritime exploration and colonization, but, unlike the travel tradition, the providence tradition focuses upon the strange and surprising aspects of these events and interprets them within a religious and philosophical framework which invests them with important meaning. And providence literature reflects the pattern of Christian experience central to the Puritan myth and organizes its *exempla* into a dramatic realization of the historical cycle, seen teleologically.

In 1704, Defoe had himself written in the providence tradition and had showed himself familiar with its ideas and conventions. In *The Storm: Or, a Collection of the Most Remarkable Casualties and Disasters Which Happen'd in the Late Dreadful Tempest, Both by Sea and Land,* Defoe interprets a spectacular storm as a judgment upon the sins of England (he uses a similar theme in *Journal of the Plague Year,* also related to the providence tradition) and says that he offers the anthology "to preserve the Remembrance of Divine Vengeance." [58] Defoe's Preface sets forth his aim: "The main Inference I shall pretend to make . . . is, the strong Evidence God has been pleas'd to give in this terrible manner to his own Being, which Mankind began more than ever to affront and despise. . . ." [59] The rendering and pointing

[58] P. 84.
[59] Fols. A5^v–A6.

of the accounts in *The Storm* suggests that Defoe well knew the matter and manner of his tradition and that, long before he undertook the art of fiction, he understood how to give anecdotes a thematic unity in the Puritan manner.

Defoe's prefatory statement in *Robinson Crusoe* that he sought to *"justify and honour the Wisdom of Providence in all the Variety of our Circumstances, let them happen how they will"* suggests that *Robinson Crusoe* shares the aims of the providence tradition, but Defoe goes beyond the tradition in contrasting the episodic appearance of events with the real orderliness of all. The dialectic of fall and recovery which is finally submerged by the total life pattern of Crusoe (an imitation, in little, of the process of history according to the Puritan myth) ultimately both subtilizes and expands the providence tradition's way of rendering *exempla,* and for this subtlety and expansion Defoe draws upon other Puritan literary traditions, particularly those of spiritual biography and pilgrim allegory. *Robinson Crusoe* is not, like *God's Protecting Providence,* merely an account of the workings of providence; unlike the stark *exempla* of Turner's *Compleat History* or the undeveloped spiritual history of Alexander Selkirk in *Providence Displayed,* it achieves a meaning that goes beyond a paraphrase of its theme. The polemical anecdotes in providence literature only illustrate a lesson, and the characters who people them (although historical) are both less humanized and less individualized than the fictional Crusoe. *Robinson Crusoe* is not adequately defined as a providence book any more than as a youth guide. But in its way of interpreting events according to a thematic scheme, and in its organizing pattern, *Robinson Crusoe* relies upon providence literature in a manner which Defoe could expect his contemporaries to recognize. When he told them that he was justifying God's ways to man, he may have spoken only part of the truth, but he was not lying. *Robinson Crusoe* rises above the polemics of the providence tradition and, ultimately, above all the Puritan subliterary traditions, but the quality of Defoe's originality should not obscure the nature of his dependence upon those traditions. The imagination which gave birth to *Robinson Crusoe* and which generated a new set of possibilities in prose fiction was steeped in the theological-moral tradition of lay polemics and was trained in the habitual patterns of the Puritan mind.

IV

Spiritual Biography

———◆•••◆———

God's control of human history manifested itself in ways other than the dramatic ones of which providence literature was made, and the seventeenth century found other forms in which to demonstrate other patterns of divine activity. Because they viewed all human events as ultimately ordered by God, Christian apologists found meaning even in seemingly trivial happenings, and they endeavored to discover patterns which organized the ordinary with the extraordinary into a coherent description of divine plan. And because they saw history as cyclical, they thought men could be instructed by these patterns. *"History . . . is of Noble, and necessary use,"* says Samuel Clarke, drawing upon Ecclesiastes 1:9, *"because by setting before us what hath been, it premonisheth us of what will be again: Sith the self same Fable is acted over again in the world, the persons only are changed that act it. . . ."* [1]

One exceptionally useful pattern of divine activity could be traced by examining in detail the experiences and motivations of a particular person, especially if that person bore unusual marks either of God's pleasure or of his displeasure. Accounts of such lives could formulate

[1] 1677 edition of *A General Martyrologie, Containing a Collection of All the Greatest Persecutions Which Have Befallen the Church of Christ, from the Creation, to Our Present Times,* fol. a1.

causes and effects to exhibit the purposeful nature of God's plan for an individual, and they could portray "examples" for the imitation or evitation of the reader, so that, like providence books, their function was not only polemical but moral. "Nature is delighted in History . . . ," writes Richard Baxter, "And the true History of exemplary Lives, is a pleasant and profitable recreation to young persons; and may secretly work them to a liking of Godliness and value of good men, which is the beginning of saving Grace." [2]

By the late seventeenth century, spiritual biography had become an important form of popular religious literature, for, according to its advocates, it demonstrated by example points argued more abstractly by the guide tradition.[3] The concreteness implicit in the form seemed particularly engaging in an age increasingly suspicious of religious or philosophical abstraction and attracted to practical examples. Clarke, quoting Dr. Sibbes, evaluates the "*four wayes . . . of teaching, Rule, Reason, Similitudes and Examples*," and concludes that examples are

[2] Baxter's preface to Samuel Clarke, *The Lives of Sundry Eminent Persons in This Later Age* (London, 1683), fol. a3ʳ.

[3] I use the term "spiritual biography" to describe "lives" published for didactic and polemical purposes. Spiritual autobiographies, discussed thoroughly by Starr (SA), were essentially a private form, intended for the use of the writer and sometimes for his close friends. John Helder (1694–1762[?]) restricted the use of his private autobiography typically: "I order," he wrote on the flyleaf of his manuscript, "this Book after my Decease to be given to the Deacons of the Congregational Church at Gilcham (to which I belong) to be kept by them with the other Books . . . for the *only* use of the Present and future Ministers . . ." (italics mine). Consciousness of audience produces substantial rhetorical differences between public and private forms and affects, too, the choice and elaboration of events. Professor Starr's strategy does not, it seems to me, allow him to make a clear distinction between subliterary forms which influence Defoe because their aims and techniques are like his, and other materials (farther in the background) which are concerned more broadly with the pattern of Christian life. Helder's manuscript is part of the Foot Collection in the library of the University of California, Riverside.

the most effective. *"The two former enjoyn,"* he says, *"but work not upon the affections; and as for Similitudes, they are for illustration, onely Examples conform us in a sweet alluring manner. . . ."* [4] Spiritual biographies updated and concretized biblical themes and offered Puritanism a kind of substitute for Catholic oral tradition. Says Daniel Burgess in his Preface to an anthology of spiritual biographies:

> *To me it seemeth no small Duty* . . . *to publish the Lives and Praises of Holy Men.* . . . *The* Memory of the Just should be blessed: *And the praise of such, is more* Gods *praise then* theirs. *As for themselves,* Saints need no Monuments. . . . *But the* Church *and* World *do need their Memorials: For* exemplified Sanctity, is the most Noble, Beautiful and Perswasive. *The Holiness that is in Gods* Children, *is of a* [?] *more excellent* kind, *than that which is in his* Holy Bible[;] *it is a living image of God; and that which is the transcendent* End, *of which the* Scripture *it self is but a* Means.[5]

By 1689, Cotton Mather might accurately claim that "the *Lives* of Pious Men have been justly esteemed among the most useful *Histories* which the Church of God Enjoyes. . . ." [6]

Spiritual biography recounted the adventures of a soul as it progressed through life to eternity, but the adventures often included nearly as many setbacks as successes, for the tradition mirrored the shifting conception of hero which permeated all forms of literature in the seventeenth century. Hagiology had, of course, a long previous history, but (as William Haller has argued convincingly) Puritanism gave spiritual biography a "spe-

---

[4] *A Collection of the Lives of Ten Eminent Divines* (London, 1662), fol. A2ᵛ.

[5] Burgess's preface to Robert Porter, *The Life of Mr. John Hieron. With the Characters and Memorials of Ten Other Worthy Ministers of Jesus Christ* (London, 1691), fols. A2–A2ᵛ.

[6] *Early Piety, Exemplified in the Life and Death of Mr. Nathanael Mather* (London, 1689), fol. A3ᵛ.

cial character."[7] Not only was the life of a saint or martyr considered significant and edifying; the travails of any Christian soul were useful and worthy of public record, for a convert or prospective convert could be inspired by the story of a common soul equally well as by that of a saint, whom he could not hope to emulate.[8] The theory of Puritan biography was not far from that of bourgeois tragedy or sentimental comedy.

In the midcentury anthologies of Samuel Clarke (*The Marrow of Ecclesiastical History, Contained in the Lives of the Fathers, and Other Learned Men and Famous Divines, Which Have Flourished in the Church since Christs Time, to This Present Age* [1650]; *A General Martyrologie* [1651]), the trend toward more modern spiritual biography is already noticeable, although the contemporary (or nearly so) lives which Clarke there chronicled were usually those of eminent Puritan divines. But his later volumes (*A Collection of the Lives of Ten Eminent Divines . . . and Some Other Eminent Christians* [1662], *The Lives of Sundry Eminent Persons in This Later Age* [1683]) demonstrate a more studied emphasis on less heroic figures, and many other spiritual biographies began to describe figures whose lives represented something less than remarkable instances of piety. John Shower's *Heaven and Hell: Or, the Un-*

---

[7] See *The Rise of Puritanism* (New York, 1938), p. 100 ff.

[8] Puritan writers continually emphasize the power of example and exhort their readers to imitation of the "saints." Common men thus become ideal subjects for spiritual biography, for they can be imitated more exactly by typical readers. Charles Morton, Defoe's mentor, says that example makes a "deeper impression than Rules, and [has] a very great influence in forming the Genius; specially of Youth, when they are stepping from Boy to Man, and are taking upon them to chuse their own way . . ." (*The Spirit of Man* [Boston, 1692], p. 22). William Gurnall, after concluding an account of an exemplary life, says that his heroine "hath not drawn up the ladder after her; use[?] her course, tread in her steps . . ." (*The Christians Labour and Reward* [London, 1672], p. 151). Note the spatial imagery in both passages, and see the discussion of such imagery in Chapters II and V of this study.

changeable State of Happiness or Misery for All Mankind in Another World. Occasion'd by the Repentance and Death of Mr. Shetterden Thomas (1700) depicts the sinful excesses of its subject, who, on his deathbed at the age of twenty-six, repented his heavy drinking, repudiated the evil influence of his friends, and requested that his mistakes be chronicled "in hope of doing Good to others." [9] And the deathbed "conversion" of Lord Rochester, though its sincerity was doubted by many contemporaries, inspired many accounts of his life which were "improved" for didactic purposes. "Having thus discharg'd the office of an Historian," writes Robert Parsons in concluding one of these accounts, "in a faithful representation of the repentance and conversion of this great Sinner; give me leave now to . . . *persuade you* . . . to follow this illustrious Person, not in his Sins any more, but in his Sorrows for them, and his forsaking them." [10]

The moral purpose of spiritual biographies comprehended lives like those of Thomas and Rochester as easily as lives of the consistently pious, for spiritual biographers, like the providence writers who interpreted divine punishments, could teach as well from negative as from positive examples, especially if the sinner ultimately saw the error of his ways and delineated the causes of his earlier sinful course. "Good examples," says Clarke in a preface to one of his anthologies, "are for imitation, bad for evitation." [11] Besides, dramatic conversions wrought by divine punishment of sinful courses could be rendered vividly to demonstrate the futility and horror of rebellion against God. Most useful of all were the lives of those who for a while pursued evil courses but who ul-

[9] The quotation is taken from Shower's title page. Shower says his treatise was "publish'd at the Desire and Direction of the Deceased."
[10] *A Sermon Preached at the Funeral of the Rt. Honorable John Earl of Rochester* (London, 1680), p. 40.
[11] *Ten Eminent Divines*, fol. A2ᵛ.

timately repented and turned their course toward heaven, for in such cases the biographer could interpret the variety of situations likely to confront readers of varying conditions and commitments. And if such variety was difficult to find in particular factual instances, spiritual biography as a total tradition could at least hope, like the providence tradition as a whole, to portray an infinite variety of experiences from which all readers might profit. Clarke's prefatory epistle to an early collection of *exempla* might well serve as an advertisement for his later anthologies of biography or even for the entire tradition of spiritual biography:

I presume that it will be superfluous for me to tell thee, what great benefit thou maist reap by acquainting thy self with these Examples: Dost thou live in places of danger & times of persecution? Here thou maist see how powerful & merciful the Lord is in supporting, or delivering his People in such times. Dost thou see the enemies of Gods Church to thrive, and prosper in their Malice, and Cruelty? Here thou maist see what the end of them is like to be, if they speedily repent not. Wouldst thou see the amiableness, & desireableness of Vertues & Graces? Here thou maist see it held forth unto thee in excellent Mirrours, or Looking-Glasses. Wouldst thou behold the ugliness, and danger of great, and horrid sins? Behold here Examples of the severity of Gods judgments against them. Wouldst thou find out, and propose some choice Patterns, and Presidents [precedents] for thine imitation? Here thou shalt find store, and variety of them.[12]

Spiritual biography shares the didactic purpose of the guide tradition, and its subject matter resembles that of the providence tradition, but its formal roots lie else-

---

[12] *A Mirrour or Looking-Glass Both for Saints, and Sinners, Held Forth in Some Thousands of Examples* (4th ed.; London, 1671; first published, 1646), fols. A3–A3ᵛ.

where. It becomes, in the hands of its best practitioners, a relatively sophisticated literary form, and, more than any tradition discussed so far, it has a direct bearing on the shape of the early novel, as I shall suggest in Chapter V. Spiritual biography strives for (though it does not always achieve) a balance between the particular and the general; it endeavors to present information about its subject's life in exact, intricate detail, and at the same time to discuss principles of religion and morality in terms understandable and appealing to readers of varying persuasions. This dual nature of spiritual biography is suggested by its rather intimate relationship to two other kinds of literature in the seventeenth century, the personal diary and the funeral sermon—one an essentially private mode, the other a public one. From the diaries which every Puritan was urged to keep for himself, spiritual biography takes much of its material, for a diary recorded in detail the ups and downs of its author's physical and spiritual fortunes, and reflected, presumably in an accurate manner, the pattern of life which spiritual biography makes public for imitational or evitational purposes. Funeral sermons also contribute some material to spiritual biography, for the sermons often close with a "life" of the deceased. But more important is the generalizing, hortatory influence of the sermons themselves. By the late seventeenth century, the funeral sermon had become less a doctrinal vehicle than a moral one, and the life of the deceased was interpreted and "improved" for the effects it could have on readers still adrift in life.

The popularity of diary-keeping among Puritans in the seventeenth century derives ultimately from the Puritan world view. Because all events were actively willed by

God, and because a proper understanding of divine intention depended upon correct interpretation of the pattern of events, every individual was obliged to observe carefully all those events which impinged on his life. But because the meaningful pattern of events was not always immediately self-evident, one needed to keep an event-by-event record so that he could later contemplate from a distance the interrelation of these events and comprehend God's total meaning in them. By keeping a diary, an individual (even a common man) helped to record human history and was, in a sense, a divine amanuensis if he observed and reported fully and accurately. The stuff of diaries might be readily absorbed, as it often was, into larger accounts of God's ways with man. Even when it was not, it instilled in its writers a continuous consciousness of the intimate relationship between human event and divine cause, and it developed or encouraged habits of close observation, formulation, and interpretation which manifest themselves in the public Puritan literature of the late seventeenth and early eighteenth century.

Practical and personal considerations also contributed greatly to the popularity of diary-keeping in Defoe's time. Keeping a diary was, first of all, an act of worship, a way of erecting a personal monument to God for his goodness, and because writing was permanent in a sense that speech was not, the recording of blessings was more pleasing to God than prayers of thanksgiving. (Diaries, like other written "memorials" of Puritanism, were a form of concretization which provided a substitute for the icons and material symbols which Puritanism rejected.) The reading of one's diary provided moral and spiritual inspiration, like that in the public literature of Puritanism, but the personal content gave diaries a greater immediacy of appeal. "Keep an exact Journal," advises John Ryther in *A Plat for Mariners* (1672), "observe what way you make, by this God may have glory; you may have past experiences to feed your faith, and hope upon for the future." [13] But most important, an accurately kept diary could provide an indication of one's spiritual standing, which was a practical necessity in a Calvinistically oriented religious life. Many Puritans thus kept diaries in scrupulous detail, recording not only the ups and downs of religious devotion but all events related to their lives, for (because God controlled everything) even seemingly trivial events often bore significant spiritual meanings, especially if the long-range pattern of events was carefully observed. Physical events were, in short, considered to be emblematic of spiritual ones.[14]

The minute detail of diaries often provided spiritual biographers with a wealth of information about their subjects—information which to modern eyes looks strange in accounts of a person's spiritual commitment. Robert Porter, for example, in an account of the life of John Hieron, meticulously lists fourteen events which Hieron had considered divine deliverances, of which the following is a fair sample:

1. *From a Cow . . . that took him on her horns. . . .*
2. *Falling out of a Chamber into a dry Fat in the lower room, yet no harm.*
3. *Fell out of a Boat into* Trent, *yet not hurt.*[15]

---

[13] *A Plat for Mariners: Or, the Seaman's Preacher* (London, 1672), fol. A3.

[14] Puritan writers continually emphasize the efficacy of historical account as an indication of divine "pattern." Flavell's comment is typical: "*Histories are usually read with delight: when once the fancy is catcht, a man knows not how to disengage himself from it. . . . . . Reader, thou only art able to compile the History of Providence for thy self, because the* memorials *that furnish it, are only in thine hands*" (*Divine Conduct: Or, the Mysterie of Providence* [London, 1678], fol. B2^v).

[15] *Hieron*, p. 2. A "fat" is a cask or vat.

Often, too, Puritan attention to minutiae was pointed up by the introspective habits of mind which diary-keeping encouraged. Richard Baxter reflects upon his boyhood aims this way: "I was much addicted to the excessive gluttonous eating of Apples and Pears; which I think laid the foundation of that *Imbecillity* and Flatulency of my Stomach, which caused the Bodily Calamities of my Life. . . . I was extreamly bewitched with a Love of Romances, Fables, and old Tales, which corrupted my Affections and lost my Time."[16] More standard biographical facts—such as parentage, employment, dates of significant happenings and decisions—usually are also incorporated in spiritual biographies. Sometimes they are supplied by diaries, sometimes by friends, and sometimes by more public sources, but these basic facts are also seen in terms of their spiritual significance.[17] Thus, the mention of one's parentage requires a full description of family piety or impiety, early religious instruction and the subject's reaction to it, and the influence of parents upon the subject's choice of calling. And often dates of important events, especially events like special providences, are considered spiritually significant by both subject and biographer, and the biographer details the celebration of their anniversaries. Of particular importance is the date of one's conversion, for it becomes his new birthday.

The day of repentance or conversion is almost always the central event in a Puritan diary, just as it is in many

[16] *Reliquiae Baxterianae: Or, Mr. Richard Baxter's Narrative of the Most Memorable Passages of His Life and Times,* ed., Matthew Sylvester (London, 1696), p. 2.

[17] In *The Life and Death of M. Bolton,* Edward Bagshaw says that he will "begin with his birth" because "I observe that throughout the sacred Bible, and writings on the persons of holy men, their places of birth are ever remembered; God loves the very ground his servants tread on . . ." (prefixed to *Mr. Boltons Last and Learned Work* [London, 1639], pp. 4–5).

forms of spiritual autobiography and in the public literary forms which describe the lives of saints. Conversion
arrests the downward cycle of events and embarks man
upon the mountainous "way" to paradise. The way remains hazardous, just as Bunyan describes it in *The Pilgrim's Progress,* and the diary-keeper often finds himself
slipping from the road into byways or being detained by
human or natural obstacles. He observes carefully each
obstacle and each of his deviations, striving for a faithfulness to particulars in detailing each experience; for he
is perpetually searching for the developing shape of his
life, trying to draw everything he does and everything he
sees into a unified vision that will simultaneously assure
him of his own election and deepen his insight into the
relationship of man to God, of this world to the world beyond his journey. All diaries thus take on first the shape
of the typical pattern of experience common to all who
repent and strive to remain true to the way they have
chosen, then of the specific individual whose relationship to God assumes particular patterns that reveal the
uniqueness of every spiritual experience. The diary thus
traces the typical downward-upward pattern of a person's spiritual life (or, put in linear terms, the running
from and then the moving toward the heavenly destination); it also comprehends the particular rhythm which
renders every man's relationship with God unique.

Diaries were not, of course, devoid of reflection and
interpretation, for the diary-keeper expected the re-
reading of his experiences to prompt him to higher pla-
teaus of virtue. Because they were a private form, however, diaries lacked the rhetorical exhortation and the
generalizing of experience which came to characterize
spiritual biography. Funeral sermons, on the other

hand, specialized in moral exhortation upon the memory of the deceased, and if biographical facts were included (as increasingly they were, late in the seventeenth century), they usually remained subordinate to interpretation and exhortation.[18] The sermons centered on standard themes—the shortness of life and the necessity of being prepared for death, the danger of postponing conversion until one's deathbed, the horrors of apostasy, the necessity of following the advice of spiritual leaders— and used the life of the deceased to point up and dramatize their message, thereby heightening the emotion of the hortatory appeal.[19]

Typical of late seventeenth-century funeral sermons is Timothy Cruso's *The Period of Humane Life Determined by the Divine Will* (1688), preached after the death of Henry Brownsword. In his preface, Cruso suggests the kind of edification to be derived from such sermons: *"Young men especially will here see (who are apt to be too much diverted by urgent temptations) how great a necessity lyes upon them, to be sober-minded; and to abound in that work, which deserves the most and best of our time; that they may not lose their souls in*

[18] Typical is John Shower's *A Funeral Sermon, Preached upon the Death of the Reverend Mr. Nathaniel Oldfield* (London, 1697). In his first forty-five pages Shower advises the following of spiritual guides (i.e., ministers); he then adds a forty-page eulogy of Oldfield. The eulogy uses biographical facts only incidentally but dwells upon the *pattern* of Oldfield's life. Shower says he does not "design to give you the History of his Parentage, Birth and Education . . . but some Account of his *Example, as a Christian,* and *as a Minister of Christ;* that being the more sensible of your Loss, you may take the more care to improve it" (p. 45).

[19] Shower, in a funeral sermon for a seventeen-year-old girl, typically tries to turn the emotionality of the occasion into Christian commitment. After the main body of his discourse, but before offering some biographical anecdotes, he says: "Therefore instead of an intemperate Mourning at [saints'] departure, let us imitate their Examples, and propound their holy Lives and Deaths as our Pattern and Encouragement" (*A Sermon Preacht upon the Death of Mrs. Anne Barnardiston* [London, 1682], p. 31).

the pursuit of Youthfull lusts." The first half of the sermon then argues that God controls the world so exactly
that he determines the precise moment of every individual's birth and death. Providential control, says Cruso,
"does not only extend to the whole Creation, or to the
whole lump of Mankind *in general,* but to every *one,*
separately by himself, and every *part,* in every individual *moment.*" The moral is, of course, that man should
be spiritually prepared for death whenever God should
will it, and the last half of the sermon warns against
complacency and exhorts early conversion lest one
should "come and *knock at Gods Door* too late!"
Brownsword's own pious childhood and youth are
cited as exemplary, for "he was born of *Holy Parents*"
and after he was orphaned he nevertheless "by a special
Providence . . . enjoy'd the benefit of a very pious Education, the impression whereof he retain'd to the very
last, and the seed which was then sown, sprung up plen-
tifully in his *Riper years.*" Cruso also chronicles Brownsword's temptations and his victories over them, and reports the remorse Brownsword felt for even his smallest
"abatements in his Zeal and spiritual fervour . . . more
than other men do the blackest Impieties." [20]

The dominant characteristics of both the personal
diary and the funeral sermon are merged in spiritual biography in a way that writers hoped would be educa-
tional, inspiring, and productive of greater piety and
higher morality. Usually, informational and hortatory
sections more or less alternate throughout the work,
though the better written biographies attempt to make
as much instruction as possible implicit in the narrative
sections. The purposeful pattern of the subject's life is
superimposed over the chronological record of events,
and the commentary and exhortation seem to draw the

[20] Fols. A3–A3ᵛ, pp. 19, 30, 27, 29.

events to their inevitable conclusion in the ultimate spiritual victory of the subject. Stylistically and artistically the biographies vary widely, from the wild, ranting, shrill harangues of the more emotional sects to the calm, reasoned way of Richard Baxter's *Autobiography* and the later anthologies of Clarke. The rhythm of spiritual success and failure varies with the "altitudos" or "backslides" of each individual and with the particular meanings of event patterns revealed to the hero or to the interpreter writing about the hero. But all spiritual biographies (like private forms concerned with the spiritual regeneration of man) share one pattern: the tracing of a rebellion-punishment-repentance-deliverance sequence described from the earliest moment of Christendom as characteristic of fallen men who are accorded God's grace.[21]

Readers of *The Pilgrim's Progress*, as well as of *Grace Abounding*, will recognize the basic pattern of spiritual biography, for ultimately the pilgrimage of an allegorical figure through life is not far from the typical journey through life of a real person, as I shall suggest more fully in Chapter V. *Robinson Crusoe* is shaped more directly by the pilgrim allegories which grow out of the spiritual biography tradition, but the line of ancestry is clear. The organizational pattern of *Robinson Crusoe* follows chronological lines, but, as in a typical spiritual biography, a thematic superstructure is the real unifying principle. Events in *Robinson Crusoe*, like those in spiritual biographies, are validated relative to the total pattern of an individual's life, and the events are "improved" ap-

[21] For excellent discussions of Christian life pattern, and the centricity of conversion, see Roger Sharrock's Introduction to *Grace Abounding* (London, 1962), pp. xxvii–xxx; and Starr (SA), p. 39 ff.

propriately in order to draw the reader himself to a special view of religion and to a personal practice of higher morality.

Arthur W. Secord's statement that "the resemblance . . . of *Robinson Crusoe* to biography is easy to exaggerate" results from a faulty understanding of what biography was for Defoe's audience and from an inaccurate appraisal of Defoe's artistic intention. "In spite of the title," says Secord, "the story is almost wholly limited to an account of Crusoe's adventures at sea and on his island."[22] Secord ignores the fundamental historical fact that Defoe follows the way of *spiritual* biography in depicting adventures which are at once most dramatic and most specifically related to the basic pattern of his subject's life. And Defoe does tell us of Crusoe's early life insofar as it is related to the pattern which emerges later in his life.[23]

Defoe's awareness of spiritual biography as a tradition is dramatically suggested by his early authorship of two brief items. One, a poem about Defoe's former pastor, Dr. Samuel Annesley, was published in 1703 and contains rather general biographical eulogy. As poetry, it rates little attention, and one could hardly predict Defoe's later interest in biography on the basis of its factual contents. But it does suggest an awareness of typical Puritan didactic application:

> *But would* you *like a Man,* or Christian grieve
> *When others die, be thankful you're alive;*

---

[22] *Studies in the Narrative Method of Defoe* ("University of Illinois Studies in Language and Literature," IX; Urbana, 1924), p. 16.

[23] The influence of spiritual biography upon the literary form of biography has not been adequately discussed. It seems to me likely that the use of extraordinary detail and the attempt to isolate a thematic pattern—characteristic of early biography—derive from the same philosophical basis as the emphasis on detail and pattern in early fiction.

Improve the Great Examples you look on,
And take their Deaths for Warnings of your own.[24]

The second, *Memoirs of the Life and Eminent Conduct of That Learned and Reverend Divine, Daniel Williams,*[25] is longer and more elaborate and suggests a more intimate acquaintance with the conventions of spiritual biography. Defoe declines to employ most of the conventions, but his decision is calculated. "I shall not," he says at the beginning, "*as is usual in Histories of this kind,* trouble my self or the Reader of these Sheets with the looking back to his Nativity, Genealogy, or Introduction into the World, or into that Sphere of Action which he was in his Childhood appointed to move in. . . . But proceed to the more weighty Affairs of his Life, and of the Times he liv'd in. . . ." At the end, he again sums up his procedures and notes their departure from "usual" practice.[26]

Defoe's knowledge of the "usual" suggests an awareness of the tradition that corresponds with his awareness of other Puritan subliterary forms. *The Family Instructor,* with its "Entirely New Way" of constructing a guide, puts some of this awareness to use, but its full potential is not realized until he turns to fiction, building novels upon a structure developed in spiritual biography and upon themes and aims developed in other Puritan traditions.

Spiritual biography, drawing also from these other traditions, is polemical biography, and it selects facts to accord with its thesis. In *Robinson Crusoe* Defoe is also selective, and it is the particular principle of selectivity involved, rather than the quantity or completeness of in-

[24] "The Character of the Late *Dr. Samuel Annesley,* by Way of Elegy," in *A True Collection of the Writings of the Author of The True Born English-man* (London, 1703), p. 111.
[25] London, 1718.
[26] Pp. 1, 84. Italics mine.

formation, which is significant. The artistry of *Robinson
Crusoe* cannot be fully described in terms of previous
biographical traditions, not even in terms of the "fictional" tradition (pilgrim allegory) which descends from
spiritual biography.[27] But a look at the biographical traditions that Defoe and his readers knew reveals ancestors
of *Robinson Crusoe* which, if they are less developed
and polished, still show us a crude form of what is to
come and enable us to isolate a family line that finds its
finest expression much later in Hawthorne, Melville, and
the symbolic novel.

[27] See Chapter V below.

V

Metaphor, Type, Emblem, and the Pilgrim "Allegory"

Most of our facile assumptions about the seventeenth-century world picture derive from the nineteenth century and, like so many fruits of nineteenth-century scholarship, cannot stand the light provided by the scholarship of our own time. Recent attempts to assess the implications of Ramism demonstrate the inadequacy of received opinion about the seventeenth-century mind and its way of perceiving its world; the old generalizations will not embrace some of the new facts, and we must be constantly willing to re-examine received opinion about aesthetics and literary forms as the truth about modes of thought becomes more clear.[1] William Haller and Perry Miller have etched outlines for a broadened understanding of seventeenth-century Puritanism, and Charles Feidelson has pursued the implications for American literature.[2] I wish now to suggest that the Puritan

[1] I am thinking particularly of Walter J. Ong's seminal *Ramus: Method, and the Decay of Dialogue* (Cambridge, Mass., 1958), and two interpretive studies of Milton based upon Ong's work: Isabel Mac-Caffrey, *Paradise Lost as "Myth"* (Cambridge, Mass., 1959), and Jackson I. Cope, *The Metaphoric Structure of Paradise Lost* (Baltimore, 1962). The full implications of Ramism for other Puritan writers have yet to be studied.

[2] See Miller, *The New England Mind: The Seventeenth Century* (New York, 1939), and *The New England Mind: From Colony to Province* (New York, 1953); Haller, *The Rise of Puritanism* (New York, 1938), and *Liberty and Reformation in the Puritan Revolution* (New York, 1955); and Feidelson, *Symbolism and American Literature* (Chicago, 1953).

93

fondness for metaphor, so brilliantly explored by Professor Feidelson, has significant implications for the beginnings of the English novel. I think that it is no coincidence that the first major early English writers of prose fiction were steeped in Puritan tradition, and I suspect that the novel as an art form owes a great debt to Puritan modes of thought and to the Puritan response to significant ideological developments of the seventeenth century.[3]

In the cosmology of the Middle Ages and early Renaissance, the Doctrine of Correspondences seemed not only valid as a general theory but as a detailed description of reality, and analogy could be a useful and an accurate epistemological tool. Until well into the seventeenth century, there was enough of the medieval view remaining that a Sir Thomas Browne could still argue cosmology from biology and could still regard the microcosm-macrocosm idea not as a figure of speech, but as an exact representation of reality.[4] But the seventeenth century also introduced the possibility of a new world view. From its inception, the new science held in its powerful hand the potential doom of both the old cosmology and the old epistemology, though the old world view did not end with a bang. The implications of Baconian thought only gradually dawned on the seventeenth century, but once that dawn had come, there was no sweeping back its light, even if men were emotionally unprepared for what it would show.

[3] When the relation between Ramism and the Puritan commitment to metaphor is fully explored, I suspect that we shall have the basis for new theories about the emergence of the novel.

[4] "To call ourselves a microcosm or little world, I thought it only a pleasant trope of rhetoric, till my nearer judgment and second thoughts told me there was a real truth therein" (*Religio Medici*, First Part, ed. James Winny [Cambridge, 1963], p. 42).

In the early years of Defoe's life, the old world was no longer intact, but one might still hear the shrill, anguished cries (and the whimpers) of men bound emotionally to the old assumptions and fearful of new ones. No longer able to argue metaphysics through the simple one-to-one relationship of analogy, defenders of the older, simpler view clung tenaciously to all they could salvage from a disintegrated world. But they began, too, to offer substitutes for what was now untenable—substitutes which still fit a body of thought processes too fully developed to be re-formed but which were cut in the styles of a newer era.

The old view assumed a symmetry of relationships between orders of things in the created world, but the symmetry was also seen to extend to the spiritual world; the book of nature thus revealed the attributes of God in a precise and definable manner. Empirical observation of data undercut the assumptions about the created world and cast doubt upon the precision of any correspondences. But it could not, by its self-defined limitations, draw absolute conclusions (positive or negative) about the relationship between the created world and the spiritual world. Puritanism exploited this limitation to support its own philosophical commitment, even when it appeared to bow to the authority of the force it circumvented.

Puritanism was not, of course, alone in its attraction to the doomed world view, but its peculiar assets provided a way of compromise more honorable than that available to more venerable and more rational religious outlooks. The Puritan mind had a rather desperate commitment to pictorialness, and the denial of correspondence posed a direct threat to its characteristic way of perceiving reality. But ultimately its crisis provided its triumph, for, unable to utilize analogy, it substituted the less precise but equally pictorial mode of metaphor. The book of nature now became not a reproduction of the spiritual world nor an exact index of the attributes of God but, rather, an imperfect emblem of the spiritual world—an emblem which needed careful interpretation but which led equally surely, if not equally easily, to truth.[5] Thus, the characters in the book of nature were no longer strictly denotative, but they no longer needed to be, in Puritanism's slippery but artful logic. Benjamin Keach, who fought vigorously for linguistic precision even while bowing to a laxer logic, distinguishes the use of analogy (which he calls similitude) from metaphor in this way: "In a similitude there is a manifest *comparison* of one thing with another, and so 'tis a *logical* Argument; but in a *Metaphor* there is one thing put for another that's like it, which nevertheless in its explication is to be handled by an *apparent* similitude." [6]

Puritan writers of the later seventeenth century, forerunners of the physico-theologians of Defoe's maturity, observed the book of nature with the care of empiricists, and they interpreted the objects they saw as expressions of the highest spiritual truths. *"The irrational and inanimate, as well as rational creatures have a Language,"* writes John Flavell in *Husbandry Spiritualized* (1669), *"and though not by* Articulate *speech, yet in a* Metaphorical *sense, they preach unto man the Wisdom, Power, and goodness of God. . . ."* [7] Men might, therefore, become conscious of spiritual matters by meditating upon the objects of creation, even objects ordinarily not regarded as emblems. Flavell, for example, meditates "Upon the pulling up of a Leek," "Upon the new

[5] For the Puritan definition of emblem, see p. 29, n. 10.
[6] *Tropologia: Or a Key To Open Scripture Metaphors* (London, 1681), I, 38. Final italics mine.
[7] Epistle Dedicatory, fol. A2.

modelling of a Garden," "Upon the singing of a Nightingale," and "Upon the fighting of two Rams," and he urges men of all employments to make similar use of objects and events they encounter in their daily lives. Ultimately, these events and objects suggested not only theological but moral truth, and an individual might discover a peculiarly personal relevance in the conclusions that his meditations brought him, for, as both creator and governor of the world, God often used this "natural" way to reveal himself to his children.

The objects of creation thus took on a multiplicity of meanings, for application of the Protestant ideal of universal priesthood introduced almost unlimited subjectivism to the old book of nature concept. The new freedom of interpretation offered, too, a convenient substitute for the iconology which the Puritans denounced but toward which they were emotionally drawn by their mental habits of conceiving abstractions pictorially. Writers, or readers, or any men could now, in a sense, "create" their own objects of meditation without violating the stricture against making graven images, for the objects they contemplated were made by God, who alone was responsible for all their significations. The interpreter was not, therefore, usurping God's creative function (as did a maker of icons, according to Puritan theology), but was merely *discovering* some of the multiplicities of meanings that God offered man through his creations.

The conception of the book of nature as metaphorical continued to feed the Puritan desire for pictorialness (just as analogy had), but ultimately this conception helped defeat the underlying aim of pictorialness: clarity. Like most aspects of Puritan literalmindedness and dependence upon the concrete, metaphorical conception ultimately brought approximation and a blurring of dis-

tinctions. Its method was substitutional rather than ana-
lytical, and it resulted in a theology (and philosophy)
less precise because more subjective; theologically, Puritanism paid a high price for its metaphorical mode of
thinking, but new artistic possibilities were opened. In
1655, John Robinson had voiced the characteristic Puritan desire to "show," rather than to conceptualize, doctrine. "Me-thinks," he wrote in *The Birth of a Day*, "I
could wish with S. *Jerom*, that I were now in the top of
such a Watch-tower, that I might discover unto you the
ruines and alteration of all things in the world, from the
beginning of the Creation to this day; and present this
lively to your eyes, which I am fain to do now only to
your minds and understandings. . . ." [8] Such a wish
could accomplish little theologically, even if it could be
fulfilled, but Milton's prospect discovered the reaches of
art.

Robinson's wish and Milton's accomplishment both illustrate another aspect of the Puritan commitment to
metaphor, the treatment not only of objects but also of
events as keys to concepts. Full comprehension of the
world in metaphorical terms must, of course, include
time as well as space, and the Puritans ultimately attached their interpretation of the observable world to
their understanding of history. The fusion of observation
with history, of space with time, was wrought through
the Puritan understanding of the ultimate source of authority. The Bible provided an interpretation of the creation within a cyclical view of history; the Bible's details
were precise, its meanings resonant, and its implications
easily extended to include contemporary observation of
object and event.

By its emphasis on natural cause, the new science had

[8] (London, 1655), pp. 5–6.

obscured or blurred the divine significance of contemporary events, and Puritanism sought to restore the significance by a metaphorical collapsing of the present into the meaningful past of biblical times. It was not only in great artistic minds that a Cromwell or a Milton could become a Samson: in the minds of typical Puritan tradesmen and housewives, England was Israel and the Puritans were the persecuted chosen people. Puritans took these identifications seriously, for the cyclical pattern of history made such identifications more than mere possibilities to the symbolistic Puritan mind, which was anxious to see significance in its observed world. In effect, Puritanism divorced its historical present from the nonteleological implications of the new science; from an earlier, securer age it took a myth poised to withstand the challenge of modernity. For the fragmented vision of object and event which the new science offered, Puritanism substituted an internally consistent world of space and time, a world where object and event had purpose and, more important, where its meanings were discoverable.

Puritanism found the roots for identifications of one time with another in typological studies of the Bible—an approach to hermeneutics which began as early as the first century (espoused especially by Philo Judaeus) and which had been popular with the early church fathers and the Schoolmen. Strictly speaking, typology dealt with objects, men, or events in the Old Testament which in some sense prefigured the New Testament. "A Type," says Samuel Mather in *The Figures or Types of the Old Testament* (1683), "is some outward or sensible thing ordained of God under the Old Testament, to represent and hold forth something of Christ in the New." [9] Men like Adam, Abraham, Moses, and David are regarded as prefigurations or "types" of the primary "antitype"

[9] (London, 1683), p. 67.

(Christ) because aspects of their characters or events in their lives paralleled the New Testament accounts of Jesus. Moses, for example, led his people out of human bondage and toward a promised land, just as Jesus through his death freed men from their bondage to sin and promised them a better, purer life beyond the grave. Then, too, some events and concepts of the New Testament are seen to be prefigured in the Old Testament. Jonah's brief stay in the whale, for example, becomes a type of Jesus' burial and resurrection, and Noah's flood, a type of the atonement. A modern viewer is likely to find even the milder conclusions of typology often far-fetched and occasionally fantastic, but careful interpreters like Mather or Benjamin Keach (whose *Tropologia: Or a Key To Open Scripture Metaphors* [1681] contained a long "Treatise of Types, Parables, &c. with an Improvement of them Parallel-wise") strove diligently to separate legitimate, and, from their point of view, intentional, parallels from simply ingenious ones, for Puritans took their typology extremely seriously. Typology offered, according to its supporters, biblical insights which produced theological truth, but ultimately it produced fruits even more important to the seventeenth century's way of understanding itself—and to a subsequent understanding of changing literary forms.

Typology had never been a very exact science, and the seventeenth century, with great ease, broadened typology's scope beyond the confines of the Old and New Testaments, for its rules were loosely formulated; typology had remained more of a useful tool of interpretation than a distinct discipline. The broadened typology simply extended to contemporary history the principle of regarding one time in terms of another: biblical objects or events now might not only prefigure other biblical events or concepts but also the events of later history. Or, put another way, the broadened typology offered contemporary history an extended mythic dimension based upon past history frozen into static form. Different interpreters might choose to emphasize different segments of the biblical myth, but nearly all Puritan thinkers represented contemporary times as reflections (sometimes distorted, often blurred) of the Judeo-Christian experience recorded by inspired writers who understood divine purposes, and as part of the continuing movement of earthly history toward an inevitable climax. The broadened typology, violating the aims but not the methods of traditional typology, thus relieved biblical history of primary interpretive attention and instead made this history the ultimate symbolic (Defoe and his contemporaries would have said "emblematic") referent of contemporary events.

For seventeenth-century Puritanism, biblical history retained its authority as myth even when contemporary history and cosmology were divorced from the older world view which biblical writers had shared. Biblical history, in fact, provided a myth which gave artificial unity to a world stripped of its standard view of its own order. Because of the fragmenting influence of the new science, western civilization might never again possess a natural myth which encompassed all metaphysical reality, but art would always have to find a myth somehow in order to give its world a comprehensive coherence. And Puritanism, still trying to cling tenaciously to its old mythic world (based originally on analogy), actually gave art a *made* myth (based on metaphor), comprised of a comprehensive written formulation of the old—a made myth which has served many non-Puritans since, from Henry Fielding to William Faulkner and John Steinbeck.[10]

[10] Non-Puritans, however, usually seem to employ the myth as structural allusion without necessarily accepting its historicity. Often, too, they fragment or stretch the myth to their own purposes. My

For Puritanism, the made myth consisted of events in a pattern, or rather in a series of patterns, which all moved teleologically towards an end of history beyond the limits of the myth but prophesied within it. It was also comprised of meanings, of concepts imaged in events (atonement, for example): if contemporary events (such as "holy" wars, plagues, and tempests) recalled biblical events, these events could also suggest *concepts* in the myth (the dual nature of man, punishment for sin, or providential intervention for man's salvation). Contemporary events thus became emblems of concepts, and the contemporary world itself became emblematic of the spiritual or conceptual world which was the ultimate referent for all creation, the ultimate reality. Contemporary events and the contemporary world now operated only suggestively on man's perception, for the old precise system of analogies was gone, but even this small guide toward certitude gladdened the hearts of men bewildered by the rapidity of changes in their world. And they clung to their myth like a child to a blanket; it was their map to a simpler, securer world. For although historical perspective shows its referent to be a made one—a formulation retreated to in a state of cosmic despair—the Puritans found it to be their one unchanging object in a world of shifting perspectives, of conceptual flux.

Seventeenth-century Puritans, committed to a metaphorical way of thinking about their world, also expressed themselves metaphorically. Whether they were

essay "Steinbeck's Wine of Affirmation in *The Grapes of Wrath*" (*Essays in Modern American Literature,* ed. Richard E. Langford [Deland, Fla., 1963]) suggests how one later writer tries to twist time and event in a part of the myth in order to provide a deeper dimension for his rather thin narrative.

writing guides to religious action, recounting remarkable events occasioned by God's intervention in history, or tracing the lives of saints or sinners, Puritan writers slipped easily into the familiar metaphorical patterns, patterns derived for the most part from the Bible and dignified by long traditions of use and enrichment. Ultimately, popular tracts and treatises expressed almost all concerns—from matters of daily conduct to the weightiest theological issues—in numerous, thick, and often extended metaphors. Often a metaphor spreads over a number of paragraphs; sometimes a single metaphor informs an entire treatise.

Even though Puritan metaphor, unlike the metaphor of earlier Anglican sermons and tracts, derived chiefly from the Bible, the possibilities of variety in metaphor were still extensive, for the Puritans found biblical events, persons, and objects to represent virtually all aspects of contemporary life. They leaned most heavily, however, upon three metaphors. The metaphor of spiritual warfare suggested the conflict between good and evil that continually raged, both in the hearts of men and in the events in which men participated. The metaphor of the journey expressed the transitory nature of man's position in this world and suggested the progress necessary to deliver him to his heavenly goal. The metaphor of the wilderness combined the implications of the first two, suggesting the conflicts and temptations of the human soul journeying toward its promised land, as well as the barren condition of an unregenerated soul fallen from its original garden state.

The metaphor of warfare probably receives its direct impetus from England's civil conflicts in mid-century, but it ultimately derives from the concept of holy war in the Old Testament. Puritan guide writers regarded the conflict between good and evil as man's central problem, and in their writings they tried to bolster the defenses of men whose weakened wills made them prey to the powerful forces of Satan, forces which had an ally in the heart of every man because of original sin. Guide writers, spiritual biographers, and pilgrim allegorists regarded the whole world as the battlefield on which the conflict was fought, and they sought to describe all of life in terms of this fundamental conflict. Book titles (Andrew Gray's *The Spiritual Warfare* or Benjamin Keach's *War against the Devil*, for example) reflect the preoccupation with the metaphor, and the implication of the metaphor pervades almost all Puritan literature of the second half of the seventeenth century. In warning men of the personal dangers the war occasioned, Richard Baxter epitomizes the breadth and depth of contemporary Puritan feeling: "The *world* is formed *into two Armies* [Good and Evil], that live in continual War. . . . This War is carried on on both sides *within us*, and *without us*; by inward solicitations and outward means. . . ." [11]

Puritanism worked out the metaphor in great detail, and played a large number of variations upon it, exploiting fully the possibilities of armor imagery (the guide tradition often described its own task in terms of armor), military ritual, bestial antagonism (lambs pitted against wolves and doves against serpents), and disguise images which suggested the subtle infiltration techniques of Satan. Because the warfare metaphor remains submerged throughout most of *Robinson Crusoe*, little attention need be given here to most of the forms of the metaphor; but one might keep in mind the Puritan emphasis upon the shape-shifting of Satan. "This *Subtil Enemy*," says

[11] *A Christian Directory* (London, 1673), p. 105.

Richard Claridge, "is to be Watched against with *All Diligence,* whether he Roar as a *Lion,* Rage as a *Bear,* Tempt and Twist as a *Serpent,* or Appear in the Similitude of an *Angel of Light.* . . ." [12] Puritans often drew out the implications of the metaphor to suggest that man's battles against nature, particularly his encounters with wild beasts, emblematized his war against the devil and ultimately reflected the world's continual conflict since Adam's fall.

The journey metaphor is even more pervasive in Puritan writings of the seventeenth century, for concern with moral conduct focused attention on the pattern of man's life—and, besides, travel metaphor had a peculiar excitement and urgency in this age of new discovery. The Bible was, again, the ultimate source of the Puritan metaphor, even though other versions of the metaphor (travel as quest, travel as learning experience) were available in western tradition. Puritanism wished to emphasize the transitory nature of man's existence on this earth—to suggest that man's real home was in heaven and that in this world he was merely a pilgrim or sojourner. The later New Testament epistles, written when Jesus' second coming was expected imminently (see, e.g., Hebrews 11:13 or I Peter 2:11), described man in these terms and probably provided Puritanism with the primary "source" for the metaphor, but it is implicit much earlier in biblical writings, even in the early Old Testament. Puritan writers, in fact, often derived their authority for the metaphor from the account in Genesis of man's expulsion from Eden, an account which fuses the themes of man's ultimate alienation from the world he lives in, his erratic pattern because of origi-

[12] *Mercy Covering the Judgment Seat* (London, 1700), p. 27.

nal sin, and his final aspiration to a higher world. "Every child of *Adam*," says Timothy Cruso, "is a miserable *Wanderer* from the birth." [13] But the Puritans also drew upon the metaphor's long tradition of use. "The saints of God are spiritual Travellers," says Benjamin Keach; "they are far from their Father's House, Heaven is their everlasting Home, and thither they are going. All the holy Patriarchs and Prophets confessed they were Pilgrims on the Earth." [14]

The travel metaphor is applied variously by Puritan writers who sometimes emphasize the uncertain, erratic nature of man's movement through life and sometimes his progress, even though confronted by formidable obstacles, toward his final destination. The emphasis depended, primarily, on whether a particular writer was discussing unregenerated man or man after conversion. Guide writers, concerned primarily with directing wayward men to the path of righteousness, found the metaphor particularly relevant, for they described their own function in spatial terms. "This is the proper work of a Guide," says Timothy Cruso in *God the Guide of Youth*, "to direct the Ignorant Traveller in a strange Land, and unknown Countrey. Such is our Case during the *time of our Sojourning* here in this World; and it is the work of the *only wise God*, to *guide our feet, and direct our steps.* . . ." [15]

Most often, the travel metaphor took on the specific

[13] *God the Guide of Youth* (London, 1695), p. 22. Often Puritan interpreters discussed New Testament and Old Testament bases of the metaphor together. Robert Bragge, for example, reads the account of the Fall in terms of a New Testament parable: "Christ's Parable of the Prodigal, belongs to *Adam*, as well as his Posterity. He quickly turn'd the back, in wandring from God; and spent, by one riotous Act, the vast Patrimony he was intrusted with. Now what he was by Choice, we are by Nature; Straglers from the very Womb" (*The Youth's Interest* [London, 1706], p. 13).

[14] *Tropologia*, II, 170.

[15] Pp. 12–13.

form of a sea journey, for in an age of growing exploration the voyage seemed the appropriate vehicle to suggest man's turbulent passage to another, better country. According to *The Young Man's Calling*, when men reflect, they "shall plainly see this Life hath been but a restless Voyage, the World a tempestuous Sea, your Bodies the frail Vessels wherein you sail, and Time the *Charon*, the Boatman to waft you over these Waters, and set you upon another shore. . . ."[16] The metaphor was often worked out in detail, with sea conditions and hazards suggesting certain human activities and difficulties, though the specific referents varied considerably from treatise to treatise. Rocks were always some sort of hazard for the soul, but they might represent an internal difficulty, such as pride or despair, or obstacles like worldly friendships or the lure of earthly goods. The compass was always a guide book or the Bible, winds might be gales of grace or the blustering passions, and such an omnipresent danger as Satan might be represented as a pirate or a monster of the deep. Often, whole sections of guide books clothed their advice in the metaphor. "Let all your tackling be of the best," advises John Ryther; "let your Judgment be well convinced and established, that's your Mast; let your affections be divine, they are your Sails; let your hope cast Anchor upon Christ, and the Scripture-promises; let your Vessel be well ballasted with humility. . . ."[17] The extent to which the metaphor was applied is hard to exaggerate; often it extended for several pages, and sometimes the organization of an entire book was based upon it. The

[16] Samuel Crossman, *The Young Man's Calling, or the Whole Duty of Youth* (London, 1683; first published, 1678), p. 2. Classical references, like the one here, are often incorporated into the Christian form of the metaphor without, however, significantly altering the form of the metaphor or evoking the classical formulation.

[17] *A Plat for Mariners: Or, the Seaman's Preacher* (London, 1672), fol. A1ᵛ.

"Aspiratio" appended to John Robinson's *The Birth of a Day* (1655) offers a fair sample of the metaphor's frequently extended application:

> Almighty God, who rulest the *Sea* of this World by thy power, & whose paths are in the roughest *waters*; We the unworthiest of all thy servants commit our frail *Barks*, with all that we have to the *Steerage* of thee our great *Pilot*, & faithful Preserver. . . . However earthly things may like *watery Billows* be every day *rowling up* & *down* in their vicissitudes about us; yet suffer, oh suffer not the heavenly truth of our Reformed Religion to *flote* about any longer so uncertainly among us, nor our selves to be as children *toss'd* to and fro with every *wind* of Doctrine. . . . Lord, *pull in* the *sailes* of our desires toward fleeting and transitory substances. . . . *Ballast* our spirits with Humility in a prosperous condition; and when we have the highest and most pleasing *gale* of the worlds favour for us, give us to *strike* our *spreading sailes* of Pride. . . . But if thou in thy just judgement against us for our manifold and heinous sins, shalt cause some *cross wind* or other to *blow* upon us, and give us over to *shipwrack* in our temporalls; Supply then, we entreat thee, their want with thy spiritualls of Patience, Faith and other suffering graces; That although the *tempest* be never so *boisterous* without, yet we may enjoy within a Christian *calmness* of spirit. . . .[18]

The wilderness metaphor derives from both the Old Testament account of the wandering Israelites and the New Testament story of Jesus' contemplation and temptation, experiences which biblical typologists regarded as almost identical in theme. Drawing upon the suggestion of trial leading to triumph in both accounts, Puritan

[18] Pp. 99–102. Italics Robinson's. Altogether, Robinson's prayer uses twenty-nine nautical terms, italicizing most of them.

writers used the metaphor to dramatize the archetypal difficulty that man faces during his travels through life, as he suffers the bleak miseries of earthly existence before attaining the promised reward. The parallel between the plight of modern Puritans and ancient Israelites had been established early in the seventeenth century, and Puritan writers exploited this convention in formulating their metaphor along the particular outlines of the Old Testament account. Thus they described the whole rhythm of the regenerated life in relation to the metaphor: man typically began life in bondage to his sins (Egypt), was redeemed by grace (release by Pharaoh after the miraculous plagues), changed his life course (Red Sea crossing), underwent trials (dissension, hunger, thirst), alternately experienced punishments and rewards for his conduct (manna, slaying of idolators), and finally achieved his heavenly reward (promised land).

Sometimes Puritan writers vigorously defended and painstakingly explained the appropriateness of the metaphor, for they wished to discount objections which could be made against their extension of biblical typology. Biblical accounts of the exodus share the "excellencies" of all Scriptural history, says William Gouge, but "they are in an especiall manner *typicall*: and set out the condition of the Church brought out of the bondage of sinne under Satan, and travailing thorow the dangers and troubles of this world unto the celestiall *Canaan*." [19] Similarly, Samuel Mather argues the intended typicality of the account by drawing upon New Testament interpreters: "The Mystery . . . is plain and obvious. *Canaan* was a Type of Heaven; it shadowed forth another and *a better Country, that is an heavenly*, Heb. 11.16. Their Rest in the Promised Land shadowed forth *another Rest remain-*

[19] *Mercies Memoriall* (London, 1645), pp. 1–2.

ing for the people of God. Heb. 4.8, 9." [20] Sometimes, too, writers turned the metaphor into simile, without feeling the necessity of arguing its relevance. "As God conducted the Children of *Israel safe* through the Wilderness, and at last brought them to the *Land of Promise*," writes Samuel Masters in 1689, "So will he *conduct* those who *Trust* in him, amidst all the *changes* and *chances* of this *mortal* Life, and at last put them in *possession* of that *Heavenly Canaan*, toward which every good man is tending in all the *passages* of his Life." [21] But frequently writers merely assumed the metaphor's relevance and applied it as a matter of course to suggest man's proper contempt for Earth. "To all the People of God," writes Joseph Cooper in 1700, "this World is a Wilderness, not a *Canaan*; an Egypt, not a Paradise; a troublesome Sea, not an Harbour of Rest!" [22] But they also noted the necessity of profiting from "wilderness" experiences in order to deserve "Canaan." "We are sure to lye down in Darkness, and to Dye in the Wilderness of our own Folly," says Cooper, "if the Lord direct us not, as by a *Pillar of Fire*, through the Night, and Thick Darkness of all our Ignorance, into the Heavenly *Canaan* of true Happiness." [23] For modern man, God had provided the Bible as the guiding pillar of fire (or as the nourishing manna),[24] but other written guides could perform a similar function. "May [God] let you find [this book]," writes Cooper in his Epistle to the Reader, "as a Pillar of

[20] *Figures or Types*, p. 202.
[21] *The Duty of Submission to Divine Providence* (London, 1689), p. 128.
[22] *Misthoskopia: A Prospect of Heavenly Glory for the Comfort of Sion's Mourners* (London, 1700), p. 251.
[23] *Misthoskopia*, p. ii.
[24] See, for example, Thomas Taylor: "Great is the Similitude between the spiritual Manna of Gods Word, and that corporall of the Israelites in the wildernesse. *That* refreshed hungry and famished bodies: *this,* hungry soules" (*The Parable of the Sower and of the Seed* [London, 1621], p. 1).

Fire to guide you through this Wilderness, to the Land of Promise."[25]

But in addition to its suggestion of the external difficulties that man must overcome, "wilderness" came to suggest an internal state, the state of a man's soul before spiritual transformation. In its "wilderness condition" the soul was disordered and unproductive, but the showers of God's grace could transform it into a "garden state." Here, too, the metaphor derived support from both Old and New Testaments: it could draw upon the contrast between the gnarled, mazey jungle and the fruitful, life-giving land (in Exodus) and upon the movement (traced in the Gospels) from the bestial wilderness of temptation[26] to the Gethsemane garden, where final triumph over sin is achieved and the Bible recovers its central symbol of perfection. The internal form of the metaphor thus collapsed time and place into a single emblem of creation and emphasized the potential of man for achieving paradisal contentment *within himself* (that is, without regard to earthly striving). But the external form of the metaphor applied until man took full advantage of the grace offered by God. As Joseph Caryl writes,

> If, where the rain of the word falleth, they that receive it, do not bud and blossom and bring forth fruit, the desolate wilderness will rise up in judgement against them, the waste grounds will condemn them. They will say, Lord, you sent rain upon us, and lo, here are our buds and our blossomes, yea, here's the fruit which we have brought forth. Will not this shame our barrenness? Hath the Lord divided the Water-course of the Gospel, and caused it to rain on us from day to day, and shall not we shew our buds and blossomes of holiness, our fruits of faith and

---

[25] *Misthoskopia*, p. xxvi.
[26] Mark says that Jesus was "in the wilderness forty days, tempted of Satan; and was with the wild beasts . . ." (Mark 1:13).

repentance, that he may come into his garden, and eat of his pleasant fruits! [27]

Often the internal and external forms of the metaphor merged almost imperceptibly into one: a man's "wilderness wandering" and the "wilderness state" of his soul became synonymous, as did man's ultimate arrival in Canaan and the "garden state" of his soul; for the body's progress, ultimately, was emblematic of the soul's condition. Writers employed the metaphor with astonishing frequency and extensiveness because it provided a convenient frame for the other two favorite Puritan metaphors, as well as a concise summary of the Puritan view of man and the world. "[The] conduct of the *Israelites* to the Land of *Canaan*," writes Ralph Robinson, "was a figure of that Conduct which God affords all his people through the Wilderness of this world to the Coelestial *Canaan*; he will never leave them till he hath put them into possession of that heavenly Country hee hath prepared for them." [28] Titles of middle and late seventeenth-century treatises reflect the popularity of the metaphor (note, for example, Thomas Bell's *Grapes in the Wilderness* [1692] or John Flavell's *Mount Pisgah* [1689]), but its total incorporation into Puritan thought is best measured by the casual way in which parts of the metaphor

[27] *An Exposition with Practical Observations* . . . [of Job:38–42] (London, 1666), p. 215. For a recent discussion of this metaphor, see George H. Williams, *Wilderness and Paradise in Christian Thought* (New York, 1962).

[28] *Safe Conduct, or the Saints Guidance to Glory* (London, 1654), p. 30. Other biblical stories were sometimes even re-read in terms of the metaphor. John Goodman, for example, describes the pattern of the prodigal son story this way: "herein is traced out the journey from *Aegypt* (a state of servitude) to the Land of Promise, through a troublesome and disconsolate wilderness; or the passage from the brink of Hell to the gates of Heaven. More particularly [the reader] will observe the unhappy onset and beginnings, the crooked and troublesome proceedings, the dangerous precipices, and the horrid and fatal mischiefs of a sinfull course, graphically described . . ." (*The Penitent Pardon'd* [4th ed., London, 1694], p. 3).

slip into the standard theological language of all forms of Puritan literature; heaven is almost always "Canaan" or "the Promised Land" and imperfect conduct is "wandering in the wilderness of this world." What was typical of Puritanism was the way the usage of the metaphor became common and almost unconscious—a usage that not only came to control the emotional associations of ideas but helped to shape the thinking process itself.[29]

When the major metaphors of Puritanism were combined, they coherently traced man's earthly existence from birth to death, highlighting spiritual triumphs and tribulations along the lines of a biblical history which clarified the patterns and deepened the dimensions of modern experience. The transformation of man's sinful Egyptian state into the freedom and security of Canaan involved a life journey along all sorts of highways and byways of human experience, paths which, in essence, led from one battleground to another, where man fought enemy after enemy who slowed his progress and tried to divert his course (or checked his growth and tried to choke out the developing fruitfulness of his soul). "This World," writes Samuel Mather, "is but a Wilderness, an howling Wilderness, full of *Lyons* and *Leopards*, sins and troubles, Cant. 4.8. full of fiery Serpents, and Scorpions, and Drought. . . ." [30]

The comprehensive metaphor which evolved was utilized by guide writers charged with protecting man from potential hazards, but spiritual biographers found an even more dramatic application of the patterns to trace the histories of individual men, whose lives thus became

---

[29] For a recent discussion of Renaissance manifestations of the pilgrim idea, see Samuel C. Chew, *The Pilgrimage of Life* (New Haven, Conn., 1962).

[30] *Figures or Types*, p. 200.

types of Christian experience. The pattern became an even more distinguishable basis of structure as the spiritual biographies were transformed into pilgrim allegories, where historical facts about individuals were replaced by epitomical experiences of human types—and where life as the basis of Puritan didacticism was replaced by a manipulable fictive world.

Earlier in the seventeenth century, the potentiality of a form based on the comprehensive metaphor was rejected by writers who, instead of developing the metaphor logically and fully, settled for a partial application. Their distinction between precept and example was quite rigid, and they did not exploit the possibility of blurring or losing the distinction by means of the metaphor. The titles of these books (John Welles's *The Soules Progresse to the Celestiall Canaan, or Heavenly Jerusalem* [1639], for example) suggest total involvement in the metaphor, but the text within shows only partial application of the metaphor. Most often, the metaphor remains implicit throughout, structures the book in a general way, and is occasionally and partially, but not consistently, applied to precepts or examples. Gradually, as the century unfolded, the metaphor was applied more relentlessly, both by guide writers and by spiritual biographers. (See, for example, Thomas Gouge's *The Young Man's Guide, through the Wilderness of This World to the Heavenly Canaan* [1670] and Isaac Penington's *A Brief Account of My Souls Travel towards the Holy Land* [1681].)

The tradition of pilgrim allegory is the culmination of the use of the comprehensive metaphor; it puts to full use the structural possibilities of the rhythm of life as seen by Puritan interpreters. In such allegories as *The Pilgrim's Progress*, the metaphor achieves its perfect formal shape, for here it is undistorted by facts about individual lives or events. These allegories, of course, retain the didactic purposes of both the guide tradition, whose method was preceptual, and spiritual biography, whose method was that of *exemplum*, but their form fuses precept and example, thus evolving a more sophisticated form than the earlier Puritan literature had achieved.

However difficult it may be, the modern critic must remember the essentially moral and religious purposes of pilgrim allegory: whatever literary results are achieved are by-products, related only indirectly to the writer's essential intentions. Pilgrim allegory, then, must be seen as an attempt to present the case for morality in a more persuasive manner than had yet been devised. The choice of allegory as a new frame for the Puritan myth is a response not to artistic questions but to practical questions of influence on the reader. These practical questions take on enormous significance because of the Puritan suspicion of anything fictional—a suspicion deriving from the Puritan conception of the world and events as emblematic. For the Puritanism of the late seventeenth century, fiction simply falsified the detailed world of fact and event—and thereby obscured the clear message that God wrote for men in "real" happenings.[91] Thus, the Puritan dilemma was this: to touch the lives of men who were less and less impressed by conventional exhortation and recitation of standard examples and who were, at the same time, becoming more and more sophisticated in their tastes, a more effective vehicle was needed. But the obvious vehicle (the fictionalized story) which most ages have used to illustrate and dramatize their message had to be avoided.

[91] "Nature is delighted in History," writes Richard Baxter, "And the World is dolefully abused by false History" ("To the Reader," in Samuel Clarke's *The Lives of Sundry Eminent Persons in This Later Age* [London, 1683], fol. A3ᵛ).

The Puritan contempt for fiction is widely known, but the gradual shift in the Puritan position has not, I think, been sufficiently recognized—nor has the role, in that shift, of pilgrim allegory been adequately studied. Everyone knows that Defoe thought it necessary to disguise his fiction as fact in order to gain acceptance, that Richardson faced fewer, though still frequent, objections, and that Fielding dared count on acceptance (even among many Puritan readers) only on the grounds of moral concern. What is not so obvious is that the (at least partial) acceptance of fiction in the middle of the eighteenth century results from two bold steps: one by the writers of pilgrim allegory (Bunyan deserves the most credit, for he is the most articulate about what he is doing and the most successful in his performance) and one by Defoe.

Except for the Puritan stricture against fiction, didactic treatises might have exchanged historical anecdote for fictional story long before Bunyan, for apologists needed the most dramatic examples they could muster to prove their various religious and moral points. Pilgrim allegory provided a compromise. It freed writers from absolute adherence to historical detail without convicting them of "creating" characters and events in the usual fictional sense.[32] By mixing the stories of individuals into a potpourri which suggested the typical in human experience, writers like Bunyan remained true to the spirit of Puritan doctrine, but they violated the letter. Their stories were "true" only in the sense that the episodes conformed to the totality of human experience, but the use of allegorical names and places (which did not pretend to correspond to "real" names or places) cir-

---

[32] Puritanism's stricture against fiction was partially based on the same premise as the stricture against icons: creation of such objects usurped a function reserved by God. Other considerations, such as the time wasted by reading such stories, also contributed to the rigidity of the Puritan position.

cumvented the charge of "feigned history." Besides, as Bunyan pointed out rather tediously in his verse "apology" for *The Pilgrim's Progress*, there was precedent for using allegory to promote virtuous ends, even in the Bible itself. "Use it I may, then," Bunyan concludes,

> . . . and yet nothing smother
> Truth's golden beams; nay by this method may
> Make it cast forth its rays as light as day.[33]

The step taken by pilgrim allegory breached Puritanism's absolute prohibition of fiction and provided later writers like Defoe with a necessary transitional precedent. But even this hesitant, compromising step would have been impossible had not theorists already begun to raise questions about the rigid Puritan distinction between history and fiction. The questions derived a certain authority from the context in which they arose, namely, in attempts to define biblical methods of illustrating a point. Commentators noted that to "prove" its points analogically the Bible used not only historical accounts but also fictional stories, particularly in the New Testament. Such "parables" seemed exempt from the usual strictures because of their high purpose. A parable is a narrative "of a Thing feigned," says Benjamin Keach, "and adapted to instruct, which yet is not a Lie. . . . If Fables, accommodated to teach and instruct, are not Lies, much less are Parables." [34] Keach tries to particularize the differences between parable and history (though defending the use of both), but other commentators note the difficulty of precision and certainty. Jesus, they note, did not always indicate whether his stories were factual or not, often beginning by simply saying

---

[33] "The Author's Apology for His Book," *The Pilgrim's Progress from This World to That Which Is To Come*, ed. James Blanton Wharey, rev. Roger Sharrock (2d ed.; Oxford, 1960), p. 6.

[34] "*Philologia Sacra*" (a section appended to the fourth book of *Tropologia* in the 1682 edition), p. 47.

"there was a certain man. . . ." The story of Lazarus
and the rich man, for example (Luke 16:19–31), might
well be based on fact, even though it is usually considered a parable. Discussing this story, Timothy Cruso
mentions a third category (or "middle way") and implies the validity of this form for teaching purposes. "It
is much disputed among Interpreters," writes Cruso,

> Whether this [story] be a *Parable* or an *History*, some
> arguing for the one, and some for the other; but there is
> a *third* sort, which go a *middle way*, to accommodate this
> difference, by understanding it as a *mixture* of both; i.e.
> a kind of *Parabolical History*, or *Historical Parable*. It may
> be partly a Narrative of *matter of fact* and partly illustrated
> with *circumstantial additions*, which are not to be look'd
> upon as real things, nor stretch'd too far beyond the *main
> design*; tho every passage will afford us proper instruc-
> tions. . . .[35]

Cruso's "middle way" was by no means universally approved, but by the end of the seventeenth century the
use of such a form had at least become a legitimate subject for debate. Those who favored fiction at all based
their stand on the didactic usefulness of such material,
which is the argument advanced by Defoe in his hedging
Preface to *Robinson Crusoe*—an argument at least partially accepted even by Charles Gildon. Although Gildon
argues at one place that "the Christian Religion and the
Doctrines of Providence are too sacred to be delivered in
Fictions and Lies," [36] he elsewhere tacitly admits the

[35] *Discourses upon the Rich Man and Lazarus* (London, 1697), pp.
1–2. The category is not original with Cruso. In 1639, William Gouge
had spoken of the prodigal son story as *"a Parabolical History,* or His-
toricall Parable" (*A Recovery from Apostacy* [London, 1639], p. 7),
and many other authors mention it.
[36] *The Life and Strange Surprizing Adventures of Mr. D—— De
F—— of London, Hosier* (London, 1719), as reprinted in *Robinson
Crusoe Examin'd and Criticis'd*, ed. Paul Dottin (London and Paris,
1923), p. 127.

validity of using fiction to teach, but he still insists that Defoe's use of fiction is unwarranted because Defoe's ideas are misguided and pernicious: "The Design of the Publication of [*Robinson Crusoe*] was *not sufficient* to justify and make Truth of what [is] fiction or fable. . . ." [37]
Once the possibility of permitting some fiction is allowed, the question becomes one of extent. Ultimately, Fielding's position is the logical extreme: he defines "history" in terms of general nature and not as fact or event at all.[38] But Defoe remains very close to the pilgrim allegorists' definition of extent. In *Robinson Crusoe*, in fact, his method, drawing upon kinds of historical experiences which he distributes in terms of a typical pattern, is almost identical with that of Bunyan. Defoe's step is a relatively small one, given the compromises offered by apologists like Cruso and artists like Bunyan, but it is essential, for it opens the possibilities for the creation of individualized fiction simply by the particularizing of typical experiences in a specific time and place.

Defoe's own thoughts on the efficacy of fictional account reflect the shifting attitudes of his time. In his Preface to *The Storm* (1704), his denunciation of fiction is adamant and total: "I should stand convicted of a double Imposture, to forge a Story, and then preach Repentance to the Reader from a Crime greater than I would have him repent of: endeavoring by a lye to correct the Reader's Vices, and sin against Truth to bring the Reader off from sinning against Sence." [39] But later

[37] P. 113. Italics mine.
[38] See Fielding's various discussions of "history" in the interchapters of *Tom Jones* and particularly his discussion of "fact" in *Joseph Andrews*, Bk. III, chap. i.
[39] Fol. A3.

his attitude is modified significantly. In Volume I of *The Family Instructor* (1715) he says that "much of the Story is Historical" but insists that the issue is really unimportant. "Resolving," he says, "not to give the least hint that should lead to [real] Persons, [the author] has been obliged to leave it Uncertain to the Reader, whether it be a History or a Parable, believing it may be either way adapted to the sincere Design. . . ." [40] In *Robinson Crusoe* he still hedges somewhat and at first claims complete historicity, but in the Preface to *Farther Adventures* he allows that the "just application of every Incident, the religious and useful Inferences drawn from every Part . . . must legitimate all the Part that may be call'd Invention, or Parable in the Story." [41] "The Fable," he concludes in the Preface to *Serious Reflections*, "is always made for the moral, not the moral for the Fable." [42]

Defoe's assertion, in the Preface to *Serious Reflections*, that *Robinson Crusoe* is "allegorical" and "historical" may have been designed primarily to avert charges of falsehood, but it points to the easy step from allegory to fiction. If an edifying purpose is sufficient to justify conversion of biographical history into allegory, the same purpose might well justify Defoe's further step: that of turning allegory (itself a fiction or falsehood, when measured by standards of exact historical detail) back into a personal, fictionalized biography. Ordinarily, however, critics take literally and in terms of modern terminology Defoe's prefatory statements about factuality, so that he appears to be either a notorious liar or an incredibly incompetent writer. Following Defoe's suggestion that "there is a man alive, and well known too, the actions of whose life are the just subject of these

[40] P. 5.
[41] Shakespeare Head edition, VIII, x.
[42] Maynadier edition, III, ix.

volumes," [43] some scholars have attempted to illuminate *Robinson Crusoe* by detailing Defoe's own life. (Conversely, some have tried to illuminate Defoe's life by examining *Robinson Crusoe*, a procedure which follows the same naïve, unhistorical assumptions.) These scholars have assumed that the "man alive" was a specific individual, viz., Defoe himself, and that *Robinson Crusoe* was meant to contain a rather literal, event-for-event allegory of Defoe's life and times. The conclusions drawn from these studies are improbable at best, and most scholars now agree that, although some general similarities exist between the lives of Crusoe and Defoe, no one-to-one relation can be established. But such conclusions, like others which confine Defoe's imagination within the frame of factual parallels, reflect unfavorably (and unfairly) on Defoe's aim and accomplishment. And, what is more important, such conclusions seriously mislead us about his contribution to an emerging literary form.

Paul Geissler seems to me to have been close to the truth when he suggested, seventy years ago, that Defoe used the term "allegorical" to indicate *Robinson Crusoe's* relationship to didactic literature—a suggestion which seems to have attracted little attention. [44] But Puritans of Defoe's time often used such terms as "allegorical" to describe any story of deep dimension and didactic application, even if the story was meaningful on a literal level —even if it was a factual account. Contemporary novelists frequently used such terms to suggest contemporary meanings derived from specific Puritan assumptions about cosmology and metaphysics. We might well approach Defoe, and Puritan prose fic-

---

[43] Preface to *Serious Reflections*, in Maynadier edition, III, ix. Note that Defoe's statement about *Robinson Crusoe*'s being "allegorical" occurs much earlier in the Preface.

[44] Geissler notes that the attempts to work out a biographical allegory of Defoe's life result from a more modern definition of allegory (*Is Robinson Crusoe an Allegory?* [Pirna, 1893], p. 23).

tion generally, through the key terms used in this chapter (metaphor, type, allegory, and emblem), if, in doing so, we keep in mind the full implications of each term. The physical world was a series of emblems, symbols made by God to clarify to men great spiritual truths: each thing and event contained a meaning which might be discovered by men who studied all aspects of that thing or event. Typology, as the Puritans practiced it, was the particular device by which time was comprehended into their emblematic scheme. Metaphor was to words what emblem was to physical objects: just as God informed the objects in his book of nature with discoverable spiritual significance, so his amanuenses in his book of revelation infused words with a significance that extended to later ages within the same divinely controlled cycle. Interpreters of Defoe's day might use this metaphorical biblical language to express patterns of thought deriving from an emblematic understanding of the world of thing and event, but metaphor was to be understood as approximate, for the precise system of analogies no longer applied, and man's understanding was now partial. When an interpreter imposed a total system on his metaphor (a system which he hoped would approximate the spiritual reality), he constructed an allegory, suggesting the comprehensive emblematic significance of each thing and event he portrayed.

Structurally, *Robinson Crusoe* relates closely to spiritual biography, just as it relates thematically to the guide and providence traditions. Its story line follows the conventional biographical pattern used in the lives of Richard Baxter, sailor Vincent Jukes,[45] or John Bunyan (in

[45] See William Gouge's sermon on the life of Jukes, *A Recovery from Apostacy.*

Grace Abounding)—a pattern which was followed, but abstracted, by the pilgrim allegorists. Books like Thomas Taylor's *The Pilgrim's Profession* (1622) or Symon Patrick's *Parable of the Pilgrim* (1665) simply generalize the kind of experiences recorded in spiritual biographies and apply to them the comprehensive Puritan metaphor, retaining the "realistic" detail even after the specifics of time and place have been eliminated. When *Robinson Crusoe's* plot is articulated in abstract terms, the structural parallel with both spiritual biography and pilgrim allegory may be clearly seen: a man first sails away from the Home appointed for him (instead of proceeding toward it), and then becomes isolated from God as a result of discontent and selfish pride. Ultimately, however, God intervenes to deliver him from destruction, and the direction of his life is altered to a course pleasing to God and leading at last to the man's ultimate Home. The man, however, still must undergo numerous battles with evil before he can rest content at the end of the journey.

Robinson Crusoe is *not*, of course, a story of such abstraction. It is rooted in particular times and places, and man's typical experience is presented as the history of a particular man. Crusoe is less a disembodied soul than a man, caught in a web of human circumstance, who wishes to regain his relationship both to his world and to his God. He has to do more than fast, pray, and convert natives; goats are to be cared for, houses and boats to be built, secular worlds to be conquered. These actions, however, are all of a piece in a world where secular activity is meaningful, where history (even the history of every man's trivialities) is somehow the record of divine activity. There is something less than perfect logic in the assumption that invented activities have the same divine significance as real activities, but Defoe's answer would have been the same as Bunyan's. The actions he ascribed to Crusoe were essentially true because they corresponded to human actions standardized to a typical pattern. Defoe does not preclude, nor does Bunyan, the charge that he has usurped the function of the Creator by making his own world of significances, but he obscures the issue by a form of pretense that he learns from Bunyan. If, like the rigorous employers of Puritan metaphor, he is guilty of helping to destroy the theological system which molded him, he nevertheless deserves credit for taking a necessary step toward one of literature's most impressive forms, the symbolic novel. And, paradoxically, Puritanism must be credited with supplying the milieu, the thought processes, and many of the techniques for a form which its followers might use for the glory of God, but which its philosophy could never approve without qualification.

VI

Robinson Crusoe's
Rebellion and Punishment

---◆◆◆◆▶-----

"To hear of a Man's living so long alone in a desert Island, seems to some very surprizing," writes Edward Cooke in 1712 about Alexander Selkirk, "and they presently conclude he may afford a very agreeable Relation of his Life, when in Reality it is the most barren Subject that Nature can afford." [1] Cooke's own account of Selkirk seems to prove his point, and similar accounts by Sir Richard Steele and Woodes Rogers hardly suggest that the subject is pregnant with artistic possibility.[2] *Providence Displayed* and similar stories in providence books are somewhat more pointed, for they structure events according to a specific philosophy of history, but these accounts still fail to rise above the level of *exemplum* or polemical anecdote. Since 1719, hundreds of books have recounted stories with a similar setting and plot, employing the most highly praised features of *Robinson Crusoe*, but they also have failed to achieve lasting renown. Cooke's point would seem sound indeed, were it not for Defoe.

At first glance, *Robinson Crusoe* seems to disprove Cooke. Defoe turns the kind of plot Cooke describes into one of the most popular books of all time, but a closer

[1] *A Voyage to the South Sea, and Round the World* (2 vols.; London, 1712), II, xviii.
[2] See *The Englishman*, Dec. 1–3, 1713, and *A Cruising Voyage Round the World* (London, 1712), pp. 124–31.

examination suggests that Cooke is not so far wrong, for Defoe's achievement does not rest primarily on his having found a story with inherent mythic appeal. Critics who attribute *Robinson Crusoe*'s appeal to setting and plot have slipped into the fallacy which Cooke describes: the confusion of vehicle with tenor, the failure to consider the effects of artistic rendering and, ultimately, the failure to consider artistic intent.[3] What Defoe distills from desert island experience is not an "agreeable Relation" at all, but rather a rigorous multilevel moral examination of life, for the narrative is structured to render dimensions which are absent in stories of similar plot. Unlike its analogues, *Robinson Crusoe* derives dramatic power from its understanding of man's struggle against nature as both physical and metaphysical. Reared upon Puritan religious tradition and Puritan habits of mind, Defoe views Crusoe's struggles for survival against a background of established metaphors for existence and spiritual alienation, and he creates a world in which man's basic conflicts take place in a personal, physical setting with cosmic, spiritual significance. Although Milton and Bunyan are usually considered to present the poetry and prose epitomes of the Puritan view of life (and Defoe is thought to present only a fractured, diluted, and ultimately materialistic view of it), *Robinson Crusoe* also embodies the Puritan view of man on a most profound level; it also portrays, through the struggles of one man, the rebellion and punishment, repentance and deliverance, of all men, as they sojourn in a hostile world.

The island section is ultimately the most crucial part

[3] Cooke probably intended only to belittle popular taste, not to argue that appeal depended on more than subject matter. But his statement still suggests that plot alone is hardly a legitimate ground of appeal, a point which critics of far greater sophistication seem often to forget, especially when dealing with Defoe.

of *Robinson Crusoe*, not because of its sheer bulk or because the adventurous episodes on the island are more "exciting" than pre-island or post-island episodes, but because Defoe uses the island setting to isolate and resolve conflicts within Crusoe—conflicts that Crusoe shares with men in all places and all times. The simplified context of the island turns Crusoe's attention inward and forces him to look at the pattern of his life, to question the cause of his exile from civilization, and to examine the warring factions in his own nature. Defoe also uses the simplified context to alert the reader to the relationship between different levels of conflicts: man with God, man with nature, man with man, and man with himself.

On the island the movement of Crusoe's life—and the movement of the novel—is reversed. Travel, which means only flight to the young Crusoe, is transformed into pilgrimage, for Crusoe's conversion introduces purpose to his wanderings and informs his actions with real meaning. The island is a fitting climax to Crusoe's early aimlessness, but at the same time its confinement provides him with a new pace which is more conducive to reflection and redemption. The island, then, represents both punishment and potential salvation. What Crusoe thinks about on the island—and what he does—pivots the novel from a story about punishment to a story about deliverance, from a story about God's judgment to a story about God's mercy.

Before Crusoe's island struggles can be meaningful, however, Defoe must first define the nature of man's predicament by suggesting his depravity and weakness. Crusoe's pre-island adventures dramatize the attraction which evil holds for weak men, just as Crusoe's post-island adventures demonstrate the power which man may exert over his environment, his fellow man, and himself, after he has achieved a proper relationship with his God. Crusoe's rhythm of life is finely calculated, and Defoe manages to suggest that the rhythm is a matter of divine calculation, not simply of human artistry. But while artfully manipulating character and event to suggest an artless recording of divinely planned reality, Defoe gradually reveals Crusoe as a carefully wrought fictive creation. By judicious selection of events that dramatize Crusoe's personality and by careful manipulation of time and point of view to show Crusoe's developing awareness of himself and his world, Defoe delineates a man of striking individuality. By employing standard Puritan metaphors and by controlling a series of allusions, Defoe defines Crusoe as a kind of Everyman whose life and thought follow a pattern typical of man's voyage through life.

"We drive our selves away from the Port, at which we would arrive," says Bishop Patrick, "by these Storms and blustering Passions. If we would be carried to the Haven we desire, let us be calm and of a still and quiet Disposition." [4] Crusoe's inability to control his irrational inclination to roam leads to his rejection of the ordered way of life recommended by his rational father and turns his course toward the *"Island of Despair"* (A79). The whole dialectic of decline and recovery in *Robinson*

[4] Symon Patrick, *Fifteen Sermons upon Contentment and Resignation to the Will of God* (London, 1719), Sermon XV, p. 425. In another place Patrick again draws upon the Pauline conception through the same metaphor: "Is not a Ship most likely to miss her Port, when the Winds are high and boisterous, and the Sea working in a kind of Rage and Fury of her Waves? Just such a Thing is the Soul of a discontented Man, whose Tempestuous Thoughts, and ever working and rolling Mind, are most likely to blow him away from that which he intends. . . . You set your self further off from what you want, by your Restlessness of Spirit. You would be nearer to it, if you was more quiet, i.e., contented in your present estate" (pp. 169–70).

Crusoe results from the tension between human reason and Crusoe's "Propension of Nature" (A2), an antithesis that resembles Paul's spirit-flesh tension more than it does the reason-passion conflict often described by critics of the "Age of Reason." Like Pauline man, Crusoe finds himself the victim of his natural propensity to evil: he is unable to choose the right course even when aware of it. "I was hurried on," he says about his decision to leave Brazil and return to sea, "and obey'd blindly the Dictates of my Fancy rather than my Reason" (A45). His "Reason," although aided by the counsel of his elders and by supernatural warnings sent by providence, is still unable to overcome what seems to be "something fatal in that Propension of Nature tending directly to [a] Life of Misery" (A2). Crusoe finds himself incapable not only of controlling his will but even of understanding his incapacity, and he can only interpret mythically: "I had several times loud Calls from my Reason and my more composed Judgment to go home," he says after his first voyage, "yet I had no Power to do it. I know not what to call this, nor will I urge, that it is a secret overruling Decree that hurries us on to be the Instruments of our own Destruction, even tho' it be before us, and that we rush upon it with our Eyes open" (A14). Crusoe considers himself "born to be my own Destroyer" (A49) and thinks it "no great Wonder" "for me to do wrong that never did right" (A39). Throughout the early part of the novel, while his spiritual and physical fortunes are in decline, Crusoe remains powerless to deal with his "fatal" propensity to evil.[5]

---

[5] Timothy Cruso describes youth's propensity to evil this way: "Folly is *born* and *bred* with us . . . and as we *increase* in age and stature, we increase our foolishness, till God renews and enlightens our minds" (*The Usefulnesse of Spiritual Wisdom with a Temporal Inheritance* [London, 1689], p. 20).

Crusoe's inner tension between reason and natural propensity ultimately reflects the war between good and evil. Crusoe's life, like that of all other men, is simply a battleground on which one phase of a general struggle takes place. Like any postlapsarian man, Crusoe finds the battle uneven as long as he depends solely upon his own resources; he cannot even grasp the grace proffered him until God specifically interposes. Until then, he may in theory choose on the side of good, for he has (according to seventeenth- and eighteenth-century Calvinist thought) free will, but in practice the result is inevitable: man is the victim of his depraved nature until God intervenes to free him.[6]

"The effect of [Adam's] sin," Defoe writes in the 1715 volume of *The Family Instructor,* "is a corrupt and Taint which we all bring into the World with us, and which we find upon our Nature, by which we find a Natural Propensity in us to do Evil, and no natural Inclination to do Good. . . ."[7] This concept of man's depravity is implicit in *Robinson Crusoe* and is fundamental to an understanding of Crusoe's actions. Natural man is not the "noble savage" pictured by some of Defoe's contemporaries. Because he is made in God's image, he has innate potentiality for good, but this potentiality can be realized only when God intervenes to save him from his fallen nature. Defoe's natural men, including Friday and his father, are savage cannibals in their ordinary state, and Defoe vividly dramatizes the horrors of their natural

[6] Unlike some of Defoe's heroes, Crusoe does not begin with a social background that may partially excuse his behavior; he is fully responsible for his actions. His "free will," however, is of the sort associated with Calvinistic thought. Man is responsible for his actions even though he seems to be virtually a pawn in the contest between good and evil. Crusoe, in picturing this contest in the form of a battle between God's providence and man's depraved nature, interprets it according to orthodox Calvinistic doctrine.

[7] P. 22. I quote from the second edition.

depravity. God interposes to convert Friday and uses Crusoe as his instrument—first, to rescue Friday from physical death, and later, to implant the Christian doctrine of salvation.[8] (Defoe leaves Friday's father an unconverted cannibal and thus retains a dramatic touchstone of man's potential savagery in his natural, unregenerated state.) In a similar way Crusoe, although he has had the advantage of being reared by a "wise and grave" (A2) father in a presumably Christian setting, is also guided by his natural propensities in his early life. God has not yet interposed, and Crusoe lacks the conversion experience that he must have in order to gain control over his nature.

Defoe traces Crusoe's depravity along lines sketched by contemporary Puritan theology; he gives Crusoe a *dilectum delictum* (or "commanding sin") which rules his life and leads him into the straits from which he needs deliverance. According to writers in the guide tradition, man's depravity usually took a specific form in a particular individual, and the form determined the kind of sinful course the individual would follow. The idea of a *dilectum delictum* apparently derives from the patristic concept of *peccatum in deliciis* (the ultimate source, too, of the "ruling passion" idea upon which Pope draws in the *Essay on Man*), but guide writers reduced it to more simple terms (darling-pleasure, minion-delight, bosom-devil, captain sin, darling corruption)[9] and argued that the entire force of man's natural depravity

---

[8] Like Crusoe, Friday is converted only after he is brought to physical extremity. One obvious factor is his debt to Crusoe for saving his life.

[9] See Robert Bolton, *Some General Directions for a Comfortable Walking with God* (5th ed.; London, 1638), pp. 35–36; Samuel Clarke, *A Collection of the Lives of Ten Eminent Divines* (London, 1662), p. 307; Timothy Cruso, *Twenty-Four Sermons Preached at the Merchants-Lecture at Pinners Hall* (London, 1699), Sermon XIII, p. 195. For discussions of Crusoe's basic sin in less technical theological terms, see Novak (*EF*, Chapter 2) and Starr (*SA*).

was often focused in this one sin. Crusoe's *dilectum delictum* is a form of the most basic of human sins, a restlessness of body and mind which leads to discontent with one's station. It was this sin which caused man's original fall, and Puritan moralists regarded it as man's first and worst enemy. It was this sin which Herbert found basic, but ultimately self-redemptive, in "The Pulley." It was this sin to which the concept of the calling tried to minister.

Crusoe's tendency toward restlessness leads to what he describes as his "Original Sin" (A225) of leaving his station. He is inexplicably "hurried" into "the wild and indigested Notion of raising my Fortune" (A16)—a notion which, in context, suggests violation of God's order rather than accrual of material wealth.[10] Later, when Crusoe begins to attain a stable life in Brazil, his restlessness returns: "increasing in Business and in Wealth," he reports, "my Head began to be full of Projects and Undertakings beyond my Reach" (A42). His "aspiring Thoughts," Crusoe decides in retrospect, are responsible for his "Ruin," a term which ultimately suggests not only his material but moral and spiritual bankruptcy. Lured by specific "Snares" laid by the devil ("Allurement[s] of Seafaring Men" [A6], companions who "entic'd me away" [A8]) but ultimately inspired by his own *dilectum delictum,*[11] Crusoe accumulates an impressive list of auxiliary sins on the way to ruin: he becomes disrespectful toward his parents and ultimately rebels against their command, he engages in the standard vices of "loose and unguided" (A17) young men, he ignores supernatural warnings, he breaks promises to God.

[10] Phrases such as this one are often mistakenly identified as part of Defoe's mercantile vocabulary. Throughout the novel, Crusoe alludes often to his original disruption of order and his attempts to re-establish order upon his island.

[11] Crusoe first seems to blame others, but Defoe quickly shifts full responsibility to Crusoe, largely through pointed biblical allusions.

Caught in his own snowballing sinfulness, he loses the "Power" to respond to his "more composed Judgment" (A14), like the disobedient children in Bunyan's *Divine Emblems*:

> Their sinful nature prompts them to rebel,
> And to delight in paths that lead to hell.
> Their parents' love and care they overlook,
> As if relation had them quite forsook.
> They take the counsels of the wanton's, rather
> Than the most grave instructions of a father.[12]

And he is even more like the Bible's disobedient children of God.

Crusoe's disobedience closely resembles that of the first man in the Garden and takes its ultimate mythic dimension from the biblical account of the Fall. Two other biblical accounts of disobedience are, however, more in the foreground, for Crusoe discovers that both an Old and a New Testament representative of disobedience are his models. The stories to which Crusoe repeatedly and pointedly alludes,[13] those of Jonah and the prodigal son, were frequently used as *exempla* by Puritan preachers to warn against restlessness, filial disobedience, and failure to follow one's calling. Typologically, the two stories are similar: they both evince a concern with selfish abdication of one's duty, and they share a pattern of rebellion, flight to a far place, punishment by

---

[12] "Upon the Disobedient Child," *Divine Emblems, or Temporal Things Spiritualized,* in *Bunyan's Allegorical Works,* ed. Charles H. H. Wright (London, n.d.), p. 870.

[13] Defoe's allusiveness has never attracted much attention. Critics have preferred to see his allusions as evidence of "sources," thus placing the emphasis upon the models themselves rather than upon Defoe's artistic use of them. Perhaps typical is the view of Allan H. MacLaine ("Robinson Crusoe and the Cyclops," *SP,* III [1955], 599–604), who suggests that the *Odyssey* served as the "source" of Crusoe's structural plan for his castle.

physical distress, repentance during danger, and a final physical and spiritual deliverance. Crusoe's account follows this general movement, and his life bears even more precise resemblances to the particulars of each story.

The implied moral of the prodigal son parable—that God rejoices over the reclamation of the lost—was less frequently emphasized by Puritan preachers and guide writers than was the more practical literal reading of the first part of the parable.[14] The prodigal son, an emblem of filial disobedience, had fallen by foolish neglect of duty. Technically, he had not disobeyed his father's orders, but his failure to honor his father's position constituted neglect of family duty. Because a father was God's deputy in the family, conduct like that of the prodigal ultimately represented rebellion against God and the divine social order. At a time when the family and other symbols of order appeared to be under severe challenge, the parable seemed dramatically relevant, and guide writers leaned heavily upon its authority.[15] It had the added advantage that the prodigal's return and reward (which were usually interpreted on a "spiritual" level, as

[14] The ending of the parable was usually interpreted, in orthodox fashion, that the wanderer is forgiven and restored to his spiritual place. It was common practice to interpret biblical events, parabolical or "factual," in terms of both their temporal and spiritual meanings. The prodigal's father might, therefore, be simply a father on a literal level, but also the Father on an allegorical level. For typical commentary, see Samuel Willard, *Mercy Magnified, on a Penitent Prodigal* (Boston, 1684).

[15] See, e.g., John Goodman's comment comparing the prodigal's conduct with man's general discontent: "Being blown up with a conceit of himself, he presently grows male-content with his condition; and finding himself restrained, the proud waves of his passion rage and swell against all that bounds and checks them, and this rage casts up mire and dirt wherewith divine providence it self is bespattered. . . . He finds his condition not to his mind, and not being willing to bring his mind to that, he is tempted to run upon adventures, and to make experiments, that he may give his mind full scope and contentment." Goodman says that such "mutinous thoughts . . . are the immediate issue of pride, and the seminalities of all rebellion against God" (*The Penitent Pardon'd* [4th ed.; London, 1694; first published *ca.* 1678], pp. 86, 87).

well as on the literal level of the story [16]) could argue repentance to those already guilty of rebellion. The parable's effectiveness lay in its forceful illustration of the
typical plight of man: alienated from God ("in a far
country") by early sin, he constantly faced ever-
worsening crises in which he might choose to swallow
his pride and return to "his father's house." "A continued
Course of Goodness may in it self be more valuable,"
says Tillotson of the prodigal's actions, "and yet Repentance after a great Fall and long Wandrings may be much
more moving and surprizing." [17]

Defoe shapes Crusoe's view of his own state along the
lines of the contemporary understanding of the parable.
Crusoe first applies the parallel in describing his first
voyage, which he had undertaken "without asking God's
Blessing, or my Father's, without any Consideration of
Circumstances or Consequences" (A6). A storm arises,
and Crusoe, suddenly aware of the wisdom of his father's
advice, resolves that he will "like a true repenting Prodigal, go home to my Father" (A7). He makes "many
Vows and Resolutions," but when the storm subsides and
his "Fears and Apprehensions of being swallow'd up by
the Sea [are] forgotten" (A9), he abandons these "wise
and sober Thoughts" (A8). He returns to the rebellious
dictates of his "Fancy" and forgets the "Vows and Promises that I made in my Distress" (A9): "In . . . one
Night's wickedness," he says of his revelry with other
sailors, "I drowned all my Repentance, all my Reflections
upon my past Conduct, and all my Resolutions for my
future" (A8).[18] Before the voyage ends, providence

---

[16] Goodman distinguishes between the "mystical" and "literal" levels
of the story (p. 85).
[17] *The Works of the Most Reverend Dr. John Tillotson* (9th ed.; London, 1728), Sermon XVI, p. 139.
[18] Crusoe says later that he had no religious reflections during his
early life of wandering in sin: "I do not remember that I had in all
that Time one Thought that so much as tended either to looking up-

sends a much worse storm (Crusoe decides, in retrospect, that God "resolv'd to leave me entirely without
Excuse" [A9]), and when his ship capsizes Crusoe has to
be rescued by a small boat. "Had I now had the Sense to
have gone . . . home," reflects Crusoe later, "I had been
happy, and my Father, an Emblem of our Blessed Saviour's Parable, had even Kill'd the fatted Calf for me"
(A14); but his "fatal" natural propensity still prevents
the proper decision.

Like the prodigal, Crusoe is guilty of the "wicked leaving [of] my Father's House" and of a "Breach of my
Duty to God and my Father" (A7). Restless and dissatis-
fied with his lot, he foolishly leaves his family to try his
fortunes abroad. Unlike the prodigal, however, Crusoe
refuses to humble himself when brought to distress, and
he continues to follow his "Inclination" even though
fearful of the results. "I have since often observed," Crusoe reports, "how incongruous and irrational the common Temper of Mankind is, especially of Youth. . . .
That they are not asham'd to sin, and yet are asham'd to
repent." [19]

In retrospect, Crusoe sees that he should also have
learned from Jonah's example, for his life is another re-
daction of Jonah's story. Like Jonah, Crusoe refuses the

wards toward God, or inwards toward a Reflection upon my own Ways.
. . . Thro' all the Variety of Miseries that had to this Day [June 27,
1659] befallen me, I never had so much as one Thought of it being the
Hand of God, or that it was a just Punishment for my Sin . . ."
(A101). In this passage, Crusoe goes on to describe his first genuinely
religious reflections upon his life. His brief decision to forsake seafaring,
after the first storm, is evidently the product of physical rather than
religious fear, and his interpretation of these events is superimposed
from a later point of view.

[19] Friday's affection toward his father (see B26 ff.) provides a dramatic contrast to Crusoe's lack of filial respect. This contrast points up
the magnitude of Crusoe's sinful disobedience to both father and Father, for Crusoe, unlike Friday, had the advantage of a Christian up-
bringing, and he ought to have had a keener sense of duty than did
"natural" man.

calling for which he was divinely appointed, and he defiantly boards a ship to run away. Like Jonah, he finally becomes aware that the storms which plague the ship are sent by God as a punishment for his sin and as a warning to change his course of life. The captain of the ill-fated ship tells Crusoe to interpret his first voyage as *"a plain and visible Token that you are not to be a Seafaring Man"* (A15). Perhaps, he suggests, Crusoe was responsible for the ship's disaster, *"like Jonah in the Ship of* Tarshish." When he learns Crusoe's life story, he is certain of his interpretation. "What had I done," he asks, "that such an unhappy Wretch should come into my Ship?" The captain's admonition and prophecy (*"whereever you go, you will meet with nothing but Disasters and Disappointments till your Father's Words are fulfilled upon you"*) causes Crusoe to reflect, and he has "many Struggles with my self, what Course of Life I should take." But until he is brought to despair, like Jonah, in a lonely, apparently hopeless situation, he remains in the rebellious grasp of his natural propensity.[20]

The parable of the prodigal son and the Jonah story both reflect the myth of the Fall (though in a postlapsarian context), and Crusoe's rebellion and punishment parallel the specifics of the account in Genesis even more closely. At the beginning of the novel Crusoe's father portrays Crusoe's station in terms of an Edenic freedom from care—"a Life of Ease and Pleasure." "He told me," says Crusoe, "I might judge of the Happiness of this State, by this one thing, *viz.* That this was the State of Life which all other People envied. . . ." It is a station "calculated for all kind of Vertues and all kinds of Enjoy-

---

[20] The biblical parallel is strengthened by Crusoe's conduct during the voyage. Seventeenth- and eighteenth-century biblical commentators usually divided the Jonah story into sections which corresponded to the pattern that Defoe gives to Crusoe's life. See, e.g., John Ryther, *A Plat for Mariners: Or, the Seaman's Preacher* (London, 1672), p. 2.

ments," characterized by "Peace and Plenty," blessed by "Temperance, Moderation, Quietness, Health, Society, all agreeable Diversions, and all desirable Pleasures." It is designed so that its members may go "silently and smoothly thro' the World, and comfortably out of it, not embarrass'd with the Labours of the Hands or of the Head . . ." (A2–3).[21] This idyllic life is Crusoe's to enjoy without specific obligation; he is required only to accept it contentedly and to eschew the desire of altering his condition. Only the tree of discontent is forbidden: if he tries to leave his station, according to his father's prediction, he will be "the miserablest Wretch that was ever born" (A6).

Adam's sin, according to Defoe's contemporaries, stemmed from his restlessness and discontent with his place in Eden. "It was," says Andrew Gray in a sermon on contentment, "*Adams* ignorance of this divine mystery of Christianity, *to be content with every estate, wherein he was placed*, that did bring him down from that high pinacle of his excellency. . . ."[22] In effect, Crusoe expels himself from his paradise by committing the forbidden act; like Adam, whose sin had condemned man to a life of wandering in the first place, Crusoe commits the archetypal sin of discontent. Homeless physically and spiritually, he wanders in a world of sin and sickness, storm and shipwreck. Unlike Adam, however, Crusoe does not immediately suffer full punishment: in a post-atonement world where grace prevails, utter desola-

[21] Timothy Cruso similarly describes the good life: "That which affords the *most conveniences* with the *fewest burdens*, is a truly competent Inheritance. . . . The case lyes plainly thus; they that have *too little*, are opprest with *necessary* cares, and they that have *too much* are tormented with *unnecessary* ones; but they that have *enough* (and no more) are *most free* from both sorts of cares, and enjoy *most comfort*" (*Usefullnesse*, pp. 12–13). Other Christian apologists describe the "middle state" similarly.

[22] "Of Spiritual Contentment," Sermon IX in *The Spiritual Warfare* (Edinburgh, 1697), p. 114.

tion and isolation result not from one sin, but from continued rebellion. Only after advice and repeated providential warnings have failed does Crusoe's condition suddenly alter, and instead of the higher station he seeks, he is suddenly reduced "from a Merchant to a miserable Slave." Ironically, his master appoints him to care for his "little Garden" (A20), and Crusoe thinks that his situation has reached its nadir. His slavery, however, turns out to be only a "Taste of the Misery I was to go thro," for failure to heed this last warning effects a total archetypal expulsion. On his Bunyanesque "*Island of Despair*" he has to toil by the sweat of his brow, far removed from the paradise with which he had been discontented and even from his "little Garden" parody of it. Ironically, his propensity to roam, to be unconfined, results in complete loss of freedom. Alone in a hostile world, he experiences the isolation of man alienated from his place in the world because he is alienated from his God.[23]

"There are amazing *Judgments* of God," writes Cotton Mather (in explaining that "Evil Pursueth Sinners"), "Where-to Young Men do in *this World* become obnoxious." "And especially," he continues,

[23] The close relationship between man and God was, of course, broken by man's first sin, and Christianity has always recognized man's loneliness and isolation as a result of this sin. Puritanism's view of man as separate, rather than as part of a community of believers, focuses this problem. Max Weber speaks, quite correctly, of "a feeling of unprecedented inner loneliness of the single individual" which was generated by Calvinistic doctrine. Every man was a lone wanderer or pilgrim: no one could help him—no fellow man, no priest, no sacraments, no church, and not even God if God had not elected him in the first place (see *The Protestant Ethic and the Spirit of Capitalism*, trans. Talcott Parsons [New York, 1958], p. 104). Puritan religious literature of the seventeenth and eighteenth centuries is full of metaphors of loneliness and isolation which express the disruption of communication between God and man in a postlapsarian world.

when a notorious *Disobedience to the Voice of their Teachers, and their Parents,* is one Ingredient of their Wickedness. . . . There is a *Strange Punishment,* for those *Workers of Iniquity.* They become Tragical Examples of Misery and Confusion under the Judgment of God upon them; Their *Tragedy* becomes an *History.* They are made Spectacles and Monuments of what the Judgments of God will do upon such *Wretches.* The Astonished Spectators cry out, *This is the Finger of God.* The Just God sets a *Brand* upon them; they are horribly Mark'd by the *Judgments* of God. They soon run themselves into horrible Circumstances. The *Tempest* of God pursues them, and Shipwracks Them. . . .[24]

Crusoe considers himself a "*Memento*" to others because of the punishment that befalls him, and he hopes that his life story will "stand as a Direction from the Experience of the most miserable of all Conditions in the World." In retrospect, he never doubts that his difficulties result from his sin. The world, as he views it, is entirely controlled by God, and, like the providence books, he interprets both his judgments and his deliverances as "Testimonies . . . of a secret Hand of Providence governing the World" (B68).

Crusoe traces a pattern of warning and punishment in all the events leading up to his shipwreck. His early ventures result in gradually worsening punishments, but he makes only feeble and brief gestures toward repentance. On his first voyage, for example, he encounters two storms, but his religious promptings barely last until he reaches land. His voyages to Guinea similarly feature warnings—physical distress, the death of his benefactor, and, finally, his sale into slavery. Confined in Sallee, he remembers his "Father's prophetick Discourse" and decides that "now the Hand of Heaven had overtaken me,

[24] *Repeated Warnings, Another Essay, To Warn Young People against Rebellion That Must Be Repented Of* (Boston, 1712), pp. 16–17.

and I was undone without Redemption" (A20). But even when he is "deliver'd" and taken to Brazil, he cannot remain content with the accumulated riches of his new station (a parody of the paradise he might have enjoyed at home), and he undertakes one last rebellious voyage.

Crusoe's island imprisonment expands the pattern of punishment. Here, he not only faces physical danger but is effectually prevented from satisfying his major inclination. "Man that will not fear God willingly," according to Samuel Crossman, "shall be made (though little to his comfort) to do so by force. That dread of God which they flee from shall pursue them and overtake them between the straits. . . ." [25]

Crusoe's shipwreck and island isolation derives meaning both from the theology of the time and from the Puritan metaphor of man's condition. The sea—still romantic, mysterious, wild, and dangerous to Defoe's contemporaries—was a standard source of punishment for man's wickedness, according to Puritan moralists, who continually point out that the waves can be "the executioners of God's threatening" [26] and that "Winds are sent to fulfill the word of Gods threat." [27] But readers of *Robinson Crusoe* in 1719 would have found Crusoe's sea troubles meaningful for reasons beyond the inherent danger of the sea and its general providential function, for Puritan moralists taught that sin was usually punished in kind. "God chuses," says Timothy Cruso, "oftentimes to *punish* Men in that wherein they most *delight*. He is never more magnified, nor the Sinner more con-

[25] *The Young Man's Calling, or the Whole Duty of Youth* (London, 1683), p. 58.
[26] John Flavell, *Navigation Spiritualized; or a New Compass for Seamen* (Newburyport, 1796; first published, 1664), p. 102.
[27] Jeremiah Burroughs, *The Sea-Mans Direction in Time of Storme* (London, 1640), p. 72.

founded, then when the Sinner's chiefest Joy is turn'd
into his *greatest* Sorrow." [28] According to Increase
Mather, the appropriateness of punishment to sin may
take a variety of forms: God may inflict upon men the
same evil that they themselves have committed; the punishments may have "*some Resemblance and Analogy
with their Sins*"; the punishments may be brought about
by "Instruments" involved in the sin; or sin and punishment may be related "in respect of those Circumstances
of Place and Time where and when the Judgment shall
take hold on them." [29] Because Crusoe's sin is restlessness and discontent with his place in the divine order,
his punishment appropriately removes the possibility of
future rebellious wandering. The instrument of his sin (a
ship) becomes the instrument of punishment, and the
correspondence of time is so striking that Crusoe himself
comments upon it. His fatal voyage from Brazil begins
on the same day (eight years later) as did his first
voyage—September 1. It was, according to Crusoe, "an
evil Hour" (A45).

More important, Crusoe's isolation epitomizes the Puritan version of the plight of man. Fallen man is alienated from God—separated from him by a wide gulf as a
result of sin. He is lonely and isolated in a world for
which he was not in the first place intended, but into
which he is cast as a result of sin. "Surely," Calvin had
said, "no more terrible abyss can be conceived than to

[28] *Discourses upon the Rich Man and Lazarus* (London, 1697), p. 13.
[29] *The Doctrine of Divine Providence Opened and Applyed* (Boston,
1684), pp. 62–73. Mather says that God may use one or more of these
methods to suit the judgments to the sins. Thomas Gouge, though his
distinctions are less precise, makes essentially the same point: "Take
special notice of the kind of thine affliction; for it is Gods usual manner
to punish Sin in kind, by way of retaliation, observing an Analogy,
Proportion, and Similitude between the quality of the Sin, and the
punishment which he inflicteth . . ." (*Christian Directions, Shewing
How To Walk with God All the Day Long* [London, 1690; first published, 1661], p. 67).

feel yourself forsaken and estranged from God; and when you call upon him, not to be heard. It is as if God himself had plotted your ruin." [30] His relationship to God disrupted, Crusoe finds a similar disordering of his relationship to his fellow man and to his environment. His punishment, like other significant developments in *Robinson Crusoe*, converts a fundamental religious metaphor into the specifics of experience, achieving a peculiar unity of physical and spiritual levels—a unity enforced and exploited much further as the downward cycle ends and Crusoe learns that "deliverance" has more than one meaning, and that to be alone may also mean to be "singled out."

Crusoe, says Irving Howe, "never indulges in introspection. I do not think there is one statement of self-analysis in the book." [31] Such a view reflects a rather blind commitment to the premises of "modern" psychology and represents a refusal to consider *Robinson Crusoe* in its own historical setting or on its own terms. Crusoe does not, of course, attempt to peer into his psyche or pull back the curtains of his subconscious. Unlike modern psychological novels, which find ultimate answers within the limits of one man's mind, *Robinson Crusoe* depends upon the broader conception of God's providential control, within which the individual human drama must be played. Man can only seek to apprehend causes which are beyond his control and to which he must acclimate himself. *Robinson Crusoe's* philosophy

[30] *Institutes of the Christian Religion*, trans. F. L. Battles (2 vols.; Philadelphia, 1960), I, 516.

[31] "Robinson Crusoe: Epic of the Middle Class," *Tomorrow*, VII (1949), 53. Many other critics have commented similarly. See, for example, Mario Praz ("Defoe and Cellini," *English Studies*, XIII [1931], 75–87), who says that there is "practically no introspection" in any of Defoe's characters.

and psychology look backward rather than forward, but, in the book's own historical terms, Crusoe's search for understanding is both introspective and self-analytical. In fact, the narrative point of view and the ultimate structure of the novel depend upon Crusoe's introspective framework. All of the novel's events are recounted by a narrator who has had more than thirty years to reflect on the "meanings" of such actions as a flight from home or such states as slavery, shipwreck, and solitude.

The subtleties of the retrospective first-person narration are easy to overlook, for the sequence seems natural and artless. Event follows event in roughly chronological order, and the more important episodes are presented scenically, to use Lubbock's distinction,[32] with elaborate descriptions of setting and liberal use of dialogue and monologue. Defoe also employs such devices of immediacy as a "journal" (presumably written daily, to record events at the time when they occurred) and the stockpiling of small details (which, by emphasizing the amount of recall, tend to blur the time factor). A later perspective on these events is, however, implicit in the selectivity employed, and often this perspective is explicit in the account.[33] Even the "journal" section is infused with later interpretation. Crusoe does not simply transcribe his daily jottings (contrary to his promise that "I shall here give you the Copy" [A79]), but "edits" them freely from a later perspective. His first journal entry is September 30, 1659, but after two days of entries (less than one page of text, which might well be "copied" from an original "journal"), Crusoe begins to contract and expand the account.[34] The next twenty-four days of the

---

[32] See Percy Lubbock, *The Craft of Fiction* (New York, 1957), p. 67 ff.

[33] For a further discussion of Defoe's handling of time, see Chapter VIII below.

[34] Crusoe himself implies in one place that some of the journal entries were recorded at a time later than the events they describe. He says

journal are collapsed into two sentences; a few pages later Crusoe interrupts the journal account for three months, substituting a general account of progress and a description of scattered, fleeting religious promptings which he felt during that time. This description is clearly retrospective: in it he mentions events which occur three years later. Many subsequent entries could be copied from a journal, but in some places a later point of view is superimposed, without previous warning.[35] Even in sections calculated to produce the illusion of present action, Defoe uses the double time scheme to suggest movement and direction in Crusoe's life pattern and, ultimately, to suggest the structure of the novel itself.

We must recognize how the retrospective point of view works in *Robinson Crusoe* to understand the schematization of Crusoe's life, for the deceptively simple chronological record is infused throughout with later interpretation. Critics have often complained of Crusoe's moral monologues, finding them tedious and superfluous, but they have not often recognized that these reflections reinforce meanings implicit in the recounting of events. Crusoe's view of life is a unified conception, arrived at

that at first he did not keep a journal, yet the journal records a few minor details even for the first few days on the island. The mixture of entries and later reflection occurs throughout the journal section. Critics have often delighted in citing "inconsistencies" of this sort as evidence of Defoe's rapid writing and careless craftsmanship. One should note, however, that it is quite possible to account for this "inconsistency" and many others in terms of Crusoe's character. An old salt with Crusoe's predilection for interpreting the events of his life would quite likely "edit" his contemporary records, using his later point of view, in the same way that he imbues all of his life story with meaning relative to a divinely arranged pattern.

[35] The long description of illness and its spiritual results is clearly retrospective, though it purports to be a journal entry of June 27. Another short religious discussion is entered for July 4; only at the end of it is the reader alerted that the ideas reflect Crusoe's later point of view: "But leaving this Part," Crusoe says, "I return to my Journal" (A111).

after a lifetime of thought and evaluation, and evident both in his after-the-fact account of episodes and in his elaborate interpretive monologues.[36] Throughout the narrative he alludes to the pattern of his life, a pattern set up by his early disobedience and flight. Retrospectively, he notes the causal sequence of events: punishment inevitably follows disobedience; failure to heed repeated warnings intensifies both the seriousness of the sin and its practical results. Like the Puritan biographers, Crusoe seeks to determine the original cause of his physical and spiritual plight, and from this cause he traces all the events in the downward cycle. But, like the heroes of spiritual biography, Crusoe is saved physically and spiritually by the specific intervention of God, and from this intervention he traces the upward cycle. Looking back upon the history of his life, he can see the purposeful pattern of events; he is able to decipher "Providence's Checquer-Work."

Retrospection is not necessarily introspection, of course; one may look back without evaluation of causes, without assessment of one's own responsibility for involvement. But Crusoe is introspective just as Puritan diarists are introspective: he searches the events of his life for threads of meaning and examines his own acts of will in terms of a philosophy revealed to him after he had surrendered himself to a purposeful universe. What he finds is not just an occasional thread but a personal fab-

[36] Starr's treatment of *Robinson Crusoe*'s relation to spiritual autobiography does not, I think, take adequate account of Defoe's use of this double time scheme. Personal diaries usually record events soon after they happen (the immediacy of which Richardson tries to capture in his "writing to the moment" device); ordinarily, a more cohesive and pointed retrospective treatment of a saint's pattern of life results only from a decision to present the life publicly. The aim of diaries is always to *discover* the pattern, but Defoe employs his time scheme to *articulate* the pattern early in his narrative. Richardson's technique of allowing the life pattern to manifest itself gradually is much closer to the methods of journals and spiritual autobiographies.

ric of meaning, which is part of the carefully woven divine quilt of history. Far from lacking introspection, Crusoe, from the time of his conversion, reflects almost constantly upon his choices and their meanings, and he relates all of his strange and surprising adventures to a pattern that his reflections reveal to him.

Crusoe's retrospection and introspection produce a good deal of personal discomfort, for the more he thinks about his past, the more he blames himself for the difficulties he encounters. When he begins to see his own responsibility, however, he begins to understand the cause-effect process in his world and develops a desire to harmonize himself with the First Cause so that he can exchange "Misery" for "Happiness." The big step in his harmonizing process is his repentance and conversion. This step comes about when his desires have been fully prepared, and it involves direct supernatural intervention in his life. Once his desire is whetted and once that intervention comes, Crusoe's life can never again be the same, nor can his view of that life. For as divine illumination dramatically touches him, as revelation is added to his discursive powers, retrospection and introspection become literally one—and the pattern of his life becomes not only changed but understood in cosmic terms.

VII

Repentance

"The greatest Calamities," says Bishop Patrick, "are sometimes the Means of Mans greatest Felicity."[1] According to contemporary theology, if God controlled all of history in relation to his plan for individual men, he not only could turn calamities to use but might actually design a plague or a shipwreck in order to further his plan of salvation, for men too weak to accept grace through their own will had to be given special opportunity through special circumstances. If a man who had been chosen among the elect could not be drawn to redemption, he had to be driven to it—placed in a position where he was released from fleshly inclination and had the opportunity to choose for good. Man, of course, liked to think that he had the power to control his depraved natural propensities and that he could choose freely at any time, but he really needed the interposition of God. "One would not willingly indeed be indebted merely to an Affliction for his Soul's Health," says Bishop Patrick, "but have some more noble Consideration. . . . But yet we are beholden to God, if he will make use of this Remedy, when there is no other left. And as we cannot be said to perish, if we be cast safely on Shoar by a Shipwreck, so we are not undone if we suffer great Losses in this World, and therby are driven to Heaven."[2]

Crusoe's exile from the civilized world makes his con-

---

[1] *Fifteen Sermons upon Contentment and Resignation to the Will of God* (London, 1719), Sermon X, p. 254.

[2] *Ibid.*, Sermon VIII, p. 189. Theologians, both Anglican and Dis-

version possible, but the shipwreck is only the first of a series of events that alert him to his human limitations and to his need of God. Like the seeds of grain which he inadvertently plants by his doorstep, the brief spiritual promptings induced by his violent turmoil in the sea and his ultimate arrival on dry land seem at first to come to nothing. Nine months pass before a violent physical distress finally humbles Crusoe into acceptance of the new birth which he had resisted for so long.

During the early months on the island, Crusoe seems even less concerned with his spiritual welfare than he had been during his travels, for his preoccupation with accumulating things leaves little time for him to think of less tangible matters. In his unregenerated state he misses the significance of almost all the events of these early months, although many of them would seem to have rather precise meanings in the context of his later understanding of his life pattern. Defoe manipulates the double time scheme quite carefully to render, rather than merely describe, Crusoe's early naïveté, while at the same time retaining occasional reminders of his later awareness, thus highlighting the change wrought by his conversion.

In the grain episode, Defoe uses the rather simple method of an explicit contrast between Crusoe's immedi-

---

senter, constantly emphasized the need for God to "prepare" individuals for conversion because of man's natural depravity. "Such is the corruption of our nature," writes Joseph Alleine, "that it utterly disables to make a saving use of outward means without inward aids. Unless the Spirit by his powerful operations work thee into a Serious teachable temper . . . , the most concerning truths and weightiest arguments can never . . . overcome thy sensual, worldly inclinations, rescue thee from the dominion of sin and satan, and bring thee back to God" (*A Sure Guide to Heaven* [London, 1689], fol. A3).

Providence books and spiritual biographies abound in accounts of sinners converted by means of a sickness. See e.g., Samuel Clarke's account of Sir Charles Coot, *The Lives of Sundry Eminent Persons in This Later Age* (London, 1683), IV, 98.

ate response and his maturer consideration.[3] Finding stalks of English grain beside his fortification, Crusoe first imagines their growth to be miraculous and considers them "the pure Productions of Providence for my Support . . ." (A89). This first interpretation is both arrogant and naïve, for Crusoe does not yet understand man's relation to God or God's ways with man; and as soon as Crusoe finds a "natural" cause for the grain, the seeds of his intuitive faith are again choked by religious doubt and indifference.[4] Retrospectively, however, Crusoe understands that the episode demonstrates the workings of providence even though natural process was not interrupted, for his conversion and later experience expands and subtilizes his understanding of God's ways. Crusoe later understands that "it was really the Work of Providence as to me, that should order or appoint, that 10 or 12 Grains of Corn should remain unspoil'd, (when the Rats had destroy'd all the rest,) as if it had been dropt from Heaven; as also, that I should throw it out in that particular Place, where it being in the Shade of a high Rock, it sprang up immediately; whereas, if I had thrown it anywhere else, at that Time, it had been burnt up and destroy'd" (A90).[5] Here, as in the account of Crusoe's early sea scares, Defoe keeps the before-after contrast on the surface of the narrative, for he needs to

[3] The *explicit* contrast is here necessary not only to set up for the reader a contrast between meaning and the young Crusoe's understanding of it, but also to explain Crusoe's vacillating efforts to perceive. Here, as during the earlier storm, Crusoe first seems to grasp the event's meaning, then retreats from his perception. Because Defoe needs to make clear Crusoe's error, the explicit contrast is necessary; in other events in which Crusoe fails even to *consider* possible meanings, no comment is needed, for Defoe's double time scheme makes Crusoe's discrepancy in perception implicit.

[4] For a discussion of the symbolic implications of this and other passages in *Robinson Crusoe* see Edwin F. Benjamin. "Symbolic Elements in Robinson Crusoe" (*PQ*, XXX [1951], 206–11).

[5] Compare Crusoe's description of the seeds' potentiality with the parable of the sower in Matt. 13:3–8, 18–23; or Mark 4:3–9, 14–20.

show Crusoe's fumbling attempts at a comprehensive vision of life—attempts which are doomed to failure as long as his philosophical assumptions are false and his will remains unregenerated. But in other episodes during Crusoe's early months on the island, Defoe develops the contrast more subtly.

Defoe shows the young Crusoe to be dimly conscious only of the most obvious signs of divine concern; less obvious but equally significant signs escape him entirely. Once he has established Crusoe's pattern of perception, Defoe counts on the reader's memory of the before-after contrast and usually allows Crusoe to describe events in his uncomprehending state. But Defoe chooses these events with great care so that they bear an intrinsic significance which the reader may perceive even when Crusoe does not. For example, Crusoe views the storms which afflict him in his early months on the island as threats only to the *things* he possesses, and he translates the message of the storms in terms of physical fear, even though they continue the pattern of his warnings at sea (which he had at least paused over, if not understood) and even though the storms now take forms with standard symbolical significance.

Once he has pillaged the ship, Crusoe revels in his acquisitions and enjoys his tent home "where I lay with all my Wealth about me very secure" (A65). But he soon desires more luxurious quarters, builds a semicircular wall to enclose a large rock projecting from a hillside, and digs a cave beneath the rock so that he has a "Cellar to my House" (A68). He now begins to see his new home as a "fortress," mighty enough to protect "all my Riches, all my Provisions, Ammunition and Stores"— "fortify'd, as I thought, from all the World" (A67). But his fortress is still under construction when a thunderstorm suggests the inadequacy of his plans. Crusoe admits his fear, but sees the event as purposeless and "natural": "It *happen'd*," Crusoe reports, ". . . that a Storm of Rain falling from a thick dark Cloud, a sudden Flash of Lightning *happen'd*, and after that a great Clap of Thunder, as is *naturally* the Effect of it" (A68, italics mine). An intuitive thought darts into Crusoe's mind "as swift as the Lightning itself," but the intuition is limited in the same way as Crusoe's discursive reasonings. He fears for his possessions, being (he tells us) "nothing near so anxious about my own Danger." And it does not even occur to Crusoe that the storm, like previous storms, could bear a message about his *spiritual* condition.

Crusoe is similarly incapable of interpreting the earthquake which occurs only a day after he finishes building his fortress, but the reader is reminded of the meaning which Crusoe misses by Defoe's juxtaposition of the episode with Crusoe's reflections on the grain growing beside his fortress, and by Crusoe's later notation that the episode produced "not the least serious religious Thought" (A92). At the time, he describes himself at the edge of his cave, "terribly frighted with a most dreadful surprising Thing indeed, for all on a sudden I found the Earth come crumbling down from the Roof of my Cave, and from the Edge of the Hill over my Head, and two of the Posts I had set up in the cave crack'd in a frightful Manner; I was heartily scar'd, but thought nothing of what was really the Cause . . ." (A91). He finally diagnoses the natural cause of the destruction, but he fails to attach any significance to the earthquake, again thinking only of what might happen to his possessions. "I thought of nothing then," he reports, "but the Hill falling upon my Tent and all my houshold Goods, and burying all at once; and this sunk my very Soul within me . . ." (A92).

Crusoe's terminology here is typical of the language

Defoe employs throughout the episodes involving Crusoe's pre-conversion state. The "sinking of his Soul"
means nothing to Crusoe at the time, but it reminds the
reader of the disparity between Crusoe's understanding
of events and their real significance. Defoe employs the
same device, with heightened irony, in Crusoe's description of his first response to landing on the island: "I
walk'd about on the Shore, lifting up my Hands, and my
whole Being as I may say, wrapt up in the Contemplation of my Deliverance, making a Thousand Gestures
and Motions which I cannot describe, reflecting upon all
my Comrades that were drown'd, and that there should
not be one Soul sav'd but my self; for, as for them, I
never saw them afterwards, or any Sign of them, except
three of their Hats, one Cap, and two Shoes that were
not Fellows" (A52). This passage has often been praised
as an example of Defoe's "realism," but its real significance lies in its illustration of Defoe's control over the
development of Crusoe's character. For here Crusoe
vaguely uses terms ("Soul," "sav'd," "Deliverance,")
which he does not at the time comprehend, while he
demonstrates his understanding of events and people
solely in terms of things. Defoe uses a similar linguistic
device to suggest Crusoe's limited awareness of his
human impotence when, after the shipwreck, he is at the
mercy of the sea, a symbol here (it is modified later in
the novel) of danger and isolation. "Tho' I swam very
well," reports Crusoe, "yet I could not deliver my self
from the Waves so as to draw Breath, till that wave having driven me, or rather carried me a vast Way on towards the Shore, and having spent it self, went back,
and left me upon the land . . ." (A49–50).

But more basic than the device of Crusoe's quasi-
conscious language during the early island episodes is
the emblematic quality Defoe attaches to the events

themselves as a potential means of communication between man and God. Both the thunder-lightning episode and the earthquake derive their meaning not only from the general storm motif set up earlier in the novel but from traditional associations as well: each episode presents a standard symbol of God's voice speaking through natural events. Defoe's contemporaries were well aware of these symbols, for providence books contained special sections on divine warnings and punishments by thunder, lightning, and earthquake; [6] and spiritual biographies often highlighted such events as turning points in an individual's relationship with God. Like these books, *Robinson Crusoe* draws upon the biblical meanings attached to such events (see, e.g., Exodus 19:6, Psalms 77:18, Psalms 104:7, Revelation 10:4, and Revelation 14:2), but Defoe appears to have in mind one account in particular. After being threatened by Jezebel, Elijah flees into a wilderness where he is fed by God but where he remains fearful, disillusioned, and anxious for death, hiding at last in a cave. God asks Elijah why he is there and then dramatically reveals Elijah's new duty. First, God sends strong winds which "rent the mountains and break in pieces the rocks," then an earthquake, then a fire, and finally "a still small voice" which overwhelms Elijah's disillusionment, renews his faith and incites him to action.[7]

Defoe employs the pattern of revelation in the Elijah

[6] See, e.g., William Turner, *A Compleat History of the Most Remarkable Providences, Both of Judgment and Mercy, Which Have Hapned in This Present Age* (London, 1697), and Samuel Clarke, *A Mirrour or Looking-Glass Both for Saints, and Sinners* (4th ed.; London, 1671).

[7] See I Kings 19. Before conversion, Crusoe misses the significance even of acts he himself performs. Sheridan Baker points out to me that Crusoe sets up a cross on the island, then uses it only as a calendar on which he forgets to record the Sabbaths. Professor Baker further notes that Defoe's derivation of "Crusoe" from "Kreutznaer" (meaning, roughly, "fool of the cross") underscores this incident specifically and Crusoe's role generally.

story to culminate the pattern of flight in Crusoe's early life. This new biblical allusion continues and reinforces the motif introduced by the Jonah and prodigal son parallels and seals off Crusoe's period of rebellion by leading directly to the vision which produces his repentance. Defoe operates characteristically in these biblical allusions, subtly leaving more and more to his reader; he lets Crusoe cite the prodigal son story explicitly, then has a sea captain obliquely allude to Jonah, and finally allows the third (and structurally most important) parallel to remain implicit. Also characteristic is the subtle shift in meaning he gives to the Elijah episode, a shift occasioned by the distinction between Elijah's character and Crusoe's. In the biblical account, God's voice is *not* in the wind, earthquake, or fire (the author of I Kings suspends reader expectation by rejecting the traditional symbols for God's voice), but quietly follows as direct communicant. Defoe returns to the traditional symbolism, thus modifying the Elijah pattern: the storm, earthquake, and fiery vision all bear God's voice, but Crusoe (unlike the disillusioned but fundamentally religious Elijah) fails to perceive the message, so that God, to effect his purpose, has to speak directly. Defoe's subtly varied interpretation highlights again the difference between the modern Crusoe and his ancient counterparts, who were quick to perceive God's message and respond to it. Modern man, as Defoe later demonstrates more fully *after* Crusoe repents, is not only no prophet, but is slower to perceive and more hesitant to act.

The vision during Crusoe's illness completes the Elijah allusion by presenting divine manifestation first as fire, then as spoken word. But the vision and the episode involving the vision have a far broader biblical base, for the episode reflects the novel's transition from symbols of punishment for rebellion to those of deliverance as a result of repentance. Crusoe experiences the vision when he has reached the nadir of both his physical and spiritual condition. He has had to reduce his rations to one biscuit cake a day, "which made my Heart very heavy" (A95), and he has exhausted himself in an attempt to get fragments of lead and plank from the wreck. Suddenly, his world begins to seem unnatural to him, but the difficulty is really in Crusoe himself. "The Rain felt Cold, and I was something chilly" (A99), he comments in his journal for June 18, 1660. Soon, he is violently ill, suffers several aguish fits, and begins to fear for his life. "Very ill," Crusoe reports on June 21, "frighted almost to Death with the Apprehensions of my sad Condition, to be sick, and no Help; pray'd to God for the first Time since the Storm off of *Hull*, but scarce knew what I said, or why; my Thoughts being all confused" (A99). Crusoe's confusion of thought parallels his lack of spiritual perception, and, predictably, he fails to recognize that his physical condition is an emblem of his spiritual need. Three times he thinks himself improved, but each time he sinks back worse than before. Weak ("I had not Strength to stand up"), thirsty ("I was ready to perish for Thirst"), and unable to minister to his physical needs, Crusoe in desperation prays again for God's mercy, though he is "light-headed" and "so ignorant, that I knew not what to say . . ." (A99). At last he falls asleep, and is confronted by a "terrible Vision" of God's fiery vengeance: a man whose countenance is "inexpressibly dreadful" descends "from a great black Cloud, in a bright Flame of Fire" and lands upon the earth. Armed with a long spear, he moves toward Crusoe and in a voice "so terrible, that it is impossible to express the Terror of it," says, "*Seeing all these Things have not brought thee to Repentance, now thou shalt die"* (A100). Crusoe's dream seems more real to him than his waking reality, and it goes far toward clarifying his perception of the unity of physical and spiritual. Crusoe reports that the "Horrors of my Soul" resulting from the vision are indescribable, for his eight years of "Seafaring Wickedness" had brought about "a certain Stupidity of Soul, without Desire of Good or Conscience of evil . . ." (A100–1). He reviews the punishments and deliverances of his life, recalling that he had suffered little remorse and had offered no thanks. "I was meerly thoughtless of a God, or a Providence," he recalls. "[I] acted like a meer Brute from the Principles of Nature." He remembers the "good Advice" and warning of his father: "Now, said I aloud, My dear Father's Words are come to pass: God's Justice has overtaken me, and I have none to help or hear me" (A101, 104).

Crusoe's illness alerts him to his human impotence, and his dream frightens him into contemplating the causative pattern of his plight and into thinking seriously about his relationship to God. Prepared by direct revelation, Crusoe now finds his discursive powers enhanced, and he tries for the first time to arrive at a full understanding of his world. The day after his vision, he is still weak and "heavy-hearted in the Sense of my miserable Condition" (A105), but his sense of misery has a new dimension and he is a paradigm of contemplative man. He walks "a little Way," sits down upon the ground and looks out upon the sea, which, "very calm and smooth," epitomizes the benevolent attitude of nature now that he has tried to understand it. Crusoe now begins to read from the Book of Nature: from the existence of natural phenomena, he posits a creator and reasons that "if God has made all these Things, He guides and governs them all, and all Things that concern them; for the Power that could make all Things, must certainly have Power to guide and direct them." Proceeding by hypothetical syllogisms, he concludes that God has "appointed all this to befal me," and his conscience tells him that these judgments result from his "dreadful mis-spent Life." "I was struck dumb with these Reflections, as one astonish'd," he reports in retrospect, "and had not a Word to say, no not to answer to my self, but rose up pensive and sad, walk'd back to my Retreat, and went up over my Wall. . . ." This time, however, his bower provides no secure retreat from reflection; his thoughts are "sadly disturb'd and he has "no Inclination to Sleep" (A105–7).

Crusoe's account of the next incident is constructed to fuse the physical and the spiritual specifically and dramatically for the reader, and at the same time to suggest Crusoe's deepened understanding of God's manipulation of the physical world for spiritual ends. Now that Crusoe has begun to understand the connection between physical and spiritual distress, God offers a solution which dramatizes the oneness of Crusoe's two kinds of needs. In quest of physical relief, Crusoe searches in a seaman's chest for tobacco (which, he remembers, Brazilians use for "almost all distempers"). "I went," he says, "directed by Heaven, no doubt; for in this Chest I found a Cure, both for Soul and Body," for along with the tobacco the chest contains Bibles "which to this Time I had not found Leisure, or so much as Inclination to look into . . ." (A107).

Defoe's choice of the seaman's chest as the central vehicle for Crusoe's relief is more than a stroke of contemporary "realism." The chest effectively epitomizes Crusoe's previous conventional behavior and dramatizes the effect of his new perception, for Defoe's contemporaries regarded the chest as a repository for valued but unused belongings. Like Crusoe, contemporary seamen were often represented as having a conventional respect for religious faith while betraying their real feelings by relegating their Bibles to the safety of their chests. John Flavell had sent his *Navigation Spiritualized; or a New Compass for Seamen* into the world with this prefatory request in verse to his readers:

> Go little book, I have much more to say,
> But sea-men call for thee, thou must away.
> Yet ere you have it, grant me one request;
> Pray do not keep it prisoner in your chest.[8]

When Crusoe removes a Bible from the chest, he shows his new separation from the conventional conduct of his early life, and when he begins to use the Bible, he soon shows an enlarged understanding. Defoe dramatizes Crusoe's mental development through his heightened awareness of language, for words which Crusoe had previously used carelessly now become meaningful to him. Crusoe first trusts God by practicing biblical lottery, the popular Puritan custom of opening the Bible at random and depending on providence to choose a relevant passage. When Crusoe begins to read, the first words he comes upon are these: *"Call on me in the Day of Trouble, and I will deliver, and thou shalt glorify me."* At first the idea of deliverance seems "so remote, so impossible in my Apprehension of Things" that he doubts the promise, but before he retires he does "what I never had done in all my Life" (A108)—he kneels to pray. A few days later, recovered from his illness, he reflects again upon the Scripture, and "it occurr'd to my Mind, that I pored so much upon my Deliverance from the main Affliction, that I disregarded the Deliverance I had received. . . . *God had deliver'd me, but I had not glori-*

---

[8] (Newburyport, 1796; first published, 1664), p. 23.

fy'd Him . . ." (A110). Crusoe then offers a prayer of
thanksgiving and on the very next day comprehends an
even more important meaning of deliverance. Again
"providentially" led to an applicable passage, Crusoe
reads from Acts 5:31: *"He is exalted a Prince and a
Saviour, to give Repentance, and to give Remission,"* and
"with my Heart as well as my Hands lifted up to
Heaven, in a Kind of Extasy of Joy," he prays for repentance. It is the first time, reports Crusoe, "in the true
Sense of the Words, that I pray'd in all my Life," for he
now prays "with a Sense of my Condition" and "with a
true Scripture View of Hope . . ." (A110–11). Now
Crusoe begins to comprehend the spiritual meaning of
deliverance. In the past, says Crusoe, he had thought
only of "being deliver'd from the Captivity I was in; for
. . . the Island was certainly a Prison to me," but now,
looking back upon his "dreadful" sins with "Horrour," his
soul seeks "nothing of God, but Deliverance from the
Load of Guilt that bore down all my comfort." His physical deliverance is worthless by comparison: "I did not so
much as pray to be deliver'd from [solitary life], or
think of it," says Crusoe; "It was all of no Consideration
in Comparison to this [spiritual deliverance]." "Deliverance from Sin," Crusoe concludes, "[is] a much
greater Blessing than Deliverance from Affliction," and
though his physical isolation remains miserable, it seems
"much easier to my Mind." His new way of life—with
his thoughts directed by Bible-reading and prayer—
gives him "a great deal of Comfort within, which till
now I knew nothing of . . ." (A111).

In retrospect, Crusoe realizes that God had patiently
prepared him for conversion by eroding his physical
condition to make it parallel his spiritual state, but the

conversion itself occurs quite rapidly when God directly intervenes through the fiery vision. The vision penetrates Crusoe's dazed consciousness because God has prepared Crusoe's mind, but the vision's artistic effect derives from its use of well-established symbols of divine vengeance. Defoe builds the vision carefully to recall the biblical promises of God's wrath not only against individuals and nations but against the world itself, at the time of the last judgment.

Crusoe's vision begins rather like the vision that calls Ezekiel to prophetic action—with a flame of fire suddenly appearing out of a cloud and taking human form. "He was all over as bright as a Flame," Crusoe reports, "so that I could but just bear to look towards him; his Countenance was most inexpressibly dreadful, impossible for Words to describe; when he stepp'd upon the Ground with his Feet, I thought the Earth trembl'd, just as it had done before in the Earthquake, and all the Air look'd, to my Apprehension, as if it had been fill'd with Flashes of Fire." As soon as the messenger lands on earth, he brandishes "a long Spear or Weapon in his Hand," and issues God's threat: " 'Seeing all these Things have not brought thee to Repentance, now thou shalt die' " (A100).

The spear is Defoe's localized form of the Old Testament "sword of the Lord" cited in prophetic predictions of God's vengeance—a representation still used by Defoe's contemporaries (see, e.g., Joseph Alleine's description of God's justice as "like a flaming Sword unsheathed" against the unconverted).[9] And the cluster of symbols of wrath—earthquake, wind, thunder, fire, sword—vividly recalls standard divine threats against the disobedient, as in Isaiah's prophecy of the woes of the city Ariel:

---

[9] *Sure Guide*, p. 93.

Thou shalt be visited of the Lord of hosts with thunder, and with earthquake, and great noise, with storm and tempest, and the flame of devouring fire.

And the multitude of all the nations that fight against Ariel, even all that fight against her and her munition, and that distress her, shall be as a dream of a night vision.

It shall even be as when a hungry man dreameth, and, behold, he eateth; but he awaketh, and his soul is empty; or as when a thirsty man dreameth, and behold, he drinketh; but he awaketh, and behold, he is faint, and his soul hath appetite. . . .[10]

But just as the Judeo-Christian myth turns symbols of destruction and despair into those of possible regeneration and hope, Crusoe's vision bears implicit suggestions of his deliverance, suggestions which take on their full significance once he has responded to God's voice. Defoe makes the vision suggest not only vehicles of God's punishment, but also his devices to protect and guide the righteous. Crusoe's perception of the flaming messenger glances at Moses' encounter with the burning bush and recalls the Israelites' deliverance from Egyptian bondage, the favorite biblical "deliverance" of providence writers and contemporary theologians. According to Exodus 3:3 ff., God called Moses to lead the Israelites by speaking through an angel which appeared "in a flame of fire out of the midst of a bush." "I have surely seen the afflic-

---

[10] Isa. 29:6–8. A later passage in Isaiah, probably written by a different author, pictures God's fiery last judgment this way: ". . . behold, the Lord will come with fire, and with his chariots like a whirlwind, to render his anger with fury, and his rebuke with flames of fire. For by fire and by his sword will the Lord plead with all flesh: and the slain of the Lord shall be many" (Isa. 66:15–16). Still another passage in Isaiah portrays man's response to God's judgment as flight into caves during an earthquake, a pattern paralleled in *Robinson Crusoe*: "And [men] shall go into the holes of the rocks, and into the caves of the earth, for fear of the Lord, and for the glory of his majesty, when he ariseth to shake terribly the earth" (Isa. 2:19). Starr (SA) interprets Crusoe's conversion by suggesting different biblical parallels.

tion of my People," God tells Moses, ". . . and I am come down to deliver them. . . ." Like the cloud and pillar of fire which guided the Israelites through the wilderness toward Canaan, Crusoe's vision leads him out of the bondage of sin toward salvation. Crusoe's vision thus pivots the novel by culminating Defoe's three major allusions to rebellion (Jonah, the prodigal son, Elijah) and by suggesting three allusions to deliverance through obedience (Elijah, Ezekiel, Moses).

Another biblical parallel, also thematically related to *Robinson Crusoe*, is suggested by the use of sickness as a vehicle for Crusoe's repentance and by Crusoe's debate with himself about the cause of his afflictions. In Job 33, at the beginning of the book's climactic section, Elihu tells Job that God's ways, though mysterious and not always comprehensible to man, are just and are ultimately for man's own good. Elihu says:

> . . . God speaketh once, yea twice, yet man perceiveth it not.
> In a dream, in a vision of the night, when deep sleep falleth upon men, in slumberings upon the bed;
> Then he openeth the ears of men, and sealeth their instruction,
> That he may withdraw man from his purpose, and hide pride from man.
> He keepeth back his soul from the pit, and his life from perishing by the sword.   (vv. 14–18)

Like Job, Crusoe first tries to justify himself when he reasons out the divine source of his afflictions: "*Why has God done this to me? What have I done to be thus us'd?*" (A106). But as in Job's dialogue, the objection is quickly answered: "My Conscience," Crusoe reports, "presently check'd me in that Enquiry, as if I had blasphem'd, and methought it spoke to me like a Voice; *Wretch! dost thou ask what thou hast done!* look back upon a dreadful mis-spent Life, and ask thy self *what thou hast not done?* ask, Why is it *that thou wert not long ago destroy'd?*" Crusoe has no friends to advise him; his only counsels are his conscience and his Bible, and his repentance is halting and awkward. "I had alas! no divine Knowledge," he laments (A100); but he studies his Bible diligently, and finds that when he sets himself "seriously to this Work" he becomes increasingly "affected with the Wickedness of my past Life" (A110).

In the process of conversion, Crusoe first discovers by his reason that God and providence exist, but he must turn to the Bible before he attains certainty of salvation. Crusoe's action thus parallels the contemporary orthodox belief that man can be brought part of the way to Christian commitment by natural religion but that he must finally be guided by revealed religion in order to attain salvation. Prompted by sickness and the vision, Crusoe tries to interpret his life in relation to the divine world plan, convicts himself of sin, and sets about to change the course of events. The Job parallel illustrates Crusoe's exaggerated sense of his human power (a motif Defoe exploits further in the second half of the novel) and of his own righteousness, even at the moment when he sincerely tries to repent; and it reinforces Defoe's thematic attempt to justify God's ways to man.

Crusoe's repentance, born in fear, has sometimes been criticized as desperate and insincere, but such criticism proceeds from a naïve understanding of the terms of Christian conversion. Crusoe's conversion must, of course, be evaluated in the light of his later conduct, for if, as some have said, Crusoe is the same man at the end of the novel as he was at the beginning, the conversion is indeed superficial. Contemporary theologians, however, although they deplored deathbed conversions and recommended an early choice of a Godly life, were quick to recognize the possibility of conversions wrought by physical extremity. If God chose to stimulate reformation through physical distress, man ought to be grateful and impressed by God's concern, rather than critical of his method. From the saved man's point of view, it was a good bargain: "Now is this so bad a Market," asks Bishop Patrick, "for a Man to escape the Flames of Hell, by the Flames of a Fever? To be delivered from the Pit of Destruction, by being cast upon a Bed of Weakness?" [11] And from God's point of view, it could also have advantages. "When we are in the Jaws of Death," argues Stephen Charnock, "God may have his Terms of us; when we are at some distance, we will have our own. The lower a Person is, the more readily will he bend to any Condition; hope of Deliverance will make him stoop. . . . If common Patience leads to Repentance, a rescue from an amazing Danger is a stronger Cord to draw us to Repentance and Obedience." [12] The results might be better, therefore, than if a man were converted earlier. "They who are reclaim'd from a wicked course," says Tillotson, "are many times more thoroughly and zealously good afterwards. . . . A lively sense of their past errors is apt to make them more . . . desirous . . . to redeem their former miscarriages by their good behaviour for the future." [13]

The Puritan concept of "Finding Times" placed great emphasis on God's interposition at a specific time and

[11] *Fifteen Sermons,* Sermon IV, p. 94. Such language is frequent in the writings of both Anglicans and Dissenters, for man's relationship with God was frequently described in terms of a contract. The source of this language, and of the idea, is probably not Hobbes, but rather the Old Testament idea of covenant.

[12] "A Discourse on the Fifth of November," *Works* (3d ed., 2 vols.; London, 1699), I, 593.

[13] *Works* (9th ed.; London, 1728), Sermon XVI, p. 139.

under specific circumstances as a corollary to the doctrine of predestination. "There are," says Flavell, ". . . seasons and gales of grace for our souls; golden opportunities of salvation afforded to men. . . . God hath given unto men a day of visitation, which he hath limited. . . ." [14] Repentance, adds Benjamin Calamy, is "never out of Season . . . yet there are some particular Times wherein we are more especially called upon to review our Actions . . . ; such are times of Affliction, . . . when we our selves are visited with any Sickness or grievous Calamity. . . ." [15] John Goodman, in his *The Penitent Pardon'd: Or, a Discourse of the Nature of Sin, and the Efficacy of Repentance* (1694), even asserts that "it is *usually* some affliction or other which first awakens habitual sinners into consideration, and the rudiments of piety and religion. Or as serious considerativeness begins conversion, so *commonly* some sharp affliction or other begins that seriousness." [16]

Spiritual biographies are filled with incidents of conversion through affliction, and most conversions are then supported by evidence of the person's continued godliness and righteous action. The most tenuous conversion stories involve repentances followed by immediate death. Technically, such a repentance, if sincere, is adequate for salvation, according to orthodox Christianity, but God alone could judge the penitent's sincerity.

The best-known deathbed "conversion" of Defoe's time was that of Lord Rochester, who, according to his eulogizers, renounced his libertine life and attitudes almost at the moment of death. Among numerous defenders of Rochester's conversion, one even compared his

---

[14] *Navigation Spiritualized,* p. 63.
[15] *Sermons Preached upon Several Occasions* (3d ed. corr.; London, 1700), Sermon X, pp. 290–91.
[16] P. 153. Italics mine.

moment of illumination to that of Paul,[17] for Christian moralists regarded the repentance of such a notorious rake as useful because of its shock effect. Scoffers reveled in the lack of evidence, and Rochester's "conversion" became a standing joke among the sophisticated in Defoe's time—a joke which illustrated the gullibility of apologists desperate for evidence of God's continuing role in history. But the Rochester incident clearly illustrates two facts important to Defoe's writing of *Robinson Crusoe*. Defoe's contemporaries regarded the conversion of a notorious sinner as an effective *exemplum*, but accounts of these conversions could only quiet the scoffers if they provided ample evidence of a reformed life after conversion. Had Defoe "delivered" Crusoe from his island immediately after his sickness and vision, he would have laid himself open to the criticisms leveled against Rochester's defenders—and to modern critics anxious to find Crusoe an "economic man." The fact that Crusoe remained on the island for twenty-seven years, however, silenced the potential objections of Defoe's contemporaries—and provides an answer for those modern critics willing to meet the book on its own historical terms.

[17] See Robert Parsons, *A Sermon Preached at the Funeral of the Rt. Honorable John Earl of Rochester* (Oxford, 1680).

VIII

Deliverance

———◆◆◆◆►———

Crusoe dates his "Hope that God would hear me" (A111) from his sincere supplications for repentance, but he does not immediately emerge a fully developed Christian. Although his attitudes are changed by his conversion, he has much to learn about the demands of a religious life, and years later he still has to admit that he has "more Sincerity than Knowledge" (B5). Conversion provides Crusoe with the requisite attitude for a reformed life, but, like his physical deliverance, complete spiritual deliverance is still far away.

Some changes in Crusoe are rapid, almost immediate. His new awareness of God's active concern and control invests his daily activities with new meaning, and his new determination to subordinate his impulses to God's will brings notable formal changes in his routine. He begins to read the Bible every morning and night (later he expands his reading to three periods per day), and instead of his occasional and conventional *"Lord ha' Mercy upon me"* (A92) [1] he prays regularly and sin-

---

[1] Crusoe often refers to his several conventional religious responses before conversion. He talks, for example, about his conventional "what pleases God" (A89), and when he first arrives on his island he offers conventional thanks for his rescue to a conventionally assumed God. He also conventionally keeps Sundays for a while. But none of these practices has real meaning for him. Typical is his response to Sabbath-keeping: "I soon neglected my keeping Sundays, for omitting my Mark for them on my Post, I forgot which was which" (A82). Note his abrupt change after conversion.

cerely "with a Sense of my Condition, and with a true Scripture view of Hope founded on the encouragement of the Word of God . . ." (A111). A little later he begins to keep a Sabbath, a practice he had earlier ignored because "I had no Sense of Religion upon my Mind" (A119). He suddenly becomes conscious also of the concurrence of dates of providential events in his life [2] and celebrates the anniversary of his "deliverance" on the island as a "Solemn Fast, setting it apart to Religious Exercise, prostrating my self on the Ground with the most serious Humiliation, confessing my Sins to God, acknowledging His Righteous Judgments upon me, and praying to him to have Mercy on me, through Jesus Christ . . ." (A119).[3] His observance of the day even becomes sacramental, within the limits of his condition: after twelve hours of fasting he eats "A Bisket Cake, and a Bunch of Grapes. . . ."

Crusoe's attitudes toward his station and toward his island environment change more slowly and subtly, but within a few months he develops from a prisoner on alien soil into a kind of ruler over his strange land, eager for ultimate deliverance but content with his lot until God wills his translation to a better place. On the day of his conversion (July 4, 1660), Crusoe finds his condition

[2] He had, for example, become a Sallee slave on the anniversary of his flight from home. Such concurrences are significant because of the view of history which informs the novel.

[3] Puritan guide writers emphasized the importance of observing certain anniversaries with days of contrition or thanksgiving. William Haller notes that anniversaries of events in a person's life replaced the traditional Christian holidays. "[Puritan] holy days," says Haller, "were the days when they fasted and humiliated themselves for defeats they themselves had brought upon the spirit or the days when they gave thanks for the victories which had been vouchsafed to them by divine Providence" (*The Rise of Puritanism* [New York, 1938], p. 151). Cotton Mather offers specific direction on how to observe such special days in *The Religion of the Closet . . . or, a Christian Furnished with, a Companion for Solitude* (2d ed.; Boston, 1706), p. 29. Also see my discussion above, Chapter IV.

"much easier to my Mind," and reports that he has "a great deal of Comfort within, which till now I knew nothing of . . ." (A111). As he increasingly accepts his lot as a just punishment for previous conduct, he grows more contented with his place. "I acquiesced," he reports shortly after his conversion, "in the Dispositions of Providence, which I began now to own, and to believe, order'd every Thing for the best; I say, I quieted my Mind with this, and left afflicting my self with Fruitless Wishes . . ." (A125). By the second anniversary of his landing on the island (which he observes "in the same solemn Manner as before" [A129]), he can objectively discuss the numerous advantages of his island existence —in sharp contrast to his half-hearted attempt to list the credits and debits of his life when he first arrived on the island.[4] "I began sensibly to feel," he reports, "how much more happy this Life I now led was, with all its miserable Circumstances, than the wicked, cursed, abominable Life I led all the past Part of my Days; and now I chang'd both my Sorrows and my Joys; my very Desires alter'd, my Affections chang'd their Gusts, and my Delights were perfectly new, from what they were at my first Coming, or indeed for the two Years past" (A129–30). Crusoe's contentment becomes almost too intense, and once he almost thanks God for his isolation.

[4] Crusoe's early attempts to cheer himself up are filled with gloom and almost cosmic despair. "I drew up," he reports during his early days on the island, "the State of my Affairs in Writing . . . to deliver my Thoughts from daily poring upon them, and afflicting my Mind; and as my reason began now to master my Despondency, I began to comfort my self as well as I could . . ." (A74). His attempts to list advantages involve conventional admissions of God's sovereignty, but Crusoe's true sentiments are artfully betrayed by his complaint against loneliness and his rationalization of its advantage: "*I have no* Soul *to speak to, or relieve me*," Crusoe says on the debit side. "*But*," he answers himself, "*God wonderfully sent the Ship in near enough to the Shore, that I have gotten out so many necessary things as will either supply my Wants, or enable me to supply my self even as long as I live*" (A75) (emphasis mine).

"Something shock'd my Mind at that Thought," reports
Crusoe, "and I durst not speak the Words: How canst
thou be such a Hypocrite, (said I even audibly) to pretend to be thankful for a Condition, which however thou
may'st endeavour to be contented with, thou would'st
rather pray heartily to be deliver'd from . . . yet I sincerely gave Thanks to God for opening my Eyes, by
whatever afflicting Providences, to see the former Condition of my Life, and to mourn for my Wickedness, and
repent" (A131). Crusoe's attitude toward his island station thus exactly parallels the ideal Christian outlook on
earthly existence: he is content with what he has but is
eager to be delivered to that higher existence which his
Bible-reading promises.

Crusoe's conversion is further dramatized by his altered conduct toward his environment itself. Until conversion, he had been almost paralyzed with fear and had
explored only a small part of one side of his island. But
less than two weeks after conversion he has new strength
and confidence, and he begins to "take a more particular
Survey of the Island itself" (A112). Only two miles from
his fortress, he enters a place of incredible beauty and
abundance, reminiscent of Milton's land of Eden just
outside the garden.[5] He first finds a brook bordered by
"pleasant *Savana's* or Meadows; plain, smooth, and cov-
ered with Grass," and by green, wild plants such as aloes
and sugar cane. Just beyond is a thicker wooded area
with "Mellons upon the Ground" and vines spread across
the trees offering "Clusters of Grapes . . . in their
Prime, very ripe and rich" (A113–14). Continuing north
in a valley surrounded by a ridge of hills, Crusoe comes
at last to a clearing "where the Country seem'd to de-

---

[5] See *Paradise Lost*, IV, 131 ff.

scend to the West, and a little Spring of fresh Water which issued out of the Side of the Hill by me, run the other Way, that is due East; and the Country appeared so fresh, so green, so flourishing, every thing being in a constant Verdure, or Flourish of Spring, that it looked like a planted Garden." [6] Crusoe is almost overwhelmed by the sight; he descends "on the Side of that delicious Vale" and surveys the land "with a secret Kind of Pleasure, (tho' mixt with my other afflicting Thoughts) to think that this was all my own, that I was King and Lord of all this Country" (A114).

In his unregenerated state, Crusoe had been incapable of exploring or even contemplating such pristine peace and plenty, but his conversion has opened new vistas of posssibility. The garden is not, however, a prelapsarian paradise but rather an earthly paradise *in posse*, for Crusoe is postlapsarian man who has to toil to cultivate his land into its full abundance. The sugar canes Crusoe finds are "wild, and for want of Cultivation, imperfect" (A113), and the "Abundance of Cocoa Trees, Orange, and Lemon, and Citron Trees [are] all wild . . . , very few bearing any Fruit, at least not then" (A115). By placing Crusoe's discovery immediately after his conversion, Defoe suggests his new inner peace and his heightened perception of potentiality, while still noting the effort necessary to transform a wilderness into a garden —or to cultivate a fallen man into fit company for the angels.

Crusoe's new religious devotion regularizes his daily routine and imposes an order in his life which had been lacking before his conversion. Earlier, his movement from place to place had been haphazard and purposeless; travel had meant flight rather than progress, and Crusoe had lacked any sense of teleology. His motion

[6] See Gen. 2:8–10.

had been "restless" and his motivation negative rather than positive; the verbs in the first third of *Robinson Crusoe* ("run away," "break loose," "forsake," "leave my father's house," "abandon my duty,") reflect a motif of rebellion and flight which become a positive value in the nineteenth century but which suggested only irresponsibility to Defoe's contemporaries. In retrospect, Crusoe can regard his early years only as "loose and unguided." [7] His early months on the island are similar, for while his wandering is effectually halted (partly by geography, but mainly by a sense of physical fear), his life remains disordered and confused. He makes no over-all plan for his activities: he feverishly rescues every detachable bit from the wreck, only to find that most of the materials and tools are unusable in his present circumstance, and the chief result of his haphazard method is a storehouse of junk.[8] Even his fumbling attempts at order go awry, for he fails to subordinate his order to that of nature: the earthquake demonstrates the inadequacy of his security measures, and he has to redistribute his goods, even though he thinks (the irony is dramatic) that "every thing was put in order" (A94).

After his conversion, however, Crusoe's more comprehensive awareness improves his sense of order. "I bestirr'd my self," he reports just after conversion, "to . . . make my Way of living as regular as I could" (A111). By the end of his second year, he can report that he has "regularly divided my Time" (A131), and he begins to

---

[7] In his unregenerate state, Crusoe was imperceptive. On the island, he wishes to "know the Vertue and Goodness of any of the Fruits or Plants which I should discover," but he finds that such knowledge eludes him because "I had made so little Observation while I was in the *Brasils*, that I knew little of the Plants in the Field" (A113).

[8] Contrast his later behavior when a Spanish ship is wrecked within his reach. Then, he plans his trips to the wreck carefully and gathers only materials useful to him.

be conscious of the order of nature itself, building his own plans accordingly. "The rainy Season, and the dry Season, began now to appear regular to me," he reports, "and I learn'd to divide them so, as to provide for them accordingly" (A119). He thus begins to till the soil methodically, spading, planting, cultivating, and guarding his crop from beasts and birds. He builds protective fences for his fields, constructs scarecrows, and begins to collect domestic animals, finally amassing a dairy that provides meat, milk, butter, and cheese; his habitation becomes less and less the "horrid," "horrible desolate," "dismal unfortunate," "wild miserable" wilderness he had first entered.[9] Just before conversion (June 29, 1660), Crusoe had been unable even to conceive deliverance from his wilderness state. "I began to say," he reports, "as the Children of *Israel* did, when they were promised Flesh to eat, *Can God spread a Table in the Wilderness*" (A108). A year later, his cultivation and exploration have produced such abundance and variety that "*Leaden-hall* Market could not have furnish'd a Table better than I" (A126). By the end of his fourth year, Crusoe returns to his original metaphor to affirm his revised thinking. "I frequently sat down," he reports, "to my Meat with Thankfulness, and admir'd the Hand of God's Providence, which had thus spread my Table in the Wilderness" (A150).[10] Defoe does not allow Crusoe

[9] The "wilderness" state of Crusoe's island is established by recounting many details of the island's plant and animal life. For example, the "confus'd Screaming" of birds when Crusoe first fires a gun (A60) aurally suggests the natural disharmony that exists in the fallen world. At this point in the novel, Crusoe is totally unable to reimpose an order on the wilderness.

[10] Later, Crusoe reaffirms his revised judgment in the same terms: "What a Table was here spread for me in a Wilderness, where I saw nothing at first but to perish for Hunger" (A171). Crusoe later alludes again to the wilderness wandering of the Israelites (B36). Also compare Crusoe's attempt to recreate Paradise with the transformation of the "wilderness and solitary place" in Isaiah. According to the Isaianic

to transform completely his island wilderness into a garden, for his ultimate paradise (like man's, according to Christian myth) is elsewhere; but regenerated, aware, and determined to follow divine guidance, he is able to tame his environment and live peacefully as a sojourner, for he has answered his God and conquered himself. Emblematically, Crusoe has beaten the sword of his vision into the ploughshare of his experience.

Crusoe continues to develop spiritually during his remaining years on the island, but his progress is erratic, and he suffers setbacks which have sometimes contributed to misunderstandings about his conversion itself, for much criticism of *Robinson Crusoe* has proceeded from the incorrect assumption that conversion induces immediate perfection. Failure to regard Crusoe's limitations has often produced critical confusion about the kind of hero Defoe created and has sometimes provoked critical disappointment in Crusoe's conduct. Following Gildon, who charged that Crusoe is a "strange whimsical, inconsistent Being" who quits his religion "upon every Whimsy," [11] many critics have found Crusoe's religion shallow and mercurial and his conduct far below the plane of his reflections. Conscious of Crusoe's spiritual lapses, they have emphasized the points at which

---

prophecy, when God's kingdom is established, gardens will be made out of deserts:

> And an highway shall be there, and a way, and it shall be called The way of holiness; the unclean shall not pass over it; but it shall be for those: the wayfaring men, though fools, shall not err therein.
>
> No lion shall be there, nor any ravenous beast shall go up thereon, it shall not be found there; but the redeemed shall walk there.
> (35:8–9)

[11] Charles Gildon, *The Life and Strange Surprizing Adventures of Mr. D—— De F—— of London, Hosier* (London, 1719), p. viii, reprinted in *Robinson Crusoe Examin'd and Criticiz'd*, ed. Paul Dottin (London and Paris, 1923), p. 70.

his grasp falls short of his reach and have concluded that his conversion is not real, that he is "exactly the same creature when he leaves the island as when he stepped onto it." [12] Crusoe's reflections are thus seen to result from a fraudulent piety given him by Defoe in an attempt to appease public taste and to exploit popular morality. Crusoe, according to Irving Howe, is not the type of man to reflect morally, and his conduct proves it.[13]

Defoe's portrait of Crusoe, however, is more orthodox theologically and more accurate psychologically than are the comments of his critics.[14] Crusoe is no Saint. He is an Everyman spiritually in the same sense that he is an Everyman physically: he is a man of ordinary capabilities who overcomes many of his limitations by a combination of divine guidance and enlightened effort. It takes eight years of aimless wandering, several brushes with catastrophe, and finally a confinement, a sickness, and a vision of damnation to make him ask God for help, for he, like other men, is blind to divine purpose and

[12] See Irving Howe, "Robinson Crusoe: Epic of the Middle Class," *Tomorrow*, VII (1949), p. 52.

[13] *Ibid.*, p. 53.

[14] Crusoe professes to have no interest in the finer points of theology, and, although his point of view is obviously Puritan, his faith is orthodox and is intended to be unobjectionable to both Anglican and Dissenter. Defoe's preface to the 1715 volume of *The Family Instructor* applies equally well to *Robinson Crusoe*: "In the pursuit of this Book care is taken to avoid Distinctions of Opinion, as to Church of England or Dissenter, and no offense can be taken here on the one Side or the other; as I hope *both* are Christians so *both* are treated here as such, and the Advice is impartially directed *to both* without the least distinction" (p. 3). Gildon's view must be regarded as anti-Puritan rather than typically Anglican; despite his "conversion" to Anglicanism the theology he displays in his attack on Defoe clearly owes a debt to deism. Defoe's attempt to appeal to a larger audience than Puritans in no way denies his own artistic debt to Puritan tradition and the Puritan mind. It is something of a mistake, I think, to conceive Defoe's heritage in terms of the audience for whom he wrote; Defoe's Puritan heritage affects, subtly but profoundly, the kind of art he was able to create. His choice of audience is, on the other hand, a wholly conscious but relatively mechanical matter.

powerless to overcome his natural depravity until God specifically interposes. But even conversion is not a magic carpet which delivers him directly to heaven's gate. Though converted, he is still human; his fallen nature, though subdued by grace, is never entirely overcome in this world, and he is still subject to temptation and occasional failure. Unlike the chain of sins which characterized his early life, however, his post-conversion sins represent lapses from his good intentions and from his general pattern of conduct; he repents of them rapidly, and his life journey continues on the new direction that he chose during his sickness.

Crusoe's physical and mental limitations are obvious.[15] He builds a boat so big and so far from the water that he cannot launch it. He can only make one plank from a tree, while his contemporaries in fact and fiction could make at least two. He cannot construct a wheelbarrow because he cannot imagine how to fashion a wheel. It takes him years to learn to make pottery. Diligent and determined, Crusoe is no paragon of brilliance in conquering his environment, even though he has almost a shipload of tools and equipment. He learns by trial and error, and he often solves his problems only after most embarrassing mistakes. These limitations have been praised, quite correctly, as examples of Defoe's art, for through them Crusoe becomes a man with whom an ordinary reader may easily identify. Similar spiritual limitations are often cited, however, as examples of Defoe's limited view or attributed to oversight and inconsistency in composition.

Properly understood, Crusoe's spiritual lapses dramatize the pitfalls of overconfidence and pride, for the last

[15] For a fine discussion of Crusoe's limitations, see H. F. Robins, "How Smart Was Robinson Crusoe?," *PMLA*, LXVII (1952), 782–89. Robins tries to distinguish carefully between Crusoe's mistakes and Defoe's.

two-thirds of *Robinson Crusoe*, like almost all of *The Pilgrim's Progress*, describes the difficulties attending a Christian convert before he reaches final deliverance. Reminders of man's mortality are carefully woven into the narrative just after Crusoe's conversion, so that Crusoe's subsequent slips and stumbles seem a natural though unfortunate result of man's depravity— weaknesses which must be contemplated and overcome if man is to reach his human potential and arrive at his final destination. The near-paradise Crusoe finds on his first exploratory journey after conversion, for example, contains reminders of man's fall and of postlapsarian conditions which modern man must endure. The vegetation is wild and needs cultivation by man's hands, and destructive animals lurk in the surrounding countryside. "I was surpriz'd," reports Crusoe when he returns to the "garden" to fetch the fruits he had piled up for future use, "when coming to my Heap of Grapes, which were so rich and fine when I gather'd them, I found them all spread about, trod to Pieces, and dragg'd about some here, some there, and Abundance eaten and devour'd: By this I concluded, there were some wild Creatures thereabouts" (A115).[16] The image of Crusoe as a new Adam thus cuts two ways: in his regenerated state Crusoe is indeed "King and Lord of all this Country," recipient of its full beauty and abundance, but the land no longer stretches forth its bounty to man's touch, and the

[16] Crusoe's postlapsarian state is also emphasized by his attitude toward clothes: "The Weather was so violent hot, that there was no need of Cloaths, yet I could not go quite naked; no, tho' I had been inclin'd to it, which I was not, nor could not abide the thoughts of it . . ." (A154). Cf. Swift's use of the device in *Gulliver's Travels*, Bk. IV, chap. iii, where the Houyhnhmns are unable to understand what clothes mean.

Crusoe's carrying of fruit from the "garden" back to his old habitation glances at the biblical account of spies returning from Canaan laden with fruit. Defoe's apparent intent is to reinforce the wilderness-Canaan motif which he exploits throughout the novel.

land's creatures, including man, no longer romp in serene harmony but are forever haunted by the initial act of disorder.

Crusoe's first post-conversion surrender to his natural propensity follows some of his greatest triumphs. His religion, born in deprivation, has more difficulty in surviving prosperity. He has just succeeded in becoming a potter and in constructing the many tools he needs to make barley loaves,[17] and he now finds that his crops have also been enormously successful. He forgets his limitations and falls into a trap which his New Testament reading should have prepared him for. "And now indeed," reports Crusoe, "my Stock of Corn increasing, I really wanted to build my Barns bigger" (A142).[18] A moment later he fantasizes about nearby lands and arrogantly contemplates taking deliverance into his own hands. Now he wishes he had not sold Xury, not because of moral regrets, but because he needs him for the venture. He tries to float the small boat which has washed ashore from the shipwreck but after three or four weeks admits that his feverish but ridiculous efforts are "fruitless Toil" (A144). Next, he decides to make a large canoe, considering the task not only "possible, but easy," and he "pleas[es] my self extreamly with the Thoughts of making it. . . ." "I went to work," he summarizes, "upon this Boat, the most like a Fool that ever Man did,

[17] Crusoe's pottery-making suggests the familiar biblical metaphor of God as potter and man as clay (See Isa. 64:8 or Rom. 9:21), a metaphor which Crusoe specifically alludes to later (A244). The significance of Crusoe's pottery-making, after many early attempts and failures, lies in an achieved success which implies God's blessing upon him and suggests that he is now God's deputy. Crusoe's making of barley loaves carries a similar implication, for this activity reflects John 6:5–14. Crusoe's "miracle" in supplying himself with bread becomes an indication of his discipleship.

[18] See Luke 12:16 ff. for the parable of the rich man whose greed in desiring "to pull down my barns, and build greater" results in his damnation.

who had any of his Senses awake. I pleas'd my self with the Design, without determining whether I was ever able to undertake it. . . . This was a most preposterous Method; but the Eagerness of my Fancy prevail'd . . ." (A145–46). Crusoe chooses a cedar tree which he imagines must surpass the ones Solomon used to build the temple at Jerusalem, and he spends almost six months in cutting the tree and fashioning his canoe, but when the job is done, he finds that he cannot get the boat into the water unless he spends "ten or twelve Years" digging a canal. At last he gives up thoughts of "the maddest Voyage, and the most unlikely to be perform'd, that ever was undertaken" and profits from his mistake. "Now I saw," he reports, "tho' too late, the Folly of beginning a Work before we count the Cost; and before we judge rightly of our own Strength to go through with it" (A147–48).[19] His content with his station now returns and is even intensified. "I look'd now," Crusoe reports, "upon the World as a Thing remote, which I had nothing to do with, no Expectation from, and indeed no Desires about." And he loses the greed which had impelled him to build larger barns. "I might have rais'd Ship Loadings of Corn," he notes, "but I had no use for it; so I let as little grow as I thought enough for my Occasion" (A148).

Crusoe has intermittent feelings of self-pity, discouragement, and dissatisfaction with his station during his middle years on the island, but his general movement is toward greater serenity and resignation to the will of God. He is increasingly impressed by God's providential care of him and ascribes even the most minute events to divine activity. One event does, however, temporarily disrupt the newfound order of his existence and almost

[19] Crusoe echoes a biblical passage (Luke 14:28) which demands that a convert forsake his selfish concerns to follow the new way.

causes him to lose his spiritual foothold before he can understand the event and use it as an aid to ultimate deliverance. Finding a footprint in the sand, he freezes "like one Thunder-struck, or as if I had seen an Apparition; I listen'd, I look'd round me, I could hear nothing, nor see any Thing" (A177). From a composed, self-assured king of his island, Crusoe is reduced in a moment to a desperately befuddled fugitive. "Like a Man perfectly confus'd and out of my self," reports Crusoe in retrospect, "I came Home to my Fortification . . . looking behind me at every two or three Steps, mistaking every Bush and Tree, and fancying every Stump at a Distance to be a Man . . ." (A178). His first impulse is to destroy completely the order he has so carefully created. "I proposed," Crusoe reports, ". . . to throw down my Enclosures, and turn all my tame Cattle wild into the Woods, that the Enemy might not find them . . . , [to destroy] my two Corn Fields, that they might not find such a Grain there . . . to demolish my Bower, and Tent, that they might not see any Vestiges of Habitation . . ." (A184). "Depriv'd" of his reason, Crusoe becomes again a victim of his natural self, his spiritual life disrupted and his thoughts confused. "I must observe with Grief," he reports, "that the Discomposure of my Mind had too great impressions . . . upon the religious Part of my Thoughts . . . [;] I seldom found my self in a due Temper for application to my Maker . . ." (A189).[20] Reflection, Christian resignation, and the pas-

---

[20] During this period of upset Crusoe again begins to think of delivering himself, even before God gives him a clear indication that his penance is completed and that he may, with God's blessing, prepare to leave. Crusoe had earlier been warned to "Wait on the Lord" (A182), but in his bewildered state he reverts to his sinful nature. "So deep," reports Crusoe, "had the Mistake taken root in my Temper, that I could not satisfy my self in my Station, but was continually poring upon the Means and Possibility of my Escape from this Place . . ." (A226). Contemporary theology was adamant against

sage of time alleviate his fears somewhat, and he is soon able to thank God for placing him in a station of life different from the "dreadful Creatures" whose depraved nature guides them to cannibalistic feasts on his island. Upon reflection, he also becomes grateful that his early activities on the island were so guided by providence that he made his abode in a place safe from the sight of visiting savages.

Crusoe at last returns this relapse into his greatest spiritual triumph, as the footprint materializes into creatures who intrude upon his philosophy and force him to expand his Christianity from an individual level to a social one. When Crusoe first determines the origin of the footprint, he is horrified at the very thought of cannibalistic banquets, and the "horrid Spectacle" of "Skulls, Hands, Feet, and other Bones of Humane Bodies" (A190) on the beach nauseates him. At first he contemplates only the "inhuman, hellish Brutality, and the Horror of the Degeneracy of Humane Nature" (A191) behind the act, but he soon envisions himself as a scourge and minister born to set right the whole heathen tradition by means of violence and murder. "Night and day," reports Crusoe, "I could think of nothing but how I might destroy some of these Monsters in their cruel bloody Entertainment. . . ." He contemplates exploding their fire-pit with gunpowder and imagines himself ambushing them with his "three Guns, all double loaded; and in the middle of their bloody Ceremony, let[ting]

man's taking matters into his own hands. "In all dangers we are first humbly to pray for [God's] aid, and then to rest our selves cheerfully on him. . . . But above all things, we must be sure to fix our dependance wholly on him, and not to rely on the creatures [i.e., other men] for help; much less must we seek to deliver ourselves by any unlawful means . . . ; such courses do commonly deceive our hopes at present, and instead of delivering us out of our straits, plunge us in greater . . ." (Richard Allestree[?], *The Whole Duty of Man* [London, 1696; first published, 1658], pp. 27–28).

fly at them, when I should be sure to kill or wound perhaps two or three at every shoot; and then falling in upon them with my three Pistols, and my Sword, I made no doubt, but that if there was twenty I should kill them all: This Fancy pleas'd my Thoughts for some Weeks, and I was . . . full of it" (A194–95). Gradually, however, it occurs to Crusoe that his plan is inspired by malice and personal fear rather than morality,[21] and he realizes that God has not called him to be a "Judge and Executioner upon these Men as Criminals" (A197). After long debate, he decides that even his selfish goals could be thwarted by such unauthorized action, and he concludes that "I was perfectly out of my Duty, when I was laying all my bloody Schemes for the Destruction of innocent Creatures, I mean innocent as to me: As to the Crimes they were guilty of towards one another, I had nothing to do with them; they were National, and I ought to leave them to the Justice of God, who is the Governour of Nations, and knows how by National Punishments to make a just Retribution for National Offences" (A200).

Later, Crusoe deepens his understanding of the proper conduct of a Christian toward other men, but he acts only after he receives direct supernatural guidance. His desire for a companion and guide inspires him to consider rescuing a savage prisoner from being eaten, but he intervenes only after a dream affirms God's approval of the act and after Friday flees into his grove in the manner that the dream promises. Guided by such supernatural "hints," Crusoe again discovers that God's will, prop-

[21] Crusoe's description of his murderous plan betrays his motives; he says his contrivances were for "destroying these Creatures, or at least frightening them, *so as to prevent their coming hither any more* . . ." (A195, italics mine). Note also that Crusoe's righteous indignation against the cannibals' conduct bears a tinge of pharisaism: Crusoe reports that he "gave God Thanks that had cast my first Lot in a Part of the world, where I was distinguish'd from such dreadful Creatures . . ." (A191).

erly understood, ultimately meshes with prudential considerations if man patiently awaits divine direction rather than taking matters into his own hands. As Friday races toward Crusoe's shelter, Crusoe perceives in a flash: "It came now very warmly upon my Thoughts, and indeed irresistibly, that now was my Time to get me a Servant, and perhaps a Companion, or Assistant; and that I was call'd plainly by Providence to save this poor Creature's life . . ." (A235).

Crusoe regards the "secret Hints" that he receives as sent, like his dreams, by God. Midway through the novel Crusoe explains his philosophy about these hints at length, noting that many times a "strange Impression" saves men from harm. "I never fail'd to obey the secret Dictate," Crusoe reports of his later conduct, "though I knew no other Reason for it, then that such a Pressure or such a Hint hung upon my Mind: I could give many Examples of the Success of this Conduct in the Course of my Life . . ." (A203). Late in the novel Crusoe receives two important sets of secret hints; the first saves him from destruction by the English mutineers (B41), and the other causes him to return to England by land rather than boarding a doomed ship (B85). The pattern of the novel is consistent: when Crusoe obeys his supernatural promptings (and thus shows himself to be in tune with divine will), he progresses toward ultimate deliverance; when he fails to follow the promptings, he slips off his forward course.

The "saving" of Friday ultimately takes on an added dimension as Crusoe realizes that Friday's appearance is providential in more than one sense. Friday's appearance vindicates God's action in allowing Crusoe to find the fear-provoking footprint, for he now finds that the presence of savages on the island, at first a terror, becomes at last a comfort. Crusoe advises that "all People who shall meet with my Story" should observe "How frequently in the Course of our Lives, the evil which in it self we seek most to shun, and which when we are fallen into it, is the most dreadful to us, is oftentimes the very Means or Door of our Deliverance . . ." (A210). Friday immediately relieves Crusoe from the discomforts of loneliness, and shortly he provides not only insurance against physical fear but also hope of eventual physical deliverance. More important, however, Friday enables Crusoe to recover his spiritual development and even to extend it. While alone, Crusoe can only dramatize his reformation by performing such religious duties as praying and reading Scripture and by controlling his thoughts. By introducing a companion—especially a non-Christian one—Defoe provides Crusoe with further occasion to demonstrate his religious sincerity; and Crusoe, his faltering spirits recovered, proves equal to the occasion.[22]

"A true Principle of Thankfulness," writes George Stanhope in *The Seaman's Obligations to Gratitude and a Good Life* (1699), "will not allow Men to be contented with their own private Virtue, but will render them zealous Promoters of God's Glory, by winning over others to his Service."[23] Fired with this sort of Puritan evangelical zeal, Crusoe begins work on Friday's religion and ethics, now fully conscious that his task is to convert heathens, not to destroy them. He first teaches Friday to abhor cannibalism, then guides him toward positive

[22] As in the 1715 volume of *The Family Instructor*, Defoe here uses zeal for converting others as a device to make probable the religious professions of his hero. I have discussed this and other aspects of the episode in my essay, "Friday as a Convert: Defoe and the Accounts of Indian Missionaries," *RES*, n.s., XIV (1963), 243–48. For another view of this episode—a view that offers a quite different interpretation of the novel—see Dewey Ganzel, "Chronology in Robinson Crusoe," *PQ*, XL (1961), 495–512.
[23] (London, 1699), p. 21.

theological and moral principles. "I was not wanting to lay a Foundation of Religious Knowledge in [Friday's] Mind" (B1) Crusoe reports proudly. In dramatic form, Crusoe presents the most important of these lessons which convert Friday into "a good Christian, a much better than I . . . such a Christian, as I have known few equal to him in my Life" (B6–7). Crusoe acknowledges his ignorance on many religious matters; he finds himself "tho' . . . an old Man, yet . . . a Young Doctor, and ill enough quallified for a casuist" when Friday poses difficult questions, but his instruction of Friday also improves his own faith. "In laying Things open to him," Crusoe reports, "I really inform'd and instructed myself in many Things . . . which occurr'd naturally to my Mind, upon my searching into them, for the Information of this poor Savage . . . so that . . . I had great Reason to be thankful that ever he came to me" (B4, 5–6). His wavering now past, Crusoe rejoices in his condition and continues "In this thankful frame . . . all the Remainder of my Time . . ." (B6).[24]

---

[24] Two later passages have sometimes been cited as evidence that Crusoe inflates the value of his religious experience. When he contemplates returning to Brazil, he has "some little Scruple in my Mind about Religion, which insensibly drew me back. . . . However, it was not Religion that kept me from going there *for the present* . . ." (B84, italics mine). Critics have been especially harsh with Crusoe for saying that "I began to regret my having profess'd my self a Papist, and thought it might not be the best Religion to die with" (B84). Readers of Puritan religious literature, however, will immediately recognize that such a statement is not so flippant as modern critics have taken it, for theologians and guide writers emphasized the importance of dying with the proper religious outlook and argued for Christian conversion primarily on the basis of an afterlife. At any rate, Crusoe's briefly wavering thoughts about Brazil soon settle. After his bout with the wolves (see below, p. 191 ff.), Crusoe says that a "Scruple came in my Way [about going to Brazil], and that was Religion; for as I had entertain'd some Doubts about the Roman Religion, even while I was abroad, especially in my State of Solitude; so I knew there was no going to the *Brasils* for me . . ." (B103).

Crusoe's later wandering, described briefly in the last paragraphs

Crusoe's lapses after conversion should not blind us to
his genuine and very substantial spiritual progress. Defoe's Puritan contemporaries, less sanguine about man's
nature than many of their modern counterparts, regarded post-conversion sins as deplorable but predictable falls from grace, for they did not assume that conversion changed human imperfection into inhuman
perfection. "There is after conversion," writes Nicolas
Estwick in his funeral sermon for a famous penitent,[25]
"much corruption and sinne in Gods people to be morti-
fied." "The dearest of Gods Saints," adds Ralph Robinson
in his *Safe Conduct, or the Saints Guidance to Glory*,
"have a *gadding* spirit within them, they love to wander,
they shut their Eyes and will not see, they stop their Ears
and will not hear; wilfulness occasions wandrings." [26]
But, Robinson points out in another place, though
"the best of Bcleevers have a spice of the Spiritual
Falling-sickness . . . when they sink into misery God
will lift them up, and when they slip into sin God will
restore them." [27] The important thing to note in *Robin-*

of *Robinson Crusoe*, has also been cited to show that his religion does
not endure. These paragraphs do represent Defoe's tentative advertisement for a possible sequel (*Farther Adventures*), but they are not
necessarily a total artistic and thematic sellout. Crusoe remains in
England during his wife's lifetime and only resumes his travels after
her death, when he has no further responsibilities in England. Further-
more, he may be regarded as having responsibilities to his island.
Puritan theologians recognized that a man's calling might change,
especially when the events of his life prepared him for a calling different from his original one.

[25] "A Learned and Godly Sermon [for] the Funerall of Mr. Robert
Bolton," *Mr. Boltons Last and Learned Work* (London, 1639), p. 55.
[26] (London, 1654), p. 41.
[27] *Ibid.*, p. 36. Theologians were, of course, quick to point out that
continued attacks of "falling sickness" might indicate that a person
was not among the elect. The test was whether a person showed
general spiritual progress and learned from his relapses. Samuel Clarke
prefaces one of his collections of spiritual biographies this way: "Sometimes we shall find some of these Worthies at the first encounter
(through the violence of temptation, and humane frailty) giving
[going?] back: But . . . they (according to the nature of true grace)

son Crusoe is that Crusoe does recover from his various attacks of "falling-sickness," conscious of his error and determined to profit from it. He sees with increasing clarity the divine plan for himself and his world, and he follows with increasing exactness the guidance of dreams and "secret Hints" sent by providence.

Viewed as an ordinary human being—an Everyman —in spiritual as well as physical and mental strength, Crusoe becomes, rather than a model of perfection, an example of human accomplishment made possible by God's providence. Before conversion, Crusoe is preoccupied with things; getting and spending are his chief concerns, and Xury represents sixty pieces of eight. Crusoe fails to see the meanings of the things that he has and of the events that befall him; the warnings of storms and the rewards of Brazilian labor entirely elude his consciousness. Later, however, he comes to understand that these things are only important as indications of something beyond them, beyond the entire physical world. After conversion, he does not reduce an Ismael to a "Moely" and send him swimming for his life, nor does he enslave an X until getting a better offer. Rather, he transforms an emblem of human sacrifice into a Friday, a convert who can help "deliver" Crusoe on both levels of the book's concern. Crusoe, who begins as a rebel wandering through life without purpose, becomes at last a pilgrim bound for paradise.

The adventure plot of *Robinson Crusoe* has often been critically discussed, but this plot takes on far greater significance when viewed in relation to the novel's thematic

have gathered strength by their relapses" (*A General Martyrologie, Containing a Collection of All the Greatest Persecutions Which Have Befallen the Church of Christ, from the Creation, to Our Present Times* [London, 1677], fol. a1ᵛ).

concerns. Crusoe's physical activities relate to his spiritual life not only because conversion alters his conduct; throughout *Robinson Crusoe* physical events reflect Crusoe's spiritual state, for Crusoe is concerned with accommodating himself to his world spiritually and physically at the same time, and his efforts to come to terms with his physical environment parallel his efforts to find a proper relationship with his God. Ultimately, his physical activities become a metaphor for his spiritual aspirations.

Defoe has constructed *Robinson Crusoe* so that its theme gives survival an added dimension. Man, placed in a primitive context, faces not only a physical world that is hostile, but a world where he is spiritually an alien; he has to fight not only the physical dangers of storms, hunger, sickness, wild beasts, and cannibals, but temptation, moral evil, and ultimately (because man's nature has become depraved) even himself—all on the single island battleground of his life.

Emphasis upon the "realistic" nature of both Defoe's choice of detail and his use of language has obscured the emblematic meaning of Crusoe's physical activities, but Defoe's "realism" is like that of Bunyan and substantiates the metaphor, rather than weakening it. Defoe, like Bunyan,[28] continually makes his hero express his spiritual condition by physical actions. The fusion of physical and spiritual concerns is implicit throughout *Robinson Crusoe*, and the general pattern of Crusoe's action is emblematic of larger matters. Crusoe's erratic straying from his course at sea, his Turkish slavery, and his ship-

---

[28] When meeting Faithful, for example, Christian rushes to catch up with him and "did also overrun him; so the last was first." "Then," reports Bunyan, "did Christian vaingloriously smile, because he had gotten the start of his brother; but not taking good heed to his feet, he suddenly stumbled and fell . . ." (*The Pilgrim's Progress*, ed. James Blanton Wharey, rev. Roger Sharrock [2d ed.; Oxford, 1960], p. 66).

wreck upon the rocks parallel his spiritual drift, his bondage to sin, and the "spiritual shipwreck" (to use the standard term of the guide tradition) of his soul, just as his island deliverance presages his being set apart and his relief from sickness parallels the cure of his soul. Similarly, his efforts to convert the island wilderness into a garden parallel his efforts to cultivate his spiritual self, weeding out the wild undergrowth of desires which, since man's fall, "naturally" choke the life of the soul.

Individual episodes also reflect Defoe's emblematic view of events and human actions. Crusoe's efforts to sustain himself physically from the wrecked ship, for example, parallel his efforts to obtain God's grace, according to the contemporary Puritan view: Crusoe must venture to the ship as best he can, once God has providentially intervened to bring it within his reach. Similarly, Defoe has Crusoe discover the miraculous "straggling Stalks" of grain beside his habitation and notes his first religious promptings which, though brief, are gradually multiplied by nurture and care, like his crop of grain. Later, his first physical act of kindness for Friday presages his subsequent spiritual aid: "I gave him Bread," reports Crusoe, "and a Bunch of Raisins to eat, and a Draught of Water . . ." (A238). Crusoe's attacks of "falling-sickness" are also indicated emblematically. His discovery of the terrifying footprint indicates that not all is as perfect as the complacent Crusoe had thought, that still to be conquered are enemies not yet dreamed of in Crusoe's philosophy.[29] And his meanders in the canoe, when he comes close to taking deliverance into his own hands, emblematize his spiritual drift from his course of total

[29] Though Crusoe is intellectually aware of man's depravity, the idea has no real meaning for him until his personal confrontation with "natural" men—the cannibals.

reliance on God—a drift which, like one of his excursions, is almost fatal because the natural current is so strong that it can scarcely be resisted.

The language of *Robinson Crusoe* is also carefully calculated to suggest the fusion of physical and spiritual. In his feverish sickness, Crusoe describes his physical condition in terms which exactly express his spiritual aspirations just before conversion. "I was," he reports, "ready to perish for Thirst, but so weak, I had not Strength to stand up, or to get my self any Water to drink" (A99); later, after a brief prayer for mercy and then a deep sleep (but before his prayer of repentance), he finds himself "much refresh'd, but weak, and exceeding thirsty . . ." (A99–100). Such verbal ambiguity, implicit in the first third of the novel, becomes explicit at the time of Crusoe's conversion, when he for the first time becomes conscious of the potentiality of words. Previously, his interpretation of "deliverance" had been purely physical, but now he begins to "construe the Words . . . in a different sense from what I had ever done before," and his physical deliverance becomes secondary, though it remains emblematic of his spiritual deliverance.

It is in this context that we may most profitably examine the novel's last major episode, the attack by wolves in the Pyrenees. This episode has been condemned severely as unnecessary and anticlimactic, an example of Defoe's pandering to popular taste, his careless craftsmanship, and his inability to provide unity of action. Viewed in relation to Crusoe's maturation and the novel's emblematic method, however, the episode takes on significant meaning and provides a dramatic climax to the previous physical and spiritual adventures.

During his stay on the island, Crusoe matures in important ways. His progress is not uniform, for certain events (such as the finding of the footprint) disrupt his composure and interrupt his development toward self-knowledge and self-control, but after conversion he clarifies his relationship to his environment and gains increasing control over himself and his world. He comes to think of himself as a "general," and as "monarch" and "governor" of his island, and he develops increasing confidence in his ability to conquer his environment and to lead men. It is particularly in the final years that Crusoe demonstrates his self-assurance and leadership ability. To Friday, he becomes both tutor and master, Christianizing and civilizing the natural savage and then ordering their combined lives rationally and responsibly. Soon God "directs" Crusoe to organized action as the cannibal barbarians prepare to destroy the life of a Christian captive—a Spaniard who had been captured after a shipwreck near another island.[30] Crusoe conducts the rescue coolly and methodically, with the finesse of a military leader but with the zeal of a crusader. "As soon as the first Shot was made," reports Crusoe, "I threw down the Piece, and took up the Fowling-Piece, and *Friday* did the like; he see me cock, and present, he did the same again; Are you ready? *Friday*, said I; Yes says he; let fly then, says I, in the Name of God, and with that I fir'd again among the amaz'd Wretches and so did *Friday* . . ." (B22). With the Spaniard rescued and Friday's father along with him,[31] Crusoe now finds his island population expanded to four, and his leadership qualities are

---

[30] Crusoe's attack on the cannibals here is justified because the life of a Christian is at stake. His previous contemplation had guided him to leave the cannibals alone unless their existence directly impinged upon the lives of men outside their own religious tradition.

[31] The "coincidence" of the reunion of Friday and his father, like the startling coincidences in *Tom Jones*, may offend modern notions of probability, but such coincidences reflect (and dramatize) Christian assumptions about the divine control of human events.

further challenged, especially since the society is hardly a homogeneous one. "My Island," Crusoe rejoices, "was now peopled, and I thought my self very rich in Subjects; and it was a merry Reflection which I frequently made, How like a King I look'd. . . . I was absolute Lord and Lawgiver. . . . It was remarkable too, we had but three Subjects, and they were of three different Religions. My man *Friday* was a Protestant, his father was a *Pagan* and a *Cannibal,* and the *Spaniard* was a Papist: However, I allow'd Liberty of Conscience throughout my dominions . . ." (B30–31).[32]

Crusoe's first acts of leadership are clumsy and ultimately ill-fated, for his monarchy is too absolute (note his royal "we" in the above quotation and his messianic assumption of a divine stance), and he tries to outplan providence. But shortly after planning to sail away and after sending his two newest subjects to find additional manpower, Crusoe faces a greater challenge and handles it masterfully. Invaded by a boatload of mutineers, he first frees their deposed captain and then conquers the mutineers, one by one, and recruits the most likely captives under his own banner.[33] At last he wins the sworn allegiance of all but the most incorrigible rebels, and the ship is placed at his disposal. He is now master of himself and an acknowledged leader of men (all his subjects call him "Governour"), but he is also conscious of the full hierarchy of command. "I forgot not," Crusoe reports, "to lift up my Heart in Thankfulness to . . . [God] who had not only in a miraculous Manner pro-

[32] Crusoe's summary is of course comic in tone, but the "Liberty of Conscience" he allows illustrates his broadened vision of Christian social relationships. See above, p. 182 ff.
[33] Crusoe imprisons five of the leaders in a cave. This action seems to recall Joshua's confinement of five heathen kings in a cave (see Josh. 10:15 ff.). Defoe may have intended the allusion to ally the mutineers' cause with a higher form of rebellion and thus to suggest the righteousness of Crusoe's own actions.

vided for one in such a Wilderness, and in such a desolate Condition, but from whom every Deliverance must always be acknowledged to proceed" (B68).

Crusoe's full development is artistically established, however, only when he demonstrates his mastery in the setting of the larger world, free of the limitations of a never-never island world where he had special rights and a special claim to leadership. Back in Europe, but not yet permanently home, Crusoe first settles his personal affairs [34] and then, on his final journey, proves that his developed talents can stand more severe tests. He becomes "Captain" of a group of English merchants and Portuguese gentlemen who have no obligation to Crusoe; they choose him as leader solely on his merit, and he justifies their confidence by guiding them safely through a life-or-death battle.

In this last major episode Defoe again allows biblical allusion to carry the weight of meaning. Leaving Madrid by land, Crusoe's company wanders toward France but is frustrated by several delays. By "Meanders" and "winding Ways," they at last reach the mountains near Pamplona and take a prospect of the country they wish to reach. "All on a sudden," reports Crusoe, "[the guide] shew'd us the pleasant fruitful Provinces of *Languedoc* and *Gascoign*, all green and flourishing . . ." (B89).

Crusoe's view of the land he wishes to enter is the climax of a series of "prospects" in the novel. The earlier prospects, however, produce only mirages, false confidence, and unfounded hope of immediate deliverance. During his first days on the island, on a pinnacle overlooking the open sea, Crusoe buoys his hope with false imaginings. "I could not forbear." he reports, "getting up to the Top of a little Mountain and looking out to Sea in

---

[34] Crusoe's handling of his estate is meticulous but unselfish. He liberally distributes his possessions to relatives, to friends, and to charity (B82–83). Cf. Jesus' charge to his disciples.

hopes of seeing a Ship, then fancy at a vast Distance I
spy'd a Sail, please my self with the Hopes of it, and then
after looking steadily till I was almost blind, lose it quite,
and sit down and weep like a Child, and thus encrease
my Misery by my Folly" (A79). Later, he twice scans
the sea to observe currents so that he may calculate how
to deliver himself. Another time, just after admitting that
the footprint has disrupted his religious devotion and
confounded his trust in God, he again thinks he sees a
ship of deliverance, but the sight is "so remote, that I
could not tell what to make of it" (A190), and his eyes
prove too tired and weak to retain such a speck of hope.
But Crusoe's final prospect—through eyes whose sight is
sharpened by a more calm, more mature spirituality—is
informed by the contemporary understanding of Moses'
prospect of the promised land, probably the ultimate inspiration of the seventeenth century's prospect tradition
in both poetry and painting. Moses, though barred by
God from entering the earthly Canaan, achieved heavenly paradise instead, and contemporary theologians regarded his prospect from Mount Nebo (atop Mount
Pisgah) as a foretaste of his reward, for Canaan was a
standard "type" of Heaven.[35] And modern man, according to theologians, could be inspired by similar prospects
(even meditative ones) to remain on course in his pilgrimage through life.[36] "Can there be," Joseph Cooper
asks in his *Misthoskopia: A Prospect of Heavenly Glory
for the Comfort of Sion's Mourners* (1700), "a more

[35] John Flavell describes Moses' prospect and subsequent death this
way: "Get thee up to Mount Nebo, saith God, and dye there, thou
shalt not go over Jordan, and yet Moses was no loser by it. Though
God shut him out of Canaan, he took him to heaven" (*Mount Pisgah*
[London, 1689], p. 7). In seventeenth-century Puritan literature,
Canaan, Jerusalem, and Sion were all metaphors for heaven.

[36] Benjamin Keach describes life's pilgrimage this way (*Tropologia:
Or a Key To Open Scripture Metaphors* [London, 1681], II, 170):

A Pilgrim in his Travels goes up-hill and down-hill; sometimes
he meets with good Way, and sometimes with bad Way; Sometimes

cordial joy, a more entrancing delight, a more strong and
everlasting consolation, than for the Soul to feed upon
hidden Manna; to have the sweet and delicious Clusters
of *Canaan* to refresh it in the wilderness; to dwell continually upon the top of Mount Pisgah, thence taking a
clear prospect of the Land of promise . . . ?" [37]

But after Crusoe's prospect he still has "some rough
Way to pass yet" (B89), and soon he and his companions discover that, like the ancient Hebrews, they have
to fight their way into their promised land. Their enemies are ravenous wolves, and the innocent company
(all making their first journey through this hostile terri-
tory) does not know how to cope with such organized
ferocity. Crusoe, however, although inexperienced with
this specific kind of danger, demonstrates his mastery,
for seeing a hundred wolves "coming on directly towards
us . . . as regularly as an Army" (B97), he senses what
to do, and, like Joshua, achieves his purpose by making
great noises with the few weapons he has and by having
the company unite in a great shout.[38] A second, even
greater battle follows as night comes on and some three
hundred wolves gather for the attack, but again Crusoe's
strategy delivers the company. The noise of the "hellish

he passeth over Stiles, and through dirty Lanes; and then through
green Fields and pleasant Pastures, and delightful Paths, till he
comes to the desired Place.

So the Pilgrim that would travel to the New Jerusalem, meets
with various Ways and Passages. 1. He must go out of the horrible
Pit of Prophaneness; that is Work enough for the first Day's Journey.
2. Through the Brook of sincere Repentance, or true Contrition,
(for every one that leaves open Prophaneness is not truly penitent).
3. Down the Valley of Self-denial, a very difficult Passage. 4. Over
the Mountains of Opposition, for the Devil and all will straitway
make head against him. 5. Over the Stile of carnal Reason. . . .
6. In to the pleasant Ways of the New Covenant. 7. So upon the
Top of the Rock of Ages, and there he may take a Prospect of his
own Country.

Seventeenth-century writers described the steps and hurdles differently
but clung to the basic metaphor.

[37] (London, 1700), p. 166.

[38] See Josh. 6.

Creatures" increases as the company approaches "the Entrance of a Wood, through which we were to pass, at the farther side of the Plain" (B98),[39] and the carcasses of two horses and two partially eaten men suddenly appear. Several volleys of shot deter the wolves temporarily, but soon the charge is renewed. At last, Crusoe contrives a trick derived from another biblical metaphor: he builds a wall of fire between the men and wolves,[40] then leads the company in a final shout which subdues the enemy. The hero of this episode is clearly a far different Crusoe from the fear-ridden young man who, unable even to follow orders, faints at the pump during an early voyage [41] and who runs about his island, when he first arrives there, wringing his hands distractedly.

The episode of the wolves, like the final dramatic episodes in pilgrim literature, demonstrates that man is not really "delivered" until he is safe at his final destination, a point contemporary theologians stressed tirelessly. "Be not discouraged," writes John Flavell in his *Mount Pisgah* (1689), "if you should meet with some difficulties, even on the borders of the Land of Promise." [42] "*The* Israelites," adds George Swinnock in *The Christian-Mans Calling* (Volume II, 1663), "*could not enjoy the land flowing with milk and hony, till they had fought with,*

[39] Here the language is very like that of Bunyan.
[40] Zech. 2:5 describes God as a "wall of fire," protecting his chosen. In comparing the world to a wilderness Benjamin Keach says this: "In a howling Wilderness a Wall of Fire is exceeding necessary to preserve from Wild and ravenous beasts: God upon this account is said to be a Wall of Fire to his People, whilst they remain in this World, amongst the Sons of *Belial* . . ." (*Tropologia*, II, 392). John Flavell argues that this biblical metaphor derives from such an "ancient custom of travellers in the desarts" (*Navigation Spiritualized; or a New Compass for Seamen* [Newburyport, 1796; first published, 1664], p. 72).
[41] When Crusoe faints, his companions show little respect. "No body minded me," reports Crusoe, "or what was become of me; but another Man stept up to the Pump, and thrusting me aside with his Foot, let me lye . . ." (A12).
[42] P. 42.

and conquered the Cananites, and forced their way through grievous obstacles and oppositions." [43] Crusoe considers his struggle with wolves the most difficult battle he has fought. "I was never so sensible of Danger in my life," Crusoe reports, ". . . and . . . I gave my self over for lost . . ." (B102).

Ultimately, Crusoe's battle here suggests one of the novel's major concerns, the war between good and evil. Crusoe's final victory over bestiality culminates a pattern which had begun early in his life with encounters against a lion, a leopard, and a nameless beast on the coast of Africa, and which had recently included a comic encounter with a bear. [44] The beasts subdued by Crusoe are standard biblical symbols of evil, forces which God's elect (lambs) must overcome during their pilgrimage. John Flavell suggests the typical Puritan use of the bestial metaphor in these doggerel lines from *Navigation Spiritualized* (1664):

> This world's a forest, where from day to day,
> Bears, wolves, and lions range and seek their prey,
> Amidst them all poor harmless Lambs are fed,
> And by their very dens in safety led.

> . . . .

> He that to raging seas such bonds hath put
> The mouths of ravenous beasts can also shut.

> . . . .

> Shun sin, keep close to Christ; for other Evils
> You need not fear, tho compass round with devils. [45]

---

[43] Fol. B2ᵛ.

[44] Friday becomes a comic figure in this scene, perhaps to emphasize his parallel with the novel's other comic figure, Xury. Crusoe's conduct relative to the two servants dramatizes the difference in his attitudes and conduct before and after conversion.

[45] Pp. 91–92. The episode of the wolves also climaxes the motif of savagery which runs through the novel. Beginning with his early

The young Crusoe misses the significance of his early encounters, but by the end of his journey he comprehends his battle in larger terms. The wolves, Crusoe reports (and he later repeats the simile), "came on like Devils . . ." (B100).

When the company is safely delivered across the mountains, men who have previously made the same journey tell Crusoe and his friends (in language suggestive of pilgrim allegory) that their experiences are "nothing but what was ordinary in the great Forest at the Foot of the Mountains" (B101), and these seasoned travelers relate better and easier ways to defeat the enemy. But Crusoe's company, happy to have negotiated the journey by any means, basks in the secure comfort of their new land, "where we found a warm Climate, a fruitful pleasant Country, and no Snow, no Wolves, or any Thing like them . . ." (B101).

Defoe is able to use the physical to reflect the spiritual quite easily in *Robinson Crusoe*, for the novel's plot follows the comprehensive metaphor which is basic to Puritan tradition and which had taken a fictional form in pilgrim allegory. The journey metaphor (for man's temporary sojourn on earth) derives ultimately

---

travels along the barbarian coast, Crusoe continually encounters the savagery of men and beasts, but by the end of the last episode he has shown himself capable of subduing bestiality in any form. Keach articulates the standard beast emblems this way: "In a Wilderness are many wild and devouring Beasts, so that 'tis dangerous to dwell in it, or pass through it: So this World abounds with cruel and unmerciful Men, who are called Wolves, Lions, Bears, Dogs, Dragons, & c. by which means God's People are always exposed to great Trouble and Danger, whilst they remain therein" (*Tropologia*, II, 391). Sometimes, as in Dante, biblical beasts such as those in Daniel 7 are made symbols of *specific* human evils, but Puritan literature usually suggested less precise symbolism for the beasts man met in the wilderness of this world.

from the Bible, but the metaphor's wide popularity in the seventeenth and eighteenth centuries results from new Puritan modes of thinking. In the Puritan tradition, the journey most often becomes a sea voyage: man before conversion is aimlessly adrift on the wide sea and after conversion sails (against prevailing winds) toward the heavenly port. The metaphor is often extended to include life's major experiences: temptations and sins become rocks; man's uncontrollable natural propensity becomes blasts, storms, and tempests which drive him from his course; failure to overcome temptation becomes shipwreck or drowning. Sermons and guide books repeat the metaphor frequently, but the most sustained use comes in pilgrim literature. Here the metaphor is fundamental to the structure; man's entire life, the subject of the pilgrim writers, is dramatized as a journey—a journey taking place in a physical world but having a spiritual import.

Like *The Pilgrim's Progress, Robinson Crusoe* is sustained by the metaphor. Pilgrim allegory and Defoe's novel are nourished by the same Puritan traditions, and they share the same theological view of the world and man's role in it. Though it devotes more attention to man's life before conversion than does most pilgrim literature, *Robinson Crusoe* presents the same story of rebellion and punishment, repentance and salvation, which is common to Puritan spiritual histories, whether in the form of providence stories, *exempla* in guide books, spiritual biographies, or pilgrim allegories. Defoe's hero, unlike Bunyan's, or even Richardson's, does not begin with the single-minded determination and the almost supernatural power to overcome satanic adversaries. What aims he has are negative—determination not to follow the approved course—but after drifting over tempestuous seas, being cast upon shores half a world apart, and coming close to perishing upon treacherous, unseen rocks, he learns an important lesson. In utter distress, desolation, and loneliness, Crusoe finds in God's grace the power to overcome a hostile world of hunger and sickness, animal and human brutality, even the power to overcome his most dangerous adversary, himself. An Everyman, Crusoe begins as a wanderer, aimless on a sea he does not understand; he ends as a pilgrim, crossing a final mountain to enter the promised land.

An Afterword

Puritan tradition provided Defoe with a framing vision for *Robinson Crusoe*, and he drew upon his knowledge of Puritan literature for much of his artistic technique. His control of structure and meaning, as I have tried to show, derives from inherited tradition and depends upon a set of associations already well established for his contemporary audience. Many of these associations have been obscured by the passage of time, so that the full depth of the contemporary response may no longer be possible; but continuing appreciation of *Robinson Crusoe* still depends upon an artistic technique oriented in historically grounded ideas and metaphors which, if no longer fully felt, still compel response because they confront questions which continue to haunt man in all centuries—his relation to nature, his relation to supernature, his relation to cosmic purpose.

In this study I have tried to illuminate a book and its background, believing that my procedure with this particular book and this particular background could supply meaningful knowledge about Defoe, about the relationship between art and life in the early eighteenth century, and, ultimately, about the form of the early novel. My aim has been to provide notes toward an understanding of the larger issues which confront critics of Defoe, critics of the early novel, and critics of the Augustan age generally. My means have been a close reading of the text and an intense examination of the his-

torical moment of creation. I hope that my attempts to
confront seventeenth-century Puritan treatises as literary
documents may help to provide a broadened understanding of what Puritanism was really about and may help to
produce an awareness of context for Puritan writers after
Milton. I hope, too, that my reading of *Robinson Crusoe*
may provide the modern reader with some new avenues
toward an understanding and appreciation of that one
book, for it seems to me that close analyses of discrete
works of art, especially early novels, is still the major demand upon literary scholarship if we are ever to redraw
the distorted outlines of an inherited literary history.

The question of Defoe's artistic awareness may perhaps never be finally settled, for, like other writers, Defoe may sometimes in his art have produced less, or
more, than was his conscious intention. But while certainty about conscious artistry may be almost impossible, Defoe's accomplishment in *Robinson Crusoe* suggests a control greater than that usually admitted by
Defoe scholars and critics. And while I would not wish
to argue that Defoe controlled all his fiction with as
much sureness, I would suggest that his other novels—
particularly *Moll Flanders, Journal of the Plague Year*,
and *Roxana*—deserve a closer reading in their historical
context than they have yet received, for even the most
"popular" of Defoe's novels are usually discussed in non-
artistic terms: they are praised for their concern with
psychological analysis and their "social realism" or are
damned for the "middle-class" outlook of their heroes
and heroines (who are taken to be synonymous with the
author). Ordinarily, discussion of the historical context
of Defoe's novels has implied that such information was
needed not to clarify meanings but to excuse the biases

and the primitive technique of a non-artist who stumbled, rather ineptly, into a new literary form. If, instead, we read the *Journal* in relation to the providence and diary traditions and note the emblematic concept of life and art embodied in Defoe's version of Puritanism, we shall find a highly unified novel with a clear thematic structure, not a series of anecdotes masquerading as art. And if we read *Moll Flanders* and *Roxana* in relation to the guide and criminal confession traditions, remembering the Puritan version of life rhythms and Defoe's handling of a double time scheme, we may find that other carefully wrought novels exist earlier than we had thought. This is not to say that if historical considerations have made us underrate Defoe, similar considerations should now make us overrate him. Defoe's limitations are substantial, but his proper "placing" in literary history demands that we evaluate his artistry on proper, not imaginary, contextual grounds.

Elaboration of one of Defoe's techniques may show just how helpful a detailed examination of the text and context of Defoe's other novels might be. In Chapters VI through VIII of this study I have tried to suggest the extent of Defoe's allusiveness—an allusiveness which, unlike that of Pope, depends on popular knowledge, not extensive learning. Since biblical narrative was a part of popular knowledge for Defoe's readers, his biblical allusiveness is extensive and even involves the structure of important segments of *Robinson Crusoe*. Similar in derivation and intent is Defoe's political allusiveness. Crusoe's twenty-eight years of isolation and suffering, for example, parallel the Puritan alienation between the Restoration and the accession of William and Mary; the allusion intensifies the sense of Crusoe's alienation from society and suggests the thematic implications of the Puritan emblematic reading of events. Defoe's allusion to

Timothy Cruso derives from the same body of popular (as distinguished from learned) information and serves a similar kind of thematic purpose. And Defoe's control over this allusion suggests a rather sophisticated awareness of artistic method.

Robinson Crusoe's lack of sexual involvement has often been remarked. His early escapades at sea and ashore include most of the youthful "vices" (drinking, swearing, blasphemy, and so on) denounced by Defoe's reform-conscious contemporaries, but Crusoe's rebellion is notably free of feminine involvement. During his twenty-eight years on the island, Crusoe is not only physically separated from women, but he seems unconcerned about his sexual isolation and fails even to mention the implications of his forced celibacy. Finally, back in England, he does marry and father three children, but he recounts the matter only briefly, in the final pages of the book.

Crusoe's rather curious unconcern about women has provoked scattered quizzical comments from critics (and a good deal of less formal humor among post-Freudian undergraduates), but no satisfactory explanation for Defoe's artistic choice has been offered. The supposed Puritan avoidance of sexual discussion—perhaps the most common explanation offered—is a blatantly unhistorical suggestion, as Defoe's later novels, and Richardson's, plainly show. Equally unsatisfactory are the innuendoes that Crusoe was somehow abnormal, for such a conclusion implies either that Defoe forgot to round out Crusoe in this one respect (which seems unlikely, given Defoe's later novelistic subjects) or that Defoe intended to portray a psychological cripple, which is hardly more probable, in the light of the other character traits which Defoe gives Crusoe. Not much more persuasive are suggestions about the requirements of plot, for, although sexual discussion might have complicated Defoe's artistic problems on Crusoe's island, sexual sins in Crusoe's youth would seem to have been extremely useful in developing the novel's theme of rebellion.

But once Defoe named his hero allusively, he could not afford to raise sexual issues at all in his novel, for, if he had, his allusiveness would have backfired badly. Timothy Cruso had achieved his reputation as a practical theologian, reformer, preacher and guide writer, despite an episode which threatened his career. According to persistent rumors, Cruso became involved in an adulterous affair during his ministry, and his professional effectiveness was, at least for a time, seriously impaired: the affair became well known, and, according to John Dunton, Cruso had to repent publicly. Apparently, by the end of his life Cruso had fully recovered his professional stature, but it is clear that his name could never be entirely freed from memories of the affair. To be effective, Defoe thus had to capitalize on the useful associations of Cruso's career without reminding readers of other, potentially defeating, associations.

Defoe's solution may have been an imperfect one. Useful because of his thematic interests and his use of standard Puritan forms and techniques, Timothy Cruso may ultimately have proved a liability for Defoe's art because his personal life carried associations which Defoe had to avoid by making his hero improbable in an important respect. But Defoe's "solution" is interesting not because of its limitations but because it grapples consciously with an artistic issue. The point is that Defoe recognizes the implications of his allusiveness and confronts his artistic problem forcefully, even if he lacks the resources to achieve a perfect solution. His gesture at making Crusoe "normal" (Crusoe's ultimate marriage and fatherhood) is too little, too late, but the failure is that of a conscious artist, not of a hack writing a page at a time. A critic might suggest that Defoe's allusion to Cruso was ultimately a mistake; he might even question the validity of Defoe's kind of allusiveness, depending as it does on a body of information which changes from century to century, or even from month to month. But whatever the strengths and weaknesses of the method, Defoe committed himself exhaustively to it and fully pursued its implications. To "place" Defoe accurately, criticism must greet Defoe in terms of the method he pursued, not in terms of other methods pursued by other writers in other ages.

If Defoe's art is related to life by its peculiar form of allusiveness, the same relationship is also expressed in another aspect of Defoe's technique—what I have called his "emblematic method." For Puritanism, things and events in the created world were emblems of spiritual matters. All "real" things and events thus had universal significance: the growth of a stalk of grain was as significant as a political revolution, for in both events God was speaking to man. Man's task, then, was to discover the meaning in things and events. Discovery might result from direct revelation, when God chose to use such means as dreams, or from quiet introspection, or from the guidance of other human interpreters—ministers, teachers, writers. In guide books, providence books, and spiritual biographies, writers recorded "history" and construed its meaning according to their lights. They "discovered" the divine patterns implicit in things and events, regarding life not as disordered, chaotic, and shapeless, but as one entire cosmic emblem of divine purpose and plan.

The emblematic way of perceiving life becomes an

artistic method as art begins to masquerade as life. Convincing themselves that their moral intent justified them, writers like Bunyan and Defoe could weld together separate human experiences into an artificial unit, or even formulate "typical" stories according to the rhythms of established divine pattern. Art thus became an attempt to reproduce life exactly; because order was implicit in the universe, the artist did not need to impose order upon life. His function was rather to discover an already existing order and to render it in such a way that the things and events in his book became emblems of the spiritual order. The Puritan artist thus assiduously described detail, just as did the diarist or spiritual biographer, in order to suggest fully the larger meanings which informed all things and events in a world of total divine control. The Puritan carried to its logical and absurd conclusion the doctrine of the supernatural inspiration of the artist. Ironically, the religion which denied to its followers the power to make icons or material symbols gave to its literary artists the greatest power of all—the power to be the prophetic spokesmen of God. The mantle did not always fit. Or, at least, Fielding did not think so.

Richardson shared Defoe's Puritan background and many of his assumptions, both philosophical and artistic. His novels, I would suggest, also use the emblematic method, even though the modern reader may tend to think *Pamela* too much like "The Perils of Pauline" and too little like "Everywoman." But a close reading of Richardson in historical context reveals the same rhythms, the same providential control of events, the same detail-become-emblem. Richardson's "writing to the moment" technique becomes, in fact, the ultimate (but inadvertent) *reductio* of the emblematic method, a point which did not escape Fielding when he had Shamela record her seduction moment by moment, as a good diarist searching for "meaning" should.

Fielding was not responding simply to Pamela's naïveté and calculation and Richardson's simplified psychology when he wrote *Shamela*, or when he wrote *Joseph Andrews* and *Tom Jones*, although he was refuting Richardson, at least indirectly, in all three books. Fielding's disagreement with Richardson was far more basic than the superficial trappings of his direct attack might suggest. In fact, his disagreement was ultimately not with Richardson himself, but with a whole tradition of fiction in which Richardson worked—a tradition containing all sorts of assumptions repugnant to Fielding.

Take, for example, the Puritan novelist's assumption about the role of the artist. For Fielding, the world was not so neatly ordered that an artist could be simply a discoverer. If the novelist performed a didactic function for society (and Fielding agreed with the Puritan novelists that he did), he performed it not by discovering patterns already implicit in things and events but by imposing patterns upon them; the maker of symbols was not God, but the artist. In Puritan novels disaster was averted and life was made meaningful by the intervention of providence; in Fielding's novels the providential role is played by something else: that "something else" is Fielding himself. Events still happen just as marvellously as when Crusoe was washed ashore or when Pamela preserved her virtue. But the cause is different. "Coincidence" becomes a joke in Fielding because Fielding makes it a joke; he reminds his reader at every turn, through his narrative voice, that this world is not the real world of thing and event but a world of art, where Fielding is the creator and sustainer of things, events, people. Fielding continually reminds us that he is in control. If he wants to save Tom Jones from the hangman whose shadow falls over Tom's every act, then Tom can be saved, for Fielding created, and controls, both Tom and the hangman. Tom Jones, in pursuit of Wisdom during his life's travels, is Fielding's creation, and the artist can make certain that he gets her. Tom is one of the elect: Fielding elected him.

Fielding was not the first to find fault with Puritan fiction or to offer an alternative. In *Gulliver's Travels* Swift parodied Defoe's allusive method, his concept of history, his emblematicism, his point of view, and his concept of hero; and he offered prose fiction a different direction— through a tradition rather like that of formal satire, in which the artist is neither a discoverer nor a creator of order but rather is one who recalls a former order, which is now lost.

I would suggest that we might profitably rethink our categories for the eighteenth-century novel and that one promising way of doing it would be to analyze the dialectic between writers like Richardson and Fielding on the one hand and Defoe and Swift on the other. If we consider the full ramifications of the oppositions involved, I suspect that we can learn much about basic differences in forms of prose fiction; perhaps, too, we will begin to see why the English novel began to run in certain directions, then retreated toward a different way. We might speculate about what the novel would have become had Fielding not been so effective in turning the course which the Puritans had channeled. But of course such speculation is futile until we learn more about exactly what Fielding's direction was and why his contemporaries found it so attractive.

But perhaps the ultimate irony to be pondered is one that takes us a long way in time: "turning the course" is not the right metaphor, in the end, for what happened in eighteenth-century England. Although the emblematic novel (with all its assumptions, techniques and implications) disappeared from England, it sprang up again in other soil. Shaped by intellectualized Puritans like Hawthorne and Melville, the Puritan novel found not only a more satisfying temporal climate but a more perfectly realized form when it attacked the attitudes and traditions which had made its form and technique possible—an irony that might well have interested the older pioneers, Richardson, Bunyan, and Defoe.

Index

A

Abbey, Charles J., 26n, 35n
Adams, Percy G., 14n
Adventure fiction: and travel literature, 18; and *Robinson Crusoe*, 18–19; and providence literature, 61
Aitken, George A.: on novels and moral treatises, 6n, 45; and Defoe's library, 7–8
Alienation: from nature, 28, 105, 123; Crusoe's, 123, 126, 139, 189, 204; from God, 123, 135, 139, 142–43; from society, 139, 204; metaphors of, 126, 139n, 141, 142–43
Allegorical language: in *Robinson Crusoe*, 139, 197n, 199
Allegory: *Robinson Crusoe* said to be, 49, 121; and spiritual biography, 89; Puritan use of, 115; and fiction, 120; and emblematic view of world, 121; Puritan definition of, 121; and metaphor, 122
Alleine, Joseph: *A Sure Guide to Heaven*, 41, 149n, 161
Allestree, Richard [?]: *The Whole Duty of Man*, 182n
Alsop, Vincent: *God in the Mount*, 52n
Ambition. *See* Station, idea of
American literature: and Puritanism, 93. *See also* individual authors
Analogy: as epistemological tool, 94; as metaphysical argument,

95–96; disappearance of, 95–96, 102; and metaphor, 96, 122
Anderson, Hans H., 24n
Anglicanism: on the concept of the calling, 36n; on deism, 51; on the doctrine of providence, 58–60; on history, 59
Annesley, Dr. Samuel (Defoe's pastor): Defoe's poem on, 90–91
Anniversaries: Puritan celebration of, 109n
Anti-type, Christ as, 99–100
Apostasy. *See* Lapses from grace
Aristotle, ix
Armor imagery, 28, 104
Art: relation to life, in *Robinson Crusoe*, 207–8
Artist, Puritan: role of, 209
Audience: consciousness of, 77n, 176n
Augustan aesthetic: redrawing of, vii
Avarice, Crusoe's, 179
Awareness, Crusoe's: improves after conversion, 149, 157, 158, 159, 164, 168, 173, 188; depends on philosophical assumptions, 151

B

Baconian ideas: influence of, 94
Bagshaw, Edward, 85n
Bahlman, Dudley W., 25n
Baker, Ernest A., xn, 2, 3n, 8n

213

Baker, Sheridan, 154n
Barnardiston, Anne, 87n
Battestin, Martin, viin
Baxter, Richard: distinguishes be-
    tween persuasion and direction
    treatises, 27n; on guide litera-
    ture, 28; on spectral evidence
    tradition, 65n; on the uses of
    history, 77; life of, 85, 122; on
    false history, 115n
—works cited: *Reliquiae Baxter-
    ianae*, 27n, 85; *Call to the Un-
    converted*, 27n; *A Christian
    Directory*, 27n, 28, 104; *Cer-
    tainty of the Worlds of Spirits,
    The*, 65n; *Autobiography*, 89
Bayly, Lewis: popularity of *The
    Practice of Piety*, 21, 26; *The
    Practice of Piety* and *Robinson
    Crusoe*, 21, 46
Beard, Thomas, and Thomas Tay-
    lor: *The Theatre of Gods
    Judgements*, 65, 66–67
Beattie, James, 2n
Bell, Thomas: *Grapes in the Wil-
    derness*, 112
Benjamin, Edwin F., 150n
Bernbaum, Ernest, 9
Bestial encounters in *Robinson
    Crusoe*, 198. *See also* Wolves,
    episode of the
Bestial metaphor, 111: Puritan
    use of, 104–5; in Bible, 198;
    illustrated, 113
Bethel, Slingsby: *The Provi-
    dences of God*, 52–53
Bible: as man's guide, 110; as
    manna, 110n; as clarifier of
    modernity, 113; approves use
    of fiction, 117
Bible passages cited
—Old Testament
    Genesis 2, 172n
    Genesis 3, 105, 137
    Exodus 3, 162–63
    Exodus 13 ff., 111
    Exodus 19, 154
    Joshua 6, 196n
    Joshua 10, 193n
    I Kings 19, 154
    Job 33, 163

Psalms 77, 154
Psalms 104, 154
Psalms 107, 63n
Proverbs 30, 40
Ecclesiastes 1, 76
Canticles 4, 113
Isaiah 2, 162n
Isaiah 29, 161–62
Isaiah 35, 174–75n
Isaiah 64, 179n
Isaiah 66, 162n
Zechariah 2, 197n
—Apocrypha
    Jesus Sirach 11, 35
—New Testament
    Gospels, 111
    Matthew 13, 150n
    Mark 1, 111n
    Mark 4, 150n
    Luke 12, 179n
    Luke 14, 180n
    Luke 16, 118 and n
    John 6, 179n
    Acts 5, 160
    Romans 9, 179n
    Hebrews 4, 110
    Hebrews 11, 105, 109
    I Peter 2, 105
    Revelation 10, 154
    Revelation 14, 154
Biblical allusion: to compress his-
    tory, 101; and popular knowl-
    edge, 204. *See also* Biblical
    characters; Biblical events
Biblical characters: and modern
    parallels, 99, 103
—Old Testament characters cited
    Abraham, 72n, 99
    Adam, 105–6: his restlessness,
        37, 130, 138; as type, 99;
        and prodigal son, 106n; and
        Crusoe, 137–39
    David: as type, 99
    Elihu, 163
    Elijah: and Crusoe, 154–55,
        163
    Ezekiel: and Crusoe, 161–63
    Isaac, 39n, 72n
    Jezebel, 154
    Job, 35n; and Crusoe, 163–64
    Jonah, 68: as type, 100; and

Crusoe, 133–34, 136–37, 155, 163
Joshua, 196
Moses, 162, 195 and n: as type, 99, 100; and *Robinson Crusoe*, 163
Noah, 100
Pharaoh, 109
Samson, 99
Solomon, 180
—New Testament characters cited
Jesus, 194n: as anti-type, 99–100; his temptation, 108; his parables, 118–19
Lazarus, 35n, 118
Paul, St., 41n, 129 and n, 167
Prodigal son. *See* main entry
Biblical events: Puritan identification with, 99, 103, 109; as commentary on modern events, 113
Biblical lottery, 159
Biography: and *Robinson Crusoe*, 6n; and spiritual biography (*q.v.*), 90 and n
Bisse, Dr. Philip, 20n
Bolton, Robert: *Some General Directions for a Comfortable Walking with God*, 31, 131n; life of, 85n
Bonner, Willard H, 47n
Book of nature: uses of, 95–98; shifting conception of, 96–98; Puritan view of, 122; Crusoe's use of, 157–58
Bourgeois tragedy, 79
Bragge, Robert: *The Youth's Interest*, 106n
Brown, Joseph Epes, xin
Browne, Sir Thomas, 94 and n
Brownsword, Henry, 87–88
Bunyan, John, 211: and *Robinson Crusoe*, 12n, 21, 22, 119, 139, 178, 189, 197n, 200; and fiction, 116, 123–24, 208; on justification for allegory, 117; as Puritan epitome, 126; on human depravity, 133; uses physical action as emblem, 189 and n; "realism" of, 189

—works cited: *The Pilgrim's Progress*, 18n, 21, 22, 86, 117, 119, 189 and n, 200; structure of, 89, 114–15, 178; *Grace Abounding*, 89, 122–23; *Divine Emblems*, 133
Burch, Charles Eaton, 27n
Burgess, Daniel, 78
Burkitt, William: *The Poor Man's Help and Young Man's Guide*, 31n
Burroughs, Jeremiah: *The Sea-Man's Direction in Time of Storme*, 29, 54, 67–68, 70, 141

C

Calamy, Benjamin, 42, 166
Calling (vocation): guide books designed for a specific, 28–31; origin of term, 35; "election" distinguished from, 43–44
—abandonment of: by Defoe, 5n; as rebellion, 36, 40; punishment for, 37; sometimes permissible, 37n, 187n; by Jonah and prodigal son, 133
—choice of: crucialness of, 33–34; factors in, 37–38; role of parent in, 38, 85
—concept of: defined, 34; Weber and Tawney on, 34–35; and Middle Ages, 35; and Catholicism, 35; places restraints on individuals, 36; supported by contemporary philosophy, 36n; emphasized in guides for youth, 36–40; and man's basic sin, 132
Calvin, John, 36, 142–43
Canaan. *See* Exodus of Israelites
Cannibals: Crusoe and, 182, 192. *See also* Natural man
Caryl, Joseph, 111–12
Castaways: before Selkirk, 3–4; accounts of, 12–13, 63–65, 73
Caves: as biblical symbol, 154, 162n
Charnock, Stephen, 36n, 165

Chew, Samuel C.: *The Pilgrimage of Life*, 113n
Chillingworth, William, 27n
Chronology: as structure, 15, 18 and n, 88, 89; in *Robinson Crusoe*, 16–17, 18, 89, 185n. *See also* Time scheme
Civil war: and Puritan warfare metaphor, 103
Claridge, Richard, 104–5
Clarke, Samuel (1599–1683), 89: on lapses from grace, 43n, 187–88n; on didactic uses of historical example, 76, 77–78, 81; on imitation and evitation, 80; on *dilectum delictum*, 131n
—works cited: *A General Martyrologie*, 43n, 76, 79, 187–88n; *A Mirrour or Looking-Glass*, 64n, 81, 154n; *A Collection of the Lives of Ten Eminent Divines*, 77–78, 79, 80, 131n; *The Lives of Sundry Eminent Persons in This Later Age*, 77n, 79, 115n, 149; *The Marrow of Ecclesiastical History*, 79
Clothes: Crusoe and, 178n
"Coincidence": and Christian understanding of history, 192n; in Fielding, 209
Columbus, Robert R., xiin
Common men, lives of: in spiritual biography, 78–81
Companions: influence of, 30, 80
Concreteness, Puritan: in spiritual biography, 77, 78; diaries as form of, 83; dependence on, 97. *See also* Detail, use of
Conversion: of others, as obligation, 30, 185; advantages of early, 41–42, 88; special times for, 42 (*see also* "Finding Times"); means of, 149 and n, 154; tests of, 164–67; of notorious sinners, 167; effects of, 168, 172–75
Cooke, Edward: *A Voyage to the South Sea and Round the World*, 2, 15n, 18n, 125–26
Cooper, Joseph: *Misthoskopia*, 110–11, 195–96

Coot, Sir Charles, 149n
Cope, Jackson I., 93n
Correspondences: doctrine of, 94–95; loss of, 95
Cosmology: seventeenth-century, as interpreted by nineteenth century, 93; clash of old and new, 94–97, 101
Covenant, Old Testament idea of: and contract metaphor, 165n
Covenant theology, 57n
Created world: as revelatory device, 97, 99. *See also* Physical
Criminal confession tradition: and Defoe's fiction, 204
Cromwell, Oliver, 99
Cross: made by Crusoe, 154n
Crossman, Samuel: *The Young Man's Calling*, 31; on choice of calling, 38; use of *exempla* in, 41n; on life as voyage, 107; on forced repentance, 141
Cruso, Timothy: on moral degeneracy, 32; with Defoe at Morton's Academy, 32, 47, 49–50; on early conversion, 33, 88; on youthful sins, 34, 129n; on filial disobedience, 39–40, 48; on rebellion against God, 39–40, 48–49; on punishment, 40, 48–49, 53–54, 141–42; on precedence of spiritual over temporal, 43–44; reputation of, 47, 206; ministry of, 47–50; writing career of, 47–50, 206; Defoe's possible allusion to, 47–50, 204–7; early death of, 48; on man as pilgrim, 48, 106; on man as wanderer, 106; on parabolical history, 118; on *dilectum delictum*, 131n; on "middle station," 138n; personal life of, 206
—works cited: *God the Guide of Youth*, 31n, 32, 39–40, 48–49, 106; *The Necessity and Advantage of an Early Victory over Satan*, 31n, 33, 34, 47–48; *The Usefullnesse of Spiritual Wisdom with A Temporal Inheritance*, 43–44, 47, 129n, 138n; *The Churches Plea for the*

Divine Presence, 53–54; *The Period of Humane Life Determined by the Divine Will,* 87–88; *Discourses upon the Rich Man and Lazarus,* 118, 141–42; *Twenty-Four Sermons Preached at the Merchants-Lecture,* 131n

Crusoe: possible source of name, 47–50, 47n

Crusoe's father: prophecy of, 20, 157; recommends ordered life, 128; and prodigal son's father, 136; on "middle station," 137

D

Daily Advertiser, 7

Dampier, William, 18n: his *A New Voyage Round the World,* 9; as "source" of *Robinson Crusoe,* 9, 11, 12n

Dates: of conversion, 85; significance of, 85; concurrence of, in *Robinson Crusoe,* 142, 169

Deathbed repentance, 165: dangers of, 42, 87; possibility of, 42, 166; of Shetterden Thomas, 80; of Lord Rochester, 80, 166–67

Defoe, Daniel: moral reputation of, xi, 6n, 9, 10n, 22; as journalist, xii, 1, 4, 5, 11; his library, 7–8, 7n; ambivalence about tradition, 24–25n; family background, 25n; and "reform" societies, 27n; and Puritan subliterary forms, 27n, 44–47, 49, 65n, 73–74, 90–92; and allusion, 47–50, 128, 133n, 155, 204–7 (*see also* Bible, Biblical characters); his life "allegorized" in *Robinson Crusoe,* 49, 121; his shifting attitudes toward fiction, 119–20; his alleged mercantile vocabulary, 132n; on modern man, 155

—prose fiction: "circumstantial method" in, x; reputation of, xii, 8n, 13, 203; conscious artistry of, xiv, 203–7; alleged lack of artistic control in, 4–5n, 13, 19, 24n, 145n, 191; aims in, 4n, 5 and n, 22, 45, 74, 176; "sources" of, 8; parody in, 139, 141; handling of time in, 144–47; alleged realism of, 153, 158, 189; and consciousness of audience, 176n

—works cited: *Farther Adventures,* x, 120, 187n; *Serious Reflections,* x, 120–21; *Moll Flanders,* xi, xiin, xivn, 203, 204; *Roxana (The Fortunate Mistress),* xi, xivn, 203, 204; *The Family Instructor,* 5, 17n, 45n, 130, 176n, 185n; and guide literature, 44–45, 91; contents of, 44–46; popularity of, 45; and fiction, 46, 120; *The Shortest Way with the Dissenters,* 16–17n; *The Storm,* 18n, 73–74, 119; *The Review,* 27n; *Religious Courtship,* 45; *The Complete English Tradesman,* 45; *The New Family Instructor,* 45; *The Complete English Gentleman,* 45; *A True Relation of the Apparition of One Mrs. Veal,* 65n; *Journal of the Plague Year,* 73, 203, 204; "The Character of the Late Dr. Samuel Annesley,"* 90–91; *Memoirs of Daniel Williams,* 91; *A True Collection,* 91n

Degree, doctrine of: and concept of the calling, 36

Deism: challenges orthodox Christianity, 51, 55, 65; called "atheism," 51, 56n; answers to, 65; effects of, 65–66; and Charles Gildon, 176n

Deliverance: instruments of, 53n, 57, 69; accounts of, 62; should be remembered, 63, 70–71; didactic uses of, 64, 68; interpretation of, 67; and teleology, 68; as indication of future, 68; as emblem for salvation, 69; as vehicle of salvation, 69; obligations resulting from, 70–72;

Deliverance (*continued*)
    exodus of Israelites as a, 72n;
    term shifts meaning for Crusoe,
    159–60; Crusoe attempts own,
    181–82n
Dent, Arthur: *The Plain Mans
    Pathway to Heaven*, 31
Depravity, human: and *Robinson
    Crusoe*, 19–20, 127, 129, 130,
    177, 178, 189, 190n; assumed
    by orthodox Christianity, 28,
    41, 52, 57, 148, 148–49n; takes
    specific forms in individuals,
    131. *See also Dilectum delic-
    tum*; Natural man
Detail, use of: in Puritan subliter-
    ary forms, 4, 16n, 61, 84, 208;
    as artistic device, 61, 144; phil-
    osophical basis for, 61n, 84, 86,
    90n, 208
Dialectic of fall and recovery. *See*
    Patterns
Diaries: contents of, 71–72n, 82–
    86, 208; reasons for keeping,
    72, 83–84; as private mode, 82,
    86; popularity of, 82–84; and
    spiritual biography, 82–86, 88;
    as revelatory vehicle, 83, 146n;
    didactic value of, 86; and *Rob-
    inson Crusoe*, 144–46; and
    Richardson's technique, 146n;
    and *Journal of the Plague Year*,
    204
Dickenson, Jonathan: *God's Pro-
    tecting Providence*, 61, 74
Dilectum delictum: in guide lit-
    erature, 131–32; in *Robinson
    Crusoe*, 131–33
"Direction" treatises: and "per-
    suasion" treatises, 27n
Disasters: as vehicles of salvation,
    148
Discovery, geographical: and Pu-
    ritan journey metaphor, 105
Discursive reason: aided by rev-
    elation, in *Robinson Crusoe*,
    147, 157; limited, in Crusoe,
    152, 164
Disguise imagery, 104
Disobedience. *See* Rebellion
Dissenters: and "abuse" of provi-
    dence, 58–60

Dobrée, Bonamy, 13
Dottin, Paul, 21n
Dreams: controlled by God, 184,
    207; Crusoe guided by, 188
Dryden, John, viii
Dunton, John, 206

E

Earthquake: as emblem, 152,
    154; biblical meanings of, 154,
    161, 162
Economic man, Crusoe as, xn, 167
Emblem: defined, 29n, 122
Empiricism. *See* New science
*English Church in the Eighteenth
    Century, The*, 26n, 35n
Environment: man's relation to,
    as emblem, 105–6, 171; Cru-
    soe's relation to, 126, 127–28,
    139, 142–43, 169, 171–75, 189,
    192. *See also* Alienation
Epistemology: Ramism and, 93;
    clash of old and new, 94–97
Estwick, Nicolas, 187
Events: Defoe's fiction allegedly
    based on, 5; as emblems, 29n,
    98, 99, 101, 102, 122, 153–54,
    190, 204, 207–8; interpretation
    of, 54, 58–60; meaning of, 83,
    89, 168, 188; reflect other
    events, 100–1
Evitation: *exempla* used for pur-
    poses of, 66–67, 77, 80; in
    spiritual biography, 82; Cru-
    soe's life as, 140
Example, power of, 41, 77–78,
    79n
Exodus of Israelites: symbolic
    value of, 26, 109, 110, 112n,
    113, 162–63; and pattern of
    the Christian life, 28, 110, 112;
    as a "type," 72n, 100, 109,
    195; as a popular "deliver-
    ance," 72n, 162; as source of
    wilderness metaphor, 108; and
    Robinson Crusoe, 162–63, 174,
    174–75n, 178n, 196–99
Experience: obligation to record,
    71–72

Exploration of Crusoe's island, 171–72

F

"Falling Sickness." *See* Lapses from grace
Farewell, Dr. Philip, 7–8
Faulkner, William, 101
Fear, Crusoe's, 12n, 171, 173, 181, 185
Feidelson, Charles, 93–94
Fiction: Puritan condemnation of, 115–21; justified by moral intent, 116, 118; shifting attitudes toward 116–19; rigidly distinguished from history, by Puritans, 117; Defoe's changing attitude toward, 119–20; and allegory, 120
Fielding, Henry, viii, 101, 116: and Defoe, 21n; *Tom Jones*, 21n, 119n, 192n, 209–10; *Joseph Andrews*, 119n, 209; *Shamela*, 208–9; and Richardson, 208–10
"Finding Times," concept of, 42, 165–66
Fitzgerald, Brian, xn
Flaubert, Gustave, viii
Flavell, John: on degeneracy of seamen, 30n; on Christian contentment, 36–37; on "Finding Times," 42, 166; on special providences, 54, 55–56, 67, 69, 71, 72n, 141; on Christian obligations, 70n, 71; on value of history, 84n; on created world, as emblem, 96–97
—works cited: *Navigation Spiritualized*, 29, 30n, 42, 69, 70n, 141, 159, 166, 197n, 198; *Husbandry Spiritualized*, 29, 96–97; *Divine Conduct*, 36–37, 54, 55–56, 67, 71, 72n, 84n; *Mount Pisgah*, 112, 195n, 197
Fleetwood, William: *The Relative Duties of Parents and Children*, 39
Footprint episode, 12n, 180–85, 190, 192, 195

Fox, Ralph, xn
Friday, 12n, 190, 192n: as natural man, 130–31; filial affection of, 136n; Crusoe's rescue of, 183–84; conversion of, 184–86; and Crusoe's spiritual development, 184–86, 188, 192; as comic character, 198n
Friday's father, 130–31, 136n, 192 and n
Funeral sermons: and spiritual biography, 82, 86–89; described, 87

G

Ganzel, Dewey, 185n
Garden: as state of soul, 103, 111; as Bible's central symbol, 111; in Sallee, 139; on Crusoe's island, 171–72, 174, 178, 190; as emblem, 172, 190
Geissler, Paul, 121
Gildon, Charles: attacks Defoe's moral and religious views, 20, 21, 59n, 175; *The Life and Strange Surprizing Adventures of Mr. D—— DeF—— of London*, 20, 118n; religious allegiances of, 20, 176n; life of, 21n; on use of fiction, 118–19
Goodman, John, *The Penitent Pardon'd*: on prodigal son, 37, 112n, 134n; on rebellion, 37, 134n; on interpreting parables, 135n; on instruments of repentance, 166
Gouge, Thomas: *The Young Man's Guide*, 31, 114; *Christian Directions*, 142n
Gouge, William: *Mercies Memoriall*, 72, 109; *A Recovery from Apostacy*, 118n, 122n
Grain episode, in *Robinson Crusoe*, 149–51
Gray, Andrew: *The Spiritual Warfare*, 104, 138
Grimmelshausen, H. J. C. von: *Simplicius Simplicissimus*, 47n
Gudde, Erwin Gustav, 47n

Guide literature, 23–50: fondness for metaphor in, 23–50 *passim*, 104, 110–11, 200; for specific occupations, 28–31; for seamen, 29–31; for youth, 31–40; and subliterary forms, 81, 115; and Defoe's prose fiction, 122, 204; and patterns of Christian life, 200; and emblematic reading of events, 207

Gurnall, William: *The Christians Labour and Reward*, 79n

H

Hagiology, 78

Hakluyt, Richard, 14n

Halewood, William H., xiin, xiiin

Haller, William: *The Rise of Puritanism*, 34n, 78–79, 93, 169n; *Liberty and Reformation in the Puritan Revolution*, 93

Hawthorne, Nathaniel, 92, 211

Helder, John, 77n

Herbert, George: "Matins," 69n; "The Pulley," 132

Hero: shifting conception of, in seventeenth century, 78

Hieron, John, 78n, 84

"Hints," supernatural: Crusoe's response to, 129, 132, 183, 184, 188

Historical events: didactic use of, 40, 65–66, 67n, 68, 77, 81, 84; reasons to record, 72 and n; significance of, 76; as emblems, 115. *See also* Trivial events

History: Christian view of, 51, 52, 55, 58, 59, 74, 76, 82–83, 98, 101, 123, 128, 146–47, 148, 167, 169n, 207; interpretation of, 58–60; uses of, 76; as cyclical, 76, 98, 99, 146; Fielding's definition of, 119; assumptions about, in *Robinson Crusoe*, 123, 128, 146–47. *See also* Teleology

Hobbes, Thomas, 165n

Holy war: concept of, 103–4

Homer: *Odyssey* of, 18n, 133n

Horace, 4

How, Ephraim, 3, 64–65

Howe, Irving, 143, 176

Hunter, J. Paul, 12n, 101–2n, 185n

Husbandman's Calling, 29

I

Icons: Puritan substitutes for, 29n, 83, 97; and emblems, 29n, 97; Puritan rejection of, 29n, 97, 116n, 208; making of, usurps divine function, 97

Imitation: *exempla* recorded for purposes of, 77, 79, 80, 82, 87n; of ordinary men, 79 and n; sometimes combined with evitation, 80–81. *See also* Evitation

Impotence, human, 54, 104: and Crusoe, 153, 157, 177

Introspection: encouraged by diary-keeping, 85; Crusoe's, 127, 143–47; eighteenth-century contexts of, 143–44; as revelatory device, 207

Island, Crusoe's: as salvation, 127; isolates Crusoe's conflicts, 127; turns Crusoe's attention inward, 127; as punishment, 127, 141

Ismael (Moely), 188

Isolation. *See* Alienation

J

James, Henry, viii

Janeway, James: gives accounts of castaways, 3n, 4n, 64; on providences at sea, 62–63; *Token for Mariners*, 63n, 69n; illustration in, fuses physical and spiritual, 69; *Legacy to His Friends*, 30n, 63n

Jerome, St., 98

Johnson, Samuel: on *Robinson Crusoe*, xiin

"Jonah" concept: defined, 68

Journey metaphor, 23–50 *passim*, 86, 103–8, 113: source in

Bible, 105; suggests erratic movement of man, 106; suggests progress of man, 106; popularity of, 199–200. *See also* Exodus of Israelites; Voyage metaphor; Wilderness
"Judgments": as punishment for sin, 40, 53, 64, 65n, 67n, 73, 140, 157, 163, 170; as warnings of future, 53; interpretation of, 54, 67 and n; didactic uses of, 66–67
Jukes, Vincent, 122
Justice, divine: imaged as sword, 161

K

Keach, Benjamin: *Tropologia*, 96, 100, 106, 195–96n, 197n; *War against the Devil*, 104; "*Philologia Sacra*," 117
Kidder, Richard: *The Young Man's Duty*, 31
Knox, Robert: *An Historical Relation of Ceylon*, 9–10, 12n
Koonce, Howard L., xiin
Kreutznaer: meaning of, 154n
Kronenberger, Louis, xn

L

Language: Crusoe's growing awareness of, 152–53, 159, 170n, 191
Lapses from grace: inevitable in Christians, 42–43, 187 and n; in spiritual biography, 78, 89; Crusoe's, 175–88, 190, 192; Crusoe's recovery from, 187–88
Leader: Crusoe as, 191–99
Lee, William, 7n
Life as sojourn. *See* Journey metaphor; Pilgrim
Limitations, Crusoe's, 168, 175–88
Lloyd, Roger, xiiin
London fire: as a providence, 67n

Loneliness: as human condition, according to Calvinism, 139n, 142–43; Crusoe's, 185
Lovejoy, A. O., 36n
Lubbock, Percy, 144
Luther, Martin, 35, 36

M

McAdoo, H. R., 27n
MacCaffrey, Isabel, 93n
McKillop, Alan D., xn, 45n, 65n
MacLaine, Allan H., 133n
Marriage partner: choice of, 33
Masters, Samuel: *The Duty of Submission to Divine Providence*, 110
Mather, Cotton: *The Religious Marriner*, 29; *Early Religion*, 31n; *Help for Distressed Parents*, 39n; *Repeated Warnings*, on sea runaways, 40n; on power of example, 41 and n; *Young Man's Preservative*, 41n; *Early Piety*, 78; on punishment of rebellion, 139–40; *The Religion of the Closet*, 169n
Mather, Increase: *An Essay for the Recording of Illustrious Providences*, 3, 4n, 57n, 62, 63–64, 63n, 66n; *Solemn Advice to Young Men*, 31n, 40; *The Doctrine of Divine Providence Opened and Applyed*, 60–61, 142
Mather, Nathanael, 78n
Mather, Samuel: defines "types," 99; *Figures or Types of the Old Testament*, 100, 109–10, 113
Melville, Herman, 92, 211
Memento: Crusoe considers self as, 140
Memorial of God's last Twenty Nine Years Wonders in England, A (1689), 72n
Merchant's Lectures, 47, 131n
"Mercies." *See* Deliverance
Metaphor: Puritan fondness for, 93–94; and Ramism, 94n; and analogy, 95–96, 101, 122; Puritan use of, 97–98, 102–14,

Metaphor (*continued*)
122; Puritan fusion of, 113–15; and emblem, 122
Middle station: as paradise, in *Robinson Crusoe*, 137–38; described by T. Cruso, 138n
Military metaphor: Puritan use of, 104
Miller, Perry, 56–57n, 93
Milton, John, 51, 93n, 98, 99, 126, 171–72, 203
Minutiae. *See* Detail, use of; Trivial events
Miracles: and special providences, 52, 57 and n, 150; Crusoe's misunderstanding of, 150
Missionary obligations of seamen, 30
Moffatt, James, xiiin
Monologues, Crusoe's: said to be irrelevant, 19, 145, 176; as part of *Robinson Crusoe's* structure, 19–20, 145–47
Moore, John Robert, 4–5n, 47n
Morality, breakdown of: feared by Defoe's contemporaries, 24–28, 31
Moralizing, in *Robinson Crusoe*. *See* Monologues, Crusoe's
Moral laxity: guide literature as response to, 26 and *passim*
Moral treatises: and *Robinson Crusoe*, 6n, 45. *See also* Guide literature
Moral urgency: in Augustan writing, 24
Morgan, Charlotte E., 45n
Morton, Charles, 58: *Advice to Candidates*, 25n; *The Spirit of Man*, 79n
Morton's Academy: Defoe as ministerial student at, 5n, 32, 47, 49

N

"National crimes": Crusoe on, 183
Natural and revealed religion,
51, 55, 164. *See also* Deism
Natural man: not a noble savage, for Defoe, 130; Friday and his father as, 130–31, 136n; early Crusoe as, 131, 157; and Crusoe's maturation, 136n, 190n
Natural propensity: Crusoe's, 19, 128–33, 136, 137, 179, 181. *See also* Depravity, human
Negative power of example. *See* Evitation
New Adam: Crusoe as, 178–79
New science: and old values, 23–24; and theology, 55, 99; and old cosmology, 94; and meaning of physical events, 98–99
Noble savage, 130
Novak, Maximillian, xiin, 5–6n, 24n, 35n, 38n, 131n

O

Obedience. *See* Rebellion
Oldfield, Nathaniel, 87n
Olearius, Adam: *The Voyages and Travels of the Ambassadors*, 3n
Ong, Walter J., 93n
Oral tradition: Puritan substitutes for, 78
Order: on Crusoe's island, 132 and n, 172–75, 181. *See also* Garden
"Original sin," Crusoe's, 19, 132. *See also* Natural propensity
Overton, John H., 26n, 35n
Oxford, Robert Harley, Earl of, 2n

P

Palmer, Samuel: *A Defence of the Dissenters Education in Their Private Academies*, 58–59, 61n
Parables: interpretation of, 100, 134n, 135n; biblical use of,

117; and *Robinson Crusoe*, 150n, 179–80, 179n. *See also* Prodigal son

Parabolical history, 118 and n

Parents: role in choice of son's calling, 38, 39n; as divine deputies, 39 and n, 134

Parsons, Robert: *A Sermon Preached at the Funeral of Lord Rochester*, 42n, 80, 167n

Past and present: linked by typology, 99–101

Patrick, Symon, 59n: *Fifteen Sermons upon Contentment and Resignation to the Will of God*, 53, 59–60, 128 and n, 148, 165; *Parable of the Pilgrim*, 123

Patterns: of Christian life, 19, 73, 77n, 82, 86, 89 and n, 90, 105, 109, 113–15, 123, 200, 204, 208; of Crusoe's life, 19, 90, 127, 128, 137n, 140, 145, 146, 147, 149, 177, 184, 189, 200; of events, meaning in, 76, 83, 84, 207, 209–10; didactic uses of, 76–79 and *passim;* of fall and recovery, 82, 84, 86, 89, 128–29, 143, 146; in individual lives, and basic Christian pattern, 86, 88; in spiritual biography and pilgrim allegory, 88–89, 114–15; of flight, 154–55

Peccatum in deliciis. See Dilectum delictum

Penington, Isaac: *A Brief Account of My Souls Travel towards the Holy Land*, 114

Philo Judaeus, 99

Physical: as emblem of spiritual, 84, 96–98, 115, 126, 156–58, 160, 188–91, 199–200, and *passim*

Physical distress: as instrument of conversion, 42, 163, 165

Physico-theology, 96

Picaresque romance: and *Robinson Crusoe*, 6n

Pilgrim: man as, 27, 48, 89, 105, 106, 109, 123, 139n, 195,

195–96n; Crusoe as, 126, 127, 128, 175, 188, 200–1

Pilgrim allegory: and *Robinson Crusoe*, 74, 89, 92, 123, 197, 199; and Puritan metaphors, 104, 114–19, 199–200; moral purpose of, 115; and pattern of Christian life, 123, 200

Poole, Matthew, 66n

Pope, Alexander, viii, 4, 204: on *Robinson Crusoe*, xin; on breakdown of traditional values, 23, 24; *God's Revenge against Punning*, 65n; *Essay on Man*, 131

Porter, Robert: *The Life of Mr. John Hieron*, 78n, 84

Potter, Crusoe as a, 179 and n

Praz, Mario, 143n

Price, Martin, 24n

Prison: Crusoe's island as, 160

Private literature: distinguished from public, 77n

Prodigal son, 32, 39, 112n: as "type" of rebellion, 37, 40, 134 and n; and Adam, 37, 106n; his repentance forced, 42; parable of, as "parabolical history," 118n; and *Robinson Crusoe*, 133–36, 137, 155, 163

Promises in distress: obligation to keep, 70; of seamen, 70; Crusoe's neglect of, 135

Prophet: artist as, 208

Prose fiction, eighteenth-century: lag in criticism of, vii; contexts of, vii, viii; alleged simplicity of, viii; and modern novel, viii; viewed as "organic," ix; kinds of, ix, xiii, 209–11; and symbolic novel, xiii, 92, 124; didactic function of, 209

Prospect: as metaphor for meditation, 43; tradition, 98, 195; to fuse space and time, 98; in *Robinson Crusoe*, 194–96

Prosperity: as evidence of salvation, 35n, 67; as result of piety, 43

Providence Displayed (1712), 3n, 18n, 61–62, 74, 125

Providence literature, 51–75: and *Robinson Crusoe,* 74–75, 122, 140; and spiritual biography, 81; contents of, 81, 149n, 154, 162; and pattern of Christian life, 200; and *Journal of the Plague Year,* 204; and emblematic reading of events, 207

Providences: special, distinguished from general, 56

Psychology of Crusoe: based on eighteenth-century psychology-philosophy, 12, 143–44

Punishment: certainty of, 48, 68; instruments of, 57, 62, 137, 140, 141, 142, 154; island as, in *Robinson Crusoe,* 127; appropriateness of, to sin, 141–43

Purchas, Samuel, 14n

Puritan: defined, 26n

R

Rainolds, John. *See* Reynolds, John

Ramism: and epistemology, 93; and metaphor, 94n; and prose fiction, 94n

Rebellion: of Defoe's son, 5n; in *Robinson Crusoe,* 5n, 19, 125–47; punishment of, 19, 33, 40, 41n, 66, 80, 140; against parents, 19, 39–40, 48, 132, 136 and n; against God, 33, 134 and n, 136; biblical emblems of, 133–35; symbolic value of, in eighteenth century, 173

Recording experiences: as religious obligation, 60, 63, 71–72. *See also* Diaries; Historical events; Trivial events

"Reform": in early eighteenth century, 25–28

Regal metaphor: in castaway accounts, 63 and n; and *Robinson Crusoe,* 169, 172, 178, 181, 192, 193

Repentance: as synonym for conversion, 27n; special opportunities for, 42; sometimes forced, 42, 54, 141, 148, 149, 165; loss of opportunities for, 68–69; as central event in diaries, 86; instruments of, 148, 156, 165–66; Crusoe's, often doubted, 164

Rescue. *See* Deliverance

Restlessness. *See* Rebellion; Station, idea of

Retrospection. *See* Time scheme

Reynolds, John: *The Triumphs of God's Revenge against Murther,* 21–22, 65, 66

Rhythms of Christian life. *See* Patterns, of Christian life

Richardson, Samuel, 116, 200, 205, 210, 211: his "writing to the moment," 146n, 208–9; and emblematic method, 208–9

Robertson, H. M., 34n, 35n

Robins, H. F., 177n

Robinson, John: *The Birth of a Day,* 98, 108

Robinson, Ralph, *Safe Conduct or The Saints Guidance to Glory,* 43, 53n, 54–55, 112, 187

Robinsonade, 125

Rochester, John Wilmot, Earl of, 42n: deathbed conversion of, 80, 166–67; conversion doubted by contemporaries, 80, 167

Rogers, Woodes: *A Cruising Voyage Round the World,* 2, 3n, 5n, 14–15, 18n, 125

Rousseau, Jean Jacques, xn

"Ruin": as moral term, 132

Ruling passion. *See* Dilectum delictum

Ryther, John: *Sea-Dangers and Deliverances Improved,* 30; *A Plat for Mariners,* 63, 68 and n, 71, 72n, 83–84, 107, 137n; *The Seaman's Preacher,* 69

S

Sabbath-keeping, Crusoe's, 154n, 168n, 169

Sachs, Sheldon, viin

Sacraments, Crusoe and, 169

Salvation. See Deliverance

Savagery, motif of: in *Robinson Crusoe*, 198–99n

Scrimgeour, Gary J., 8n

Sea: as vehicle of conversion, 29–30; symbolic value of, in eighteenth century, 141, 153

Seaman's chest: symbolic value of, 158–59

Sea providences, 62–65, 71–72n, and *passim*

Secord, Arthur W.: on "sources" of *Robinson Crusoe*, 2n, 6n, 8–13, 18n, 47n; his influence, 13n; on *Robinson Crusoe* and subliterary forms, 14n, 16, 45n, 90; on structure of *Robinson Crusoe*, 19

Selkirk, Alexander: as castaway on island, 1–2, 15, and *passim;* published accounts of, 2–3n, 61–62, 125 and n; as "original" of Crusoe, 2–14

Sen, Sri C., xiiin

Sentimental comedy, 79

Sexual isolation, Crusoe's, 205

Shakespeare, William, xn

Shape-shifting of Satan: Puritan emphasis on, 104–5

Sharrock, Roger, 89n

Shelton, William: *Divine Providence*, 52

Sherlock, William: *A Sermon Preach'd on the Second of September*, 67n

Shipwreck: as metaphor, 29, 69, 70, 108, 189–90; divine control of, 53, 57, 69; as vehicle of punishment, 57; as vehicle of salvation, 69; Crusoe's pillaging of, 173 and n

Shower, John: *Heaven and Hell*, 79–80; *A Sermon Preacht upon the Death of Mrs. Anne Barnardiston*, 87n; *A Funeral Sermon, Preached upon the Death of Nathaniel Oldfield*, 87n

Shugrue, Michael, 6n

Sibbes, Dr. Richard, 77–78

Sickness. See Physical distress

Similitude. See Analogy

Singling out (election), 68, 143, 166

Smith, J. Harry, xiiin

Smith, Thomas: *A Discourse Concerning Divine Providences*, 52, 53

Social relationships: and Crusoe's religion, 182–83, 192–97

"Societies of Reformation": popularity of, 25; Defoe and, 27n

Sojourner, man as. See Pilgrim

Source study: of *Robinson Crusoe*, 6–13, 73, 133n

Spatial imagery, 23–50 *passim*, 79n, 93–124 *passim*

Special days: Crusoe's observance of, 169 and n

Spectral evidence: tradition of, 65n

Spence, Joseph, xin

Spiritual autobiography, xiii, 72, 77n, 85–86, 146n. See also Diaries

Spiritual biography, 76–92: and *Robinson Crusoe*, 74, 122–23, 146; Defoe and, 90–91; contents of, 104, 114, 149n, 154, 166; and pattern of Christian life, 114, 200; and pilgrim allegory, 114–15, 123; and emblematic reading of events, 207; and detail, 208

Stanhope, George, *The Seaman's Obligations to Gratitude and a Good Life*, 29, 30, 70, 185

Starr, G. A., xiii–xiv, 26n, 77n, 89n, 131n, 146n, 162n

Station, idea of: Crusoe and, 19, 132, 136, 138, 142, 170–71, 180, 181n; neglect of duties of, 28; and concept of the calling (*q.v.*), 36; and Christian contentment, 36–37, 132, 138. See also Rebellion

Steele, Richard (1629–1692): *The Tradesman's Calling*, 29, 39n; *The Religious Tradesman*, 39n

Steele, Sir Richard (1672–1729), *The Englishman*, 2–3n, 125

Steinbeck, John, 101 and n
Sterne, Laurence, viii
Stevenson, Lionel, xn
Storms. See Tempest
Subliterary traditions. See Diaries; Guide literature; Moral treatises; Providence literature; Spiritual autobiography; Spiritual biography; Travel literature
Sutherland, James, xiiin
Swift, Jonathan, viii: on breakdown of traditional values, 23, 24; Gulliver's Travels, 178n, 210; and Defoe, 210
Swinnock, George: The Christianmans Calling, 31, 197–98
"Sword of the Lord," 161
Sylvester, Matthew, 27n, 85n
Symbolic novel. See Prose fiction, eighteenth century

T

Tawney, R. H., 34–36, 39n
Taylor, Thomas: The Theatre of Gods Judgements, 65, 66–67; The Practice of Repentance, 67, 68; The Parable of the Sower and of the Seed, 110n; The Pilgrim's Profession, 123
Teleology: assumed by orthodox Christianity, 52, 73, 77, 101, 102, 207; and Robinson Crusoe, 146, 172
Tempest: as emblem, 29, 152; as metaphor, 37, 66, 108, 128 and n; symbolic value of, in Robinson Crusoe, 151–52, 154; biblical meanings of, 154, 161, 162. See also Punishment: instruments of
Thatcher, Anthony, 3–4
"Thatcher's Relation," 64
Thematic structure: and subliterary traditions, 18–19, 61, 89, 90n; and Robinson Crusoe, 18–20, 89
Things: as emblems, 122, 188,

207–8; early Crusoe preoccupied with, 151–53. See also Physical
Thomas, Shetterden, 80
Tillotson, Archbishop John: on growing degeneracy, 24; on prosperity and salvation, 35n; on providence, 52, 57–58; on prodigal son, 135; on zeal of new converts, 165
Tillyard, E. M. W., xiiin
Time: reading, as waste of, 85, 116n; fused with space, 98, 111, 122; blurred by typology, 99–101
Time scheme: in Robinson Crusoe, 128, 136 and n, 144–47, 149–53, 204. See also Chronology
Tonge, John: God's Revenge against Murther, 65n
Traditional values: breakdown of, 23–27, 34; and Defoe, 24n
Travel literature: contents of, 2–3n, 16 and n, 73; and Robinson Crusoe, 6–19; conventions of, 14–16; tone of, 15–16; structure of, 15–17; and adventure fiction, 17–18, 18n; defined, 18n
Travel motif: as learning experience, 105; as quest, 105; as flight, 127, 172–73. See also Journey metaphor; Pilgrim
Trent, W. P., xn, 6n
Trevelyan, G. M., 25
Trevor-Roper, Hugh, 34n
Trivial events: significance of, 76, 84, 85, 180, 207–8; as emblems, 97, 123. See also Detail, use of
Turner, William: A Compleat History of the Most Remarkable Providences, 3n, 4n, 41n, 60, 62, 63, 64–65, 66n, 74, 154n
Typology: links present with past, 99; defined, 99–100; and specific biblical events, 100, 108, 133, 195; broadening of, 100–1, 109; fuses space and time, 122

V

Vice, suppression of: in early eighteenth century, 25
Vision, Crusoe's, 155–57, 161–63
Voyage metaphor, 30–31, 62: illustrated, 33, 107–8, 128 and n; symbolic details of, 107; popularity of, 200

W

Wadsworth, Benjamin: *Early Seeking of God*, 33
Wafer, Lionel: *A New Voyage & Description of the Isthmus of America*, 16n
Wagenknecht, Edward, xn
Wandering: as term for sin, 113, 138. *See also* Pilgrim; Wilderness
Warfare metaphor, 28, 103–5, 113, 130
Watson, Francis, 5n
Watt, Ian, viii–ix, xn
Weavers Pocket Book (1695), 29
Weber, Max, 34–36, 139n
Welles, John: *Soules Progress to the Celestiall Canaan*, 28, 114
Wesley, Samuel, 58, 61n
Whiting, Nathaniel, *Old Jacobs Altar Newly Repaird*, 57n
Whole Duty of Man, The (1658), 182n
Wilderness: as metaphor, 103, 108–13, 178n; as biblical symbol of confusion, 154; Crusoe's

island as, 174 and n. *See also* Exodus of Israelites; Garden
Willard, Samuel, 134n
William and Mary, reign of, 52, 204
Williams, Daniel: on degeneracy, 24; *The Vanity of Childhood and Youth*, 31n, 32; life of, written by Defoe, 91
Williams, George H.: *Wilderness and Paradise in Christian Thought*, 112n
Wolves, episode of the, 191–99
Women, Crusoe and, 205–7
Woodward, Josiah: *The Seaman's Monitor*, 29, 71–72n
Work, doctrine of, 35n, 43
Works, salvation by, 35n
World: hostile. *See* Alienation
Wrath: biblical symbols of, 161
Wright, Andrew, viin

X

Xury (Crusoe's servant), 17, 179, 188, 198n

Y

Youth guides, 31–42

Z

Zeal, Christian: as evidence of salvation, 185 and n

THE RELUCTANT PILGRIM

Defoe's Emblematic Method and Quest
for Form in *Robinson Crusoe*

by J. Paul Hunter

designer:	Cecilie Smith
typesetter:	Vail-Ballou Press, Inc.
typefaces:	Caledonia (text) and Bookman Old Style (display)
printer:	Vail-Ballou Press, Inc.
paper:	Warren's Olde Style Wove
binder:	Vail-Ballou Press, Inc.
cover material:	Columbia Fictionette